Illustrated Library of

Arts and Crafts

FULLER & DEES

TIMES MIRROR

New York • Los Angeles • Montgomery

Table Of Contents

More than any other craft, basketry has functioned to serve the needs of primitive man. It is now used as much for decorating as for usefulness.

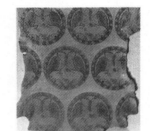

Artists and craftsmen, excited by the texture and versatility of leather, have begun to experiment and break away from the western tradition, which has been used for 200 years.

A truly American craft, decorating handmade, tinplated kitchenware originated in the Colonial America during the eighteenth century.

Jewel-like colors used in a delicate precise technique are usually associated with the art of enameling.

Collage is an excellent medium for both the beginner and the experienced artist because there is no particular style or restriction of materials.

©FULLER & DEES MCMLXXIV
3734 Atlanta Highway, Montgomery, Alabama 36109
Library of Congress Cataloging in Publication Data
Main entry under title:

The Illustrated Library of Creative Arts and Crafts

1. Handicraft.
TT157.I43   745.5   74-22068
Complete Set ISBN 0-87197-076-7
Volume III ISBN 0-87197-079-1

Etching

The beautiful effect of lines cut into a surface to create a design is unequalled in any art form.

Jewelry Making

Many intricate and beautiful cast metal pieces have been found among the artifacts of ancient cultures, indicating great skill and interest in jewelry making.

Flower Making and Preserving

Flower making is an excellent art form for amateurs because of the variety of materials which can be used. Methods of preserving are also varied and simple.

Dough Art

Materials for this art form are readily available in any kitchen, with a few special items from a hardware or paint store.

Antiquing

Inexpensive or badly worn furniture may be transformed into beautiful pieces with this interesting technique.

FULLER AND DEES

PRESIDENT
James Lueck

PROJECT EDITORS
Pat Warner
Nell McInnish

THOMAS A. CHACHARON & ASSOCIATES AND SYNTHEGRAPHICS CORPORATION

EXECUTIVE EDITOR
Richard G. Young

CONSULTING EDITORS
Thomas A. Chacharon
Sidney Lewis

PROJECT EDITOR
Bonnie Oberman

ART DIRECTOR
Will Gallagher

PICTURE EDITOR
Holly Harrington

ASSOCIATE PICTURE EDITOR
Barbara Metzger

LAYOUT STAFF
John Mahoney
Deloras Nicholas
Joseph Petek

COPY RECORDERS
Nancy Bonfield
Linda Noel

ASSIGNMENT PHOTOGRAPHY
Larry Gregory
Wayne Lennenbach

ILLUSTRATIONS

Joanna Adamski-Koperska
Victor Brecher
Joe Chmura
John Draves
Ken Hirte
Margalit Matso
Will Norman
Joe Petek
Gabriel
David Meyer

LEE WARDS

CONSULTANTS
Ward Beck
Ken Bieschke

CONTRIBUTING AUTHORS

George Blair (Pottery and Clay Modeling)
Instructor of Ceramics
Art Department
Northern Illinois University

Charles Alan Guerin (Leather Craft; Etching)
Teaching Assistant
Northern Illinois University

K. Riccio Guerin (Mobiles; Collage)
Teaching Assistant
Northern Illinois University

Lily D. Klump (Flower Making and Preserving)
Author of Handicraft Books

Norman E. Magden (Enameling)
Assistant Professor of Art History
Art Department
Northern Illinois University

Miriam W. Meyer (Dough Art)
Author, Illustrator of published works on plants and wildflowers

Daniel J. O'Neill (Antiquing)
Partner, O'Neill's Upholstery
Delanson, New York

Lee Barnes Peck (Co-author, Jewelry Making)
Associate Professor of Art
Art Department
Northern Illinois University

Naomi Greenberg Peck (Co-author, Jewelry Making)
Lecturer in Art Education
Rosary College

Pages 568, 571, 574-579 THE DECORATIVE ART OF DRIED FLOWER ARRANGEMENT by Georgia S. Vance, Doubleday & Co., New York, 1972

This detail of a gold and inlaid, enameled medallion is from the twelfth dynasty of ancient Egypt. (Courtesy, The Metropolitan Museum of Art, Contribution from Henry Walters and the Rogers Fund, 1916.)

Basketry

Beautiful contemporary baskets and sculptural forms can be created by using simple coiling and twining techniques.

Because the materials used in ancient basketry, such as vegetable fibers, are not preserved over long periods of time, it is difficult to establish exactly when basket making originated. Most of the prehistoric examples of basket work have been found in dry deserts and dry caves. Examples of coiled and twined baskets dating from approximately 8000 B.C. have been found in the Nile Delta region of Egypt. Specimens dating from about 7000 B.C. have been found in early American Indian graves in the Great Basin of the Rocky Mountains. Impressions of weaving patterns in mud and on pottery have been helpful in determining the existence of specific basket techniques in various cultures. Such impressions reveal the existence of basketry in a late Neolithic Chinese culture (about 3000 B.C.). Twined baskets 5000 years old have been found on the coast of Peru. The first evidence of basketry in Europe was found in the area of the Swiss Lake Dwellers and dates from 2500 B.C. Bronze Age baskets dating from 2000 B.C. have been found in the British Isles in peat bogs. Indeed, basketry has been practiced by cultures at all levels of development.

Among the most intricate and sought after baskets were those created by the Pomo Indian women of northern California. The most prized of the Pomo baskets, the ceremonial feather basket, had thousands of feathers decorating the surface. In addition to the feathers, tiny flat shells, beads, or pieces of metal were often added. The size of

Figure 2. Contemporary adaptations of historic design are seen in a ceremonial basket with feathers (above) by Lois Granhold and in a seed pod basket (above right) by Joann Skabo. Of historic note is a bamboo carrying basket (right) from China. (Courtesy, Field Museum of Natural History.) The Egyptian basket (bottom) is about 4000 years old. (Courtesy, The Metropolitan Museum of Art.)

these ancient baskets ranges from Indian burial baskets no larger than the head of a pin to grain baskets several feet in height and diameter.

Baskets have many uses, and basketry served many needs of primitive man; one of the most important was to provide watertight containers. In fact, Hupa Indians of California made a cooking basket so closely twined that it was used for cooking soup. Other uses of basketry include construction of and adornment for walls, roofs, and doors; rugs, chairs, and hammocks; household utensils in the preparation, cooking, and storage of food; transportation items such as rush balsas, mat rafts, sails, cradles, and coffins; equipment for hunting and fishing, such as corrals, dip nets, creels, bait baskets, and traps; clothing ranging from hats, collars, skirts, and belts to footgear; shields, helmets, body armor, and other articles of war; and rattles, drums, and other musical instruments.

The fibers used in basketry were usually untwisted strands. Bones or sticks were used as tools for sewing in the same fashion as is the modern awl. Materials used by various cultures depended largely on the wild plants indigenous to the area.

Figure 1. This Hopi twined tray (opposite) is a fine example of American Indian design in basket making. Aesthetics were a consideration even in the most functional of such objects. (Photo, Don Dedera.)

Common Terms Used In Basketry

Awl: a pointed tool used for making small holes suitable for the passage of binder fibers in coiled basketry.

Binder: the material connecting one row of core elements to another row in coiled basketry.

Bird's Eye: a technique in twining in which three crossing wefts produce a design having a dot inside two curving wefts.

Butterfly: a method of winding yarn into units suitable for weaving or twining.

Cane: a plant of the rattan family mechanically processed to a uniform diameter; used for warp and weft elements in baskets.

Chevron: a "V"-like design made from two rows of double weft twining turned in the same direction.

Coil: one element or row of core strands usually bound in a circular fashion.

Core: the strand or strands of fiber forming the inner structure of a coiled basket.

Crochet: a process in which fibers are looped through each other.

Double Weft: two strands of weft or weavers passing on both sides of and twisted between warp strands; the result is a woven fabric.

Dovetail: a method of joining areas of color in tapestry weaving or twining; weft strands connect around a common warp strand.

Ghiordes Knot: the knot used to create a pile or shag surface.

Imbrication: a supplemental surface texture or decoration used on coiled baskets.

Interlocking: a method of joining weft strands to each other between areas of color in weaving or twining.

Raffia: a fiber from palm trees found in Madagascar; it is processed for use in basketry.

Reed: a tall bamboo-like grass processed to a uniform thickness for basketry.

Rod: a single fiber strand or a branch of a tree.

Slit: the openings created in slit weaving or twining.

Soumak: a technique used in weaving and twining to create surface texture.

Split: a branch or shoot of a tree which has been divided into flat strips or sections.

Spoke: used to indicate the warp or vertical elements of a basket.

Stitch: the binding of two or more core elements to each other.

Tapestry: a flat surface weft-faced weave made of isolated areas of pattern or color.

Twining: the hand process of interlacing the two elements of warp and weft to produce a fabric.

Warp: the vertical or structural strands of a woven or twined fabric.

Weaving: the process of moving a single weft strand over and under warp elements.

Weavers: another name for the weft in a twined basket.

Weft: the horizontal or fastening strands of a woven or twined fabric.

Wicker: the name applied to a basket made of willow.

Basic Equipment And Supplies

Many materials are available to the modern basket maker. The contemporary artist using basketry techniques to create sculptural forms can choose from natural and manmade yarns, cords, and fibers readily available from weaving and craft supply stores. Most yarns and cords should be at least two-ply to sustain the constant pulling required in a firm self-supporting form. Any fiber should be tested for strength and durability before it is used for basketry. Careful selection of core elements in coiling and of warp or spokes in twining is critical to achieving the desired result. Coiling binders and twining wefts or weavers need not be as large as the cores and warps but must be able to hold up under friction and tension without fraying or pulling apart.

Those who construct traditional baskets will have no difficulty locating materials. Natural materials are abundant throughout the world. Experience enables one to determine the proper type of material for a particular project. Some basketry materials grow in the backyard or along country roadsides. Others, such as cane, reeds, and raffia, which are not as readily available, can be purchased at most large craft supplies stores.

NATURAL MATERIALS

Reed

The most common commercially available natural material used in basketry is reed. Reeds are available in round sizes and splits or flat strips ranging from the smallest diameter 000 (1 millimeter, or 1 mm) to the largest diameter 16 (5 mm). Both the scale of the basket and the techniques employed help to determine the suitable reed. Small baskets require finer reeds and large baskets heavier ones. The preparation or soaking time required depends upon the size and quality of the reeds. Smaller reeds may need only to be dipped; larger sizes may need soaking for 30 minutes or more. It is important that any reed be soaked long enough so that it bends easily and does not split or break. Soaked reeds are covered with a damp cloth until used. Do not keep reeds wrapped in a damp cloth for several days as they will begin to mold.

Cane

Cane, a member of the rattan family, can be obtained from certain craft suppliers. Cane and rattan are most frequently used in larger basket work. They characteristically have a glossy deep gold surface which distinguishes them from reed. Both cane and rattan are available in round and split sizes and are soaked in the same manner as reed.

Willow

A more common basket material found in the United States is willow. More difficult to use than reed or cane, willow should not be used by the beginner.

Other Natural Materials

Basketry materials are normally categorized by the portions of the plants most suitable for basketry. Essentially, any plant material which can be made pliable through soaking is appropriate for some type of basketry work. The following list

Figure 3. A horizontal pattern was used in weaving this Apache burden basket. Natural materials were used for the basket and the decorative hanging strips. (Photo, Don Dedera.)

contains only the most common plants found in the United States.

Grasses and Stems: bulrush or cattail, cane, broom corn, Canadian blue grass, reed grass, milkweed, basket rush, and sedge.

Shoots: white birch, cottonwood, hazelnut, mulberry, poplar, three leaf sumac, willow, and weeping willow.

Fibrous Roots: alder, bracken, cedar, elm, hemlock, and black locust.

Vines: clematis, honeysuckle, English ivy, and wisteria.

Runners: grapevine and Virginia creeper.

Barks: basswood, paper birch, red and white cedar, white pine, redbud, and black walnut.

Leaves: cattail, holy grass, squaw grass, corn husks, iris, palm leaves, and yucca.

Ferns: maidenhair fern.

TOOLS

Most tools required in basketry can be found in the home or are inexpensive and available in any hardware store. These materials include: (1) an awl for piercing rods and core elements to insert new rods or for sewing of the binder fibers; (2) pruning sheers for gathering materials and trimming rods; (3) a utility knife for splitting, piercing, and cutting rods and weavers as well as for general usage; (4) round-nose pliers for bending spokes in borders and pulling through binding elements (the ends should be covered with adhesive tape so as not to bruise the fibers); (5) measuring tape; (6) cloth for covering dampened fibers; (7) large pan or basin for soaking the materials; (8) singeing lamp for singeing off the fine hairs on cane and reed; (9) large-eyed needle for sewing and binding; (10) spring-type clothespins for temporarily securing parts and handles; (11) a small hammer for pounding weavers in place; and (12) scrap cardboard.

Basic Procedures For Coiled Basketry

Coiled basketry is the oldest of the techniques employed in basketry. It is comprised of two elements: the core, consisting of a bundle of fibers coiled spirally, and the binder or sewing thread of a similar material. Natural basketry fibers such as reeds and grasses must be soaked in water for a few hours and kept damp as they are worked. The fastening of cores with binders is usually accomplished with an awl or needle. The awl is used to make a hole or opening large enough for the binder material to pass through. A large-eyed tapestry needle is used with yarns or other similar materials.

Figure 4. This Hopi coiled plaque is an example of one of the oldest techniques used in basketry. (Photo, Don Dedera.)

BEGINNING THE BASE

There are three main ways to begin the base of a coiled basket. The core elements in the first two methods of forming the center are tapered or staggered to a gradual point whether they be natural reeds, rope, or yarns. This helps to keep the starting center tight and capable of being coiled

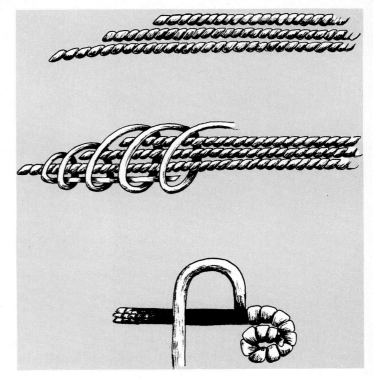

Figure 5. To begin the snail center and rosette, stagger the core elements to a gradual point (top). Then, lay the binder at the tapered end and wrap around the core elements (center). The core elements should be wrapped tightly with the binder so that the wrapped core will bend easily and coil into a spiral (bottom).

around itself. To start, lay the binder alongside the tapered core elements and wrap it around them, beginning from the farthermost point of the tapered end. Continue wrapping until the wrapped core can be bent and coiled around itself to form a spiral.

The first method, known as a snail center, radiates outward with each stitch or binder and subsequent coil. The center of the snail type remains flat and has a consistent number of stitches over the entire base. In the second method, called rosette, the first completed spiral of the core is fastened with binding stitches that pass through the center until a full revolution is made with the core. The center is thicker than the rest of the base. The third method, called four cross, is made by laying four elements of core fibers crosswise at their center to form a woven square. The fastening is begun by wrapping one of the elements with a binder and bending it sideways to meet the second element. This second element is joined with the first and wrapped together such that it includes the third and eventually the fourth ele-

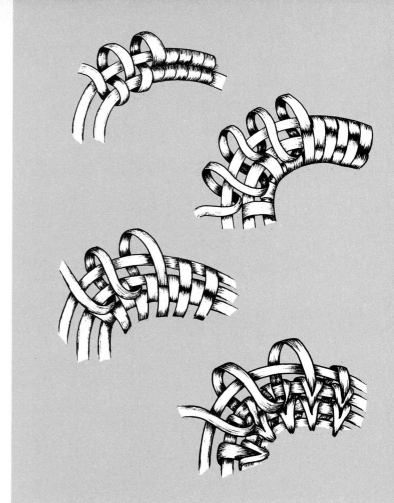

Figure 6. The snail center (top left) remains flat and the size of the stitches is the same for the entire base. The rosette center (top right) is thicker than the rest of the base because the first two core spirals are bound with stitches. The four-cross center (bottom) is formed by crossing four core elements in a sqaure and wrapping the binder.

ment. The core becomes larger as each element is added in the wrapping process. The center forms an initial square base; the actual coiling process begins with binding stitches on the side where the wrapping began.

THE STITCHES

The actual stitching of the binder can be done in several ways, depending upon the desired surface texture, design, and firmness of the form.

Figure Eight

The most common stitch is the Figure Eight or Navajo Stitch. It requires more time than most of the other stitches but gives a very firm form. The binding passes between the new and the old coil in a figure eight movement.

Lazy Squaw or Long and Short Stitch

The Lazy Squaw Stitch is made with one long stitch which goes down behind the new and the old cores, under the old core, out to the front and then up over the old and the new cores. This is fol-

Figure 7. A variety of stitches can be used to bind the coiled elements together. Some of these binding techniques include (top to bottom) the Figure Eight Stitch, Lazy Squaw Stitch, Single Rod Coil, and Split Stitch.

lowed by one or more short stitches which wrap around the new core foundation only. The strength of the form is weakened if several short stitches are made between long stitches. As each row builds outward, the next long stitch is inserted under a short stitch of the previous row.

Single Rod Coil

The binding fiber wraps around both the new and the old coil, interlocking with stitches of the old coil as it passes under the old coil.

Split Stitch

The Split Stitch, a variation of the Single Rod Coil, is a decorative stitch. The "V" pattern can be used to create a very delicate lace-like design. Each binding stitch passes through the center of the stitch below it in the old foundation coil.

Lace Stitch

The Lace Stitch produces a light airy effect because the rows of foundation cores are held apart by vertical wrappings around each long binding stitch joining coils. The initial binding stitch could be considered similar to a one-sided Long

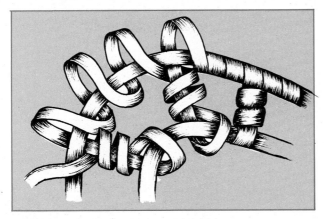

Stitch which is wrapped between coils and followed by one or more Short Stitch wrappings. The core elements are normally smaller in diameter than those used for the other types of stitches.

The binder passes over the new core and down under the old core, as in the Lazy Squaw. However, instead of being carried up and over the old core to the top of the new core, the binder passes between coils and wraps around the Long Stitch. Wrapping begins at the top of the old core and continues around the Long Stitch upward toward the new core. The number of times the Long Stitch is wrapped determines the distance between coils. Vertical wrappings between cores are spaced by the short wrappings between Long Stitches on the new core.

This stitch is used by the Fuegian Indians of South America. It produces a mesh-like fastening with the core elements slightly exposed. Begin by

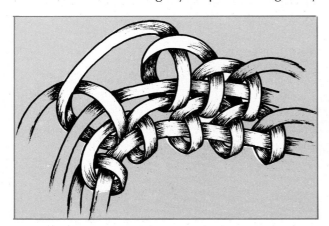

forming a small loop with the binder on top of the new core element and hold it in place with the thumb. Pass the binder under the top of the stitch of the old core below. It does not go under the old core, only under the stitch fastening the core. As it passes under the stitch, it also passes below the new core and is then brought up through the loop being held by the thumb. Pull tightly on the binder to complete the stitch.

BEGINNING NEW BINDERS AND CORE ELEMENTS

Whenever a length of binder becomes short, place a new binder alongside the new core; bind over the new binder with the remaining length of the old one. The new binder should be bound by the old one for approximately 1 inch to fasten it securely in place. At the point where the old binder becomes too short to manipulate, place it alongside the new core and use the new binder to bind the old end along with the core. If a core element consisting of several fibers is not long enough to complete the form, add elements one by one in a staggered fashion to keep the core diameter the same throughout. Core elements of a single fiber strand are taper cut and joined to a new core length which has also been tapered at the end. The angle of the two tapered ends should be identical to avoid a lump in the core. Depending upon the fiber, glue or tape can be used to secure the two ends until they are fastened by the binder.

Figure 8. Place a new binder next to the old one (top) and bind over it. If additional fibers are needed to complete the length of the core (bottom), add them in a staggered fashion.

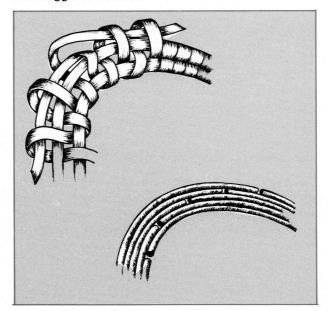

ENDING A COILED BASKET

The outermost edge of the coiled basket should be ended parallel to the point where the basket began. Cut off each core element approximately 1/4" longer than the previous one for a tapered ending. The binder is continued with the same stitch as before the cores were tapered. When only one core element remains unbound, pass the binder around this single core and the old core below. Continue binding around the two until the new core is completely covered. Insert the end of the binder under the binder that covers the core below; use a needle or an awl.

DESIGN AND COLOR IN COILED BASKETRY

Coiling techniques afford great flexibility and freedom of design and color. A mixture of any or all of the stitches within one form results in interesting textural patterns. Various sizes and types of fibers can be used as binders to create additional textures. Core elements that are exposed or change size also provide interesting variety, especially if the form is uneven or asymmetrical. Color binders are carried along with core elements in the same way as new binders are begun and ended. They exchange places with the binder and are used whenever the color changes with the design.

Shaping is controlled by the placement of the core elements. If a form is to slope inward, the new core is placed toward the inside. An outward movement places the new core toward the outer edge of the old core. Pulling tightly or relaxing the tension on the core decreases or increases the diameter of the form. Most traditional basket forms tend to be circular, with the core element making a continuous spiraling motion. Oval baskets can also be formed using coiling techniques. Begin the center base with the core element bent into a hairpin shape proportioned to the length of the oval form desired. Begin in a Figure Eight Stitch at the bend and work toward the ends to fasten the cores together. When the binding reaches the short end of the hairpin shape, the other end or new core is curved around and bound to the oval center base; use any of the binding stitches. The rest of the form can be continued in the same manner as a circular form.

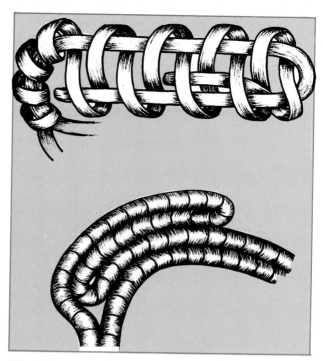

Figure 9. For an oval basket, the center base is begun with the core element bent into a hairpin shape (top). Core elements (bottom) turned back and bound on themselves establish an irregular design.

Coiling techniques can be used to create purely sculptural forms capable of supporting themselves. The strength of various fibers, the individual techniques, and both structural and decorative characteristics should be explored before sculptural form is attempted. Core elements can be turned back and bound on themselves to establish a different pattern of movement and thereby change the form itself. The core element can be wrapped with a binder and allowed to float unbound to create holes in the form. The basic techniques should be considered a point of departure in any form being created. Do not hesitate to experiment and develop original techniques. There is no right or wrong way to utilize a technique — the only limitation is whether or not the desired goal is attained.

Basic Procedures For Twined Basketry

Twining is probably the most versatile of the textile techniques. It was first used for basket forms, then became a textile technique prior to the invention of actual loom weaving. The vocabulary of twining is similar to that of weaving. The two basic elements of warp and weft produce the weave.

Twined baskets and sculptural forms are easily shaped by either increasing or decreasing the number of warps being woven. To decrease a form, join two warps. Cut off one of the two warps after it has been twined over for an inch or more. To increase the form with yarns and cords, twist the double weft and place half a double length warp strand in the open twist. Twist weft again with the other half of the warp strand placed into the opening. Follow this procedure whenever the form increases in size. Insert additional warp spokes alongside previous spokes to increase when using natural materials. Increasing can be done totally within one section to create a flaring out or bulge at that point. Gradual expansion of a form is done by adding new warps at regular intervals. Whenever a weft becomes too short to be used, the ends are placed beside a warp, and a new looped weft is begun over the same warp. Short weft ends are always carried beside a warp and twined over.

Figure 10. To increase a form (top), twist a double weft around each warp and lay it in a looped double warp. Place the weft ends along side a warp (bottom) and begin a new looped weft.

THE WEAVES

Several methods of twining are described here. It will be helpful to follow the illustrations as one reads about the techniques.

Double Weft or Single Paired Weft

A weft fiber is doubled at the center or two weft yarns are tied together to create the double weft. If yarns are used for the double weft, wind these into workable units known as butterflies. Use a long strand of yarn and loop it in the center. Working from the center, place half of the strand between the index and forefinger. From this point pass the yarn under the thumb and over the little finger. Wind on two fingers in a figure eight motion. Leave enough yarn unwound to wrap around the cross of the figure eight twice. Wrap the end around the cross once and pull the end of the yard through the loop made by the wrapping. Repeat a second time to bind securely the yarns

Figure 11. To fashion a butterfly unit (top), loop the yarn around the thumb. Wind a figure eight with the yarn (bottom). Then, wrap the point where the eights cross.

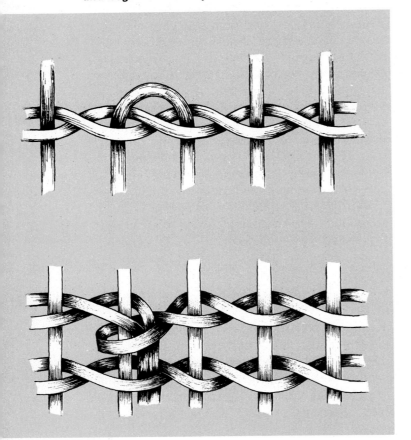

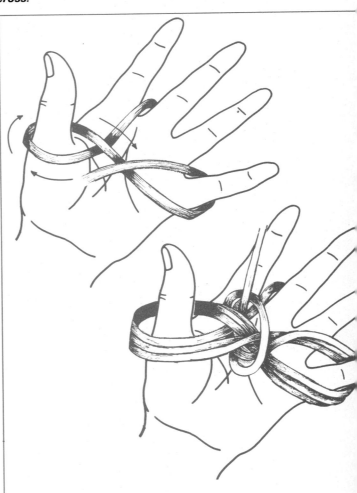

into a butterfly shape. Place the other half of the weft between the index and forefinger and wind it in the same manner. The yarn then pulls out from the center strand held between the two fingers. Place the center loop of the weft over one warp spoke.

The process of twining is that of a simple twisting motion of the weft between warp spokes. Clockwise turns of the double weft occur with each motion. The positioning of the two strands in the hand should produce an even-tensioned weave. Hold the back weft up with the index finger while the front weft is held out and down with the thumb. Join the two wefts and hold them together with the ring and little fingers; they provide tension for both wefts. As the two wefts are held in position with the fingers, pull a warp spoke in front of the down weft or through the half cross. The wefts have changed position at this point: the weft which was in front is now behind a warp,

Figure 12. When twining, the back weft is held up with the index finger, and the front weft is held out and down with the thumb (top). Hold the two wefts in position (bottom) and, with the other hand, place the warp in front of the down weft.

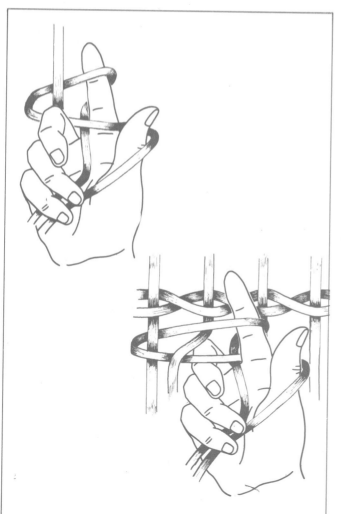

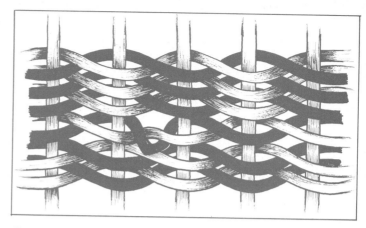

Figure 13. For a checkerboard effect, twine continuously for the desired height, thus producing stripes. Then, make a complete twist between two warp spokes to start a new row.

and the weft behind is now in front. Now reposition the fingers to repeat the process. Always hold the weft on top of the warp out and down with the thumb, and the weft behind the warp up with the index finger. Continue this process around the warp spokes of the basket to produce a weave with each weft lying at a slight diagonal.

Whenever two weft yarns of different colors are tied together to produce the weave, vertical stripes develop around the basket. A checkerboard effect can be accomplished by twining continuously for the desired height (producing stripes), then making one complete twist between two warp spokes causing two consecutive warps to have the same weft color facing the outside. This offsets the stripe sequence. Each time a full twist is made, the color sequence reverses. Full twist or complete revolutions of the two weft colors between warps keep one color constantly on the outside and another color on the inside. Half or normal twists cause the colors to appear alternately side by side.

Vary the twisting by turning the two wefts counterclockwise. Hold the wefts in the hand in the same manner as above, but roll the weft on top of the warp upward and the weft under the warp downward. This is a reverse movement from the previous method and produces a weave with the wefts laying at the reverse angle.

Open or lace-like effects are also possible in twining. The weft is usually pushed down to produce a solid weave; openings can be made by leaving spaces between rows of weft. Double twisting of the weft between two warps produces an effect known as rope twining. These double

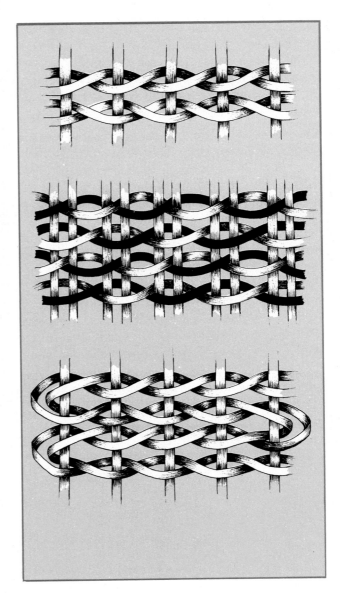

Figure 14. To achieve the rope twining effect, make double twists of the weft fibers between two warp fibers (top). For a lace-like effect, cross pairs of warp fibers and twine two weft fibers between the split warp (bottom).

Figure 15. A double weft can be twined around the warp to produce a chevron design (top). A double weft can also be twined to create a false twill pattern (center). The top and bottom wefts are folded around the outside warp to begin the next row (bottom).

twists of the weft force the warps apart causing open spaces. Make lace-like patterns by combining or crossing warps into pairs or groups and twining over them. On the second row of twining, split the warp pairs and join them with the warps to either side to form new pairs. This splitting of warp pairs back and forth creates delicate patterns.

Whenever double weft twining is worked back and forth instead of in a circular manner, a chevron design can be produced. Make a chevron or right-angle "V" by twining clockwise from left to right across the work and clockwise going back from right to left. Make a false twill pattern with a two-color weft twined back and forth and twined clockwise in one row and coun-

terclockwise in the next row. In turning to weave back, fold the bottom over to the top of the outside warp and the top weft under the outside warp. Join both wefts on the top between the last two pairs. This simple turning of the edge makes the proper movement around the outside warp with the weft ready to be twisted for the second warp to be pulled through.

Taniko Twining or Wrapped Twining

Two weft strands are used in this technique. They can be a continuous strand looped in the center or two strands of different colors tied together. Carry one weft yarn horizontally across the warps, usually on the inside of the basket. Carry the second weft on the outside and wrap it around the

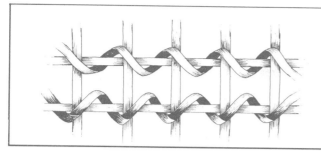

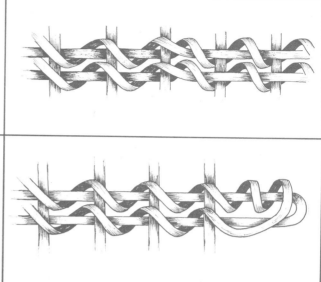

Figure 16. Two weft strands are used in Taniko twining. One weft is carried in a horizontal line and the other is looped around the horizontal weft and each warp (top left). A change in color can be made by crossing the weft under tension (top right). A flat twined piece is worked by turning the looped weft and weaving backward (right).

horizontal weft between each warp or pair of warps. It passes over a warp, then around the inside weft and back out over the next warp. The direction of the wrapping weft around the horizontal weft should be consistent, the movement being either over and under or under and over.

When the inside horizontal weft is held under tension, the outer weft wrappings incline to the right or left depending upon the direction of the weave. The inside wrappings are vertical around the horizontal weft. When the warps are closely spaced and the inside weft pulled tightly, none of the inner weft color shows on the outside. The inside of the basket has a salt and pepper effect when both weft colors show. Textural and color patterns can be made by changing the weft under tension. By carrying the outside weft horizontally under tension and wrapping with the inside weft, a mixing of the two patterns occurs. Complete reversal of the positions of the two weft colors, the outside to the inside and vice versa, creates areas of color patterns.

A flat twined piece is worked in the same manner as a circular form with the exception of turning and weaving backward. At the turning edge, carry the front wrapping weft over the last warp thread and wrap it around the bottom hroizontal weft twice. Then fold the horizontal weft back under all of the warps and place it again in a horizontal position. Carry the front weft back over the first warp and wrap it around the back horizontal weft between the first and second warps. The angle of the wrappings in weaving back will lie in an opposite direction from the previous row.

Bird's Eye Twining

Three weft fibers, usually of different colors, are used in bird's eye twining. Carry one weft horizontally on the back of the warp and two wefts on the face or top of the warp. Pull the bottom weft up into a loop between each warp. The two top warps cross as they pass through this loop. The lower color of the top becomes the high color and the high color becomes the lower color. The top two wefts continue to pass over a warp and cross each other as they move through the loop formed between warps by the back weft. Each time all three fibers are pulled tight to make an even-tensioned weave. The effect can be changed by switching one of the top wefts with the back weft.

Figure 17. In bird's eye twining, three weft fibers are used. Pull the horizontal weft into a loop between two warps; then, cross the other two wefts as they pass through the loop. Pull tight.

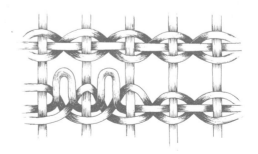

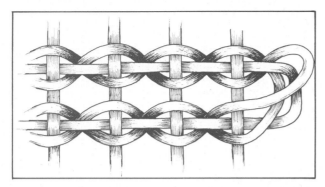

Figure 18. At the turning edge for bird's eye twining, the horizontal weft is turned in a U-shape and placed under the first warp.

The two wefts can also be carried on the back and the single horizontal weft on the top for a reversal of the weave. A decorative surface texture is created whenever the single horizontal weft is pulled tightly each time and the two wefts left slack.

In turning around on a flat twined piece, the two wefts cross beyond the last warp and under the back weft. Fold the back weft backward and place it in its horizontal position under the warp. The two top wefts turn back over the first warp and cross under the loop of the back weft, which is pulled up between the first and second warps.

Three-Strand Twining

Three weft yarns are used for this technique. The three strands are secured by taping or knotting to a warp. Place two wefts on top of the warp and one below the warp. Carry each weft over two warps and under one warp. Roll the upper of the two wefts clockwise across the next warp and behind the third warp. The lower of the two wefts moves across the first warp and behind the second warp. Bring the weft below the warp to the top between the first and second warps and

Figure 19. Three-strand twining is made by passing two wefts over the warp and one under. Only one weft goes under any one warp.

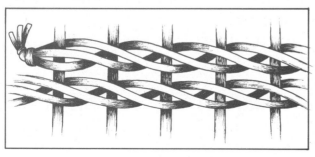

carry it across two warps. This begins the sequence of the three strand twining. Make a continuous clockwise rolling motion, with each weft moving individually over two warps and beneath a different warp. Three different colors, textures, or sizes of fibers produce an interesting weave.

Turning around on a flat woven piece requires careful observation of the positions of each strand. Carry the weft strand which has passed over the last two warps around and under the last warp. Bring the weft strand beneath the last warp back over the last two warps. Take the weft which has passed over one warp only (the last warp) under the last warp and bring it out, moving over two warps. Each weft is in position for the backward twining in a counterclockwise rolling motion.

WOVEN BASES

Many different methods can be used in beginning the base of a twined basket. The shape desired has considerable relationship to the technique chosen to begin the base. Each method forms a slightly different structure. Important is the selection of spokes or yarns large enough and sturdy enough to support the basket. Bases should be slightly domed in the center with the basket resting on the outer edge.

If a woven base is being made, an odd number of spokes must be used to create the continuous over and under weave. This odd number of spokes must be maintained as the weaving progresses and more spokes are added. Twined baskets do not require an odd number of spokes because of the nature of the technique.

The simplest round base is made of two groups of spokes or warps crossing at right angles. Each group of warps consists of four warp spokes crossing at their center. These spokes are bound together by a single weaver woven or a double weft twined three or four times around the four parts of the crossing warps. The warps are then divided into groups of two and the weft worked over the pairs three or four times. Divide the pairs and weave over each warp individually. If the base is being woven instead of twined, insert an extra or odd-numbered spoke alongside another

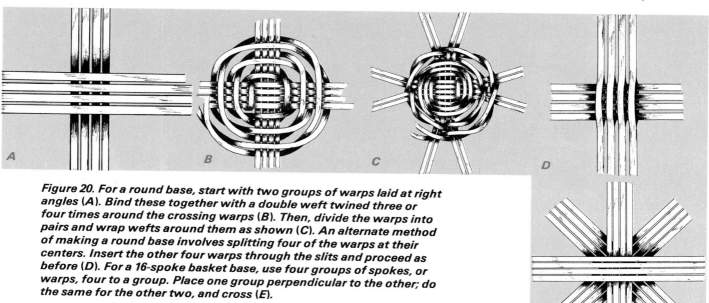

Figure 20. For a round base, start with two groups of warps laid at right angles (A). Bind these together with a double weft twined three or four times around the crossing warps (B). Then, divide the warps into pairs and wrap wefts around them as shown (C). An alternate method of making a round base involves splitting four of the warps at their centers. Insert the other four warps through the slits and proceed as before (D). For a 16-spoke basket base, use four groups of spokes, or warps, four to a group. Place one group perpendicular to the other; do the same for the other two, and cross (E).

spoke to make the weaving progress properly. Add spokes as needed to maintain a tightly woven base. An alternate method is started by piercing or splitting four rods at their centers. Insert four other rods through the split centers of the first four rods. The weaving or twining progresses as in the first method.

A 16-spoke basket base is made of four groups of spokes, each group consisting of four spokes. Place four parallel warp spokes at a right angle to four other parallel warps in the center of both. Cross the second two groups of four spokes in the same manner and place them diagonally across the center of the first two crossed groups. Hold the groups together at the center and tie them temporarily with a string to make handling easier. Weave a single weft or twine a double weft over each of the four groups three or four times. Then divide each group of four spokes into pairs. Weave over the pairs three or four times before dividing them and working them individually. It may be necessary to add more spokes for baskets with large bases. There must always be an odd number of spokes if the base is being woven.

Oval Bases

Three basic methods can be used to form an oval base. The main difference is the method used to secure the short side spokes at right angles to the

longer end spokes. Place four or more long spokes parallel to each other to form the length and ends of the basket. Place short cross spokes for the basket sides at their centers under the long spokes. Space these apart and at right angles to the long spokes. Bind with a single strand weaver. Do the first method of binding with loops which secure the short spokes to the long spokes. The weaver passes on top of the long spokes, looping around and under the right-angled short spokes twice. It passes on to each short spoke, looping around each in a continuous strand. Continue to use this single strand weaver for the base over and under each side and end spoke if the base is

Figure 21. For an oval base, lay the spokes (left). Wrap the weaver around the four spokes to secure them to the horizontal spoke (right).

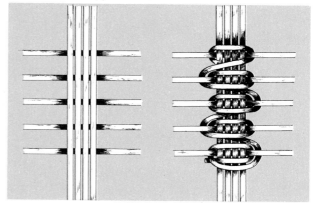

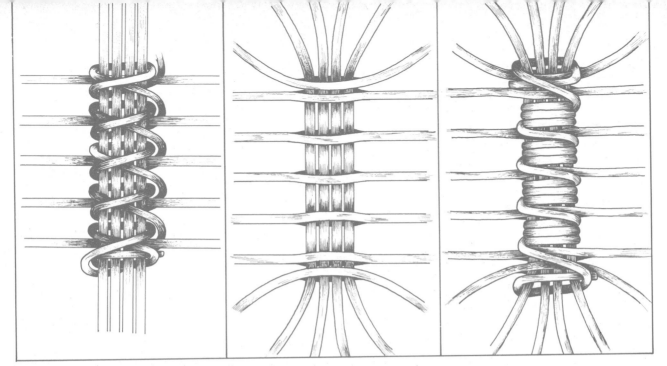

Figure 22. An oval base can be made either by wrapping the weaver in an "X" pattern (left) or by splitting the spokes and wrapping the weaver (center and right).

woven. If the base is to be twined, secure the binding weaver around the last spoke and begin the twining with a double weft.

The second method binds the spokes in place with an "X" passage of the weaver. Place the short spokes on top of the long spokes at right angles. The binder moves to the right diagonally across the short spoke, under and across the long spokes, up diagonally to the left across the short spokes, down diagonally across the back of the long spokes and on to bind the next short spoke in the same manner.

Wrapping binds the spokes to each other in the third method. Split each short spoke in the center and slide it onto the long spokes. Place two short spokes side by side for reinforcement at the ends of the long spokes. Secure the weaver at one end and wrap it over and over the long spokes. Make an equal number of wrappings between the short spokes, to space them evenly apart before crossing to the next section.

Square or Rectangular Bases

Most traditional square or rectangular bases are woven from flat splints, although round materials or yarns can be used. The weave can be a simple plain weave of over one and under one, or a more complicated twill weave. Twill weaves create a diagonal pattern effect. Examples of twill weaves

include an over two-under one movement or an over three-under one pattern. Each weft passes over a different grouping of warps, stepping one splint up with each new weft. Warp and wefts are cut long enough to form the base and sides of the basket. The two elements are interwoven in the center of both. Since the material for both is the same, warp becomes weft and weft becomes warp as they are woven over each other. The same number of vertical splints as there are horizontal splints is required to weave a square base. Rectangular bases have more vertical splints. The extending splints around the square are bent upward to form the sides of the basket. The sides can either be woven or twined.

The bases of square and rectangular baskets can be completely twined. A series of warps are placed parallel to each other. Tape them temporarily in position across one end. Using a double

Figure 23. A square or rectangular base can be made by making a simple (left) or a twill (right) weave.

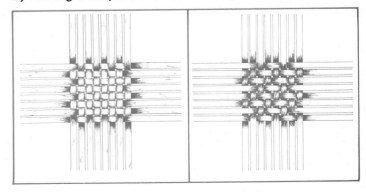

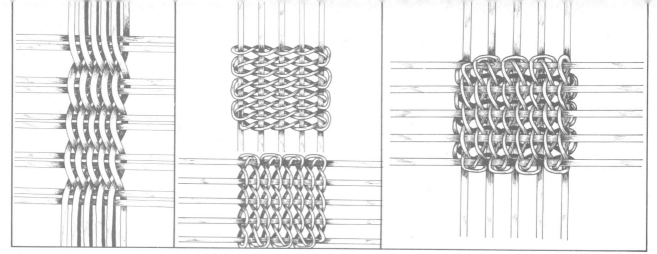

Figure 24. The base of a rectangular basket can be completely twined by weaving a double weft through parallel warps (left). Two sections can be twined (center) and splinted together at right angles (right) for a sturdy base.

weft, with beginning ends extending outward to form paired warps, twine across the parallel warps at a right angle. Allow enough weft beyond the last twined warp for a paired side warp. Use two new wefts for each horizontal row until the square or rectangle has been woven. Use the paired wefts which extend beyond both sides of the woven base as paired warps for a straight side or use them individually for sides slanting outward. Bend the double wefts and parallel warps up to become the warp of the sides. Weave or twine the sides of the basket.

A very sturdy base is made of two overlapping twined sections forming a double thickness. Twine a double weft back and forth across the center of vertical warps. Continue the twining to a height equal to the width of the woven vertical warps forming a square. Twine a second set of vertical warps of the same number as the first in the same way. Place the two twined sections on top of each other with the warps at right angles. Twine around all of the splints, binding the two layers into one. If the basket is to be square, bend the splints up and weave or twine the sides. For a rounded basket, draw the sides up gradually and add extra splints at the four corners to fill in the spaces.

BORDERS

Borders are used as a decorative finish to the top edge and occasionally the bottom edge or foot of a twined basket. The finish used most frequently is the track or woven border. Before the border is begun, make certain that the sides are level at the top. Measure around the basket from the bottom to the top with a ruler or yardstick. Tap any uneven sides down with a small hammer. Make the actual border with the warp spokes. The spokes, if of natural materials, must be thoroughly dampened to prevent their splitting or cracking when bent to begin the border. Bend each warp spoke, sideways, one at a time, at a right angle directly above the last row of weaving. Once bent, the warp becomes weft, to move in and out around the warp spokes to its side.

The simplest of the track borders is begun by bending a warp spoke sideways and moving it in front of the next or first spoke and behind the second spoke. Leave the end on the inside of the basket. Bend each consecutive warp spoke sideways and pass it in the same manner in front and behind the next two spokes. The last two warp spokes follow the same movement to complete the finished edge. Use the awl to loosen the first two warps which began the border so that the last two warps can pass in sequence in front and behind. After weaving all warps around, go back and tighten the border by pulling on each end of a spoke. Then cut the ends of each spoke at an angle slightly beyond the spoke holding them to the inside. Don't make the cut too short or the border may become unwoven.

Wider track borders are made by passing each warp spoke over more warps. Various methods of movement produce slightly different borders. Examples of other methods of weaving the warp spokes around the border include: (1) behind one, in front of one, behind one, in front of one, and behind the next one tucking in the end; (2)

behind one, in front of two, and behind the next one tucking in the end; (3) behind two, in front of two, and behind the next one tucking in the end; and (4) in front of two, behind three, in front of two, and behind the next one tucking in the end.

Always carry the method of movement completely around the border with the awl to open up the beginning portion, allowing the last few spokes to complete the cycle. Do not hesitate to use an original system of weaving the warp spokes around the border. Always make sure the ends rest securely next to the last spoke of each movement as they are being cut.

If yarn is used for warp in a soft basket or sculptural form, the ends can be woven back into the fabric and no border is necessary. Two adjacent warp yarns cross positions and are woven back into the fabric with a needle. The right warp end is woven back up alongside the left warp. The left warp end is woven back up alongside the right warp.

Projects You Can Do

Many functional and decorative items can be created with basketry techniques. The beginner will discover the simplicity of the techniques and hopefully find a craft which can be done with minimal equipment and supplies. Because of the limited materials required, most projects can be carried. Those choosing to do basketry using natural materials have limited portability, however, because of the necessity for soaking fibers. For that reason, two of the three projects that follow utilize yarns and cords instead of grasses and reeds.

COILED NAPKIN RINGS

It is advisable to experiment with each of the coiling techniques before attempting a project requiring control of design and form. Each napkin ring can be a sampler of the technique as well as a

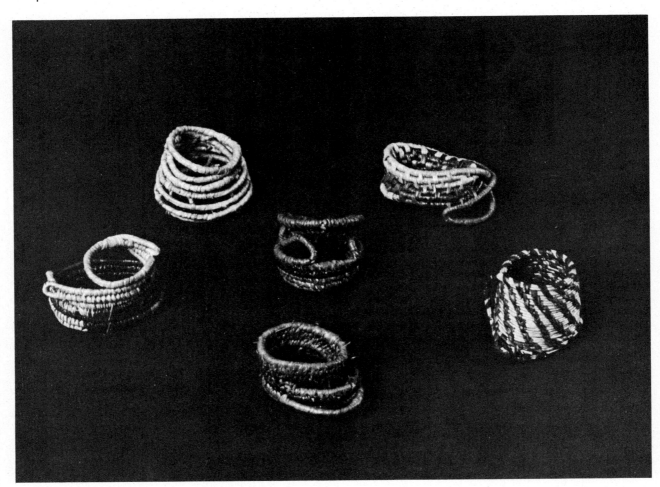

functional item. Experiment with color to create interesting designs within each ring.

Materials

The following materials are needed for this project: a reed 1 mm in size for core elements, assorted colors of raffia for binders, a large-eyed needle, and scissors. Instead of reed and raffia, a heavy 2- or 3-ply jute can be substituted for the core and yarn for the binders.

Procedures

Make six napkin rings by using a different coiling technique for each ring. Begin by wrapping six tapered 1 mm reed core elements with raffia for 6". Form the wrapped section into a circular ring and begin binding the old core to the new core. Continue coiling around the ring until the desired width has has been obtained. Cut the core elements one by one and complete the napkin ring by securing the binder thread under the binder of the old core.

COILED CHEST ORNAMENT

After the basic skills of coiling have been mastered, the designing of a particular object can be undertaken. Ideas for designs are abundant in nature and in the design motifs of various cultures. Whatever the inspiration, do not attempt to duplicate a specific form or pattern. Rather, interpret the essence of the form. Because basketry is a simple technique, many people begin with an idea and allow the materials to dictate the ultimate result. The chest ornament is constructed in pieces which are then assembled.

Materials

For this project, the following items are needed: heavy 2- or 3-ply jute for the core element, assorted metallic cords and yarns, decorative fabric trims and laces, metal rings, beads or buttons, a small plexiglass mirror, and hooks and eyes.

Procedures

Measure for fit around the neck with a tape measure. The size and approximate weight of the

Figure 25. A different coiling technique was employed to make each of the napkin rings (opposite). Assorted colors of raffia were used to create the designs and bind the core elements together.

piece should be considered when fitting the piece around the neck. The neck portion is constructed by using any of the coiling techniques. If the ornament is to be a collar form, it can be constructed in one piece. Be sure to add enough length to the neck piece so that a hook and eye can be attached. The hook and eye form the fastening device.

Figure 26. A variety of materials can be used to create unusual basketry objects. Decorative lace and a small plexiglass mirror were incorporated into the design of this coiled chest ornament.

Whenever a mirror is incorporated into the design of a body ornament, as in the one shown, set the mirror within a coiled frame. Begin the frame by forming a tight coil and working outward, keeping the disc flat. This flat disc must fit the back of the mirror to prevent scratching it. When the correct diameter is obtained, place the mirror on top of the disc and continue coiling. Gradually pull tighter on the core element, forcing it to move inward on top of the mirror. These inward rows of coiling over the edge of the mirror form a frame which secures the mirror in place. End the rows of coiling when the desired frame width has been reached.

Decorative fabric trims and laces as well as beads, buttons, or other similar objects can be worked in as the coiling progresses. Trims and laces, when carried along with the core element, create unusual and interesting areas of pattern or texture when they show between each binding stitch. Beads or buttons can be sewn onto the surface or secured in place with a binding stitch. Decorative materials should not detract from the beauty of the individual coiling stitches, however.

When connecting one portion of the ornament to another, experiment with the various coiling stitches to determine the most satisfactory one. Many other types of adornment, such as bracelets, earrings, rings, hair ornaments, and belt buckles, can be created with coiling techniques.

TWINED SCULPTURE

Twining is probably one of the oldest and most diverse of the textile techniques. Many objects woven on a loom can be twined with ease. However, the traditional loom is essentially limited to the construction of two-dimensional surfaces which, upon removal from the loom, can be manipulated into three-dimensional forms. Because twining is not restricted to the framework of a loom, it is possible to develop a form three-dimensionally. It is often easier to work on and to be able to see a form from all sides when it is being twined than to attempt to imagine a flat form on a loom in three dimensions.

Materials

Materials necessary for this project are: assorted colors and textures of yarns, cords, or rope.

Figure 27. When using the twining technique to make a three-dimensional form, it is important to choose a warp material that is strong enough to support the sculpture. Additional warp can be twined in place if the original warp element is cut too short.

Procedures

Decide upon the size of the sculptural form and select the material to be used for the warp elements. Use a warp material which will be strong enough to support the form. (A strong warp is required for any hanging or standing form.) Examine the diagrams of the various methods for beginning the base of a twined basket and decide upon a technique. Cut the warp elements longer than the required length, allowing enough extra length for take-up or shrinkage in the twining process. It is practically impossible to calculate the exact amount of additional length required because of the unique characteristics and sizes of different fibers. Large diameter fibers will require more additional length than fibers of a small diameter. After the actual twining is begun, additional warp elements will be required to increase the circumference of the form. If a warp element is too short, twine a new warp in place, and carry the old warp alongside.

The sculpture shown was begun from the top with a woven square center. Additional warp elements were twined in place at regular intervals, causing the sides of the form to expand. The three-dimensional ridges were twined by using the double weft technique. As the weft strands are turned, a warp element is pulled between the two wefts in a loop. The warp end is not pulled completely through. Each warp loop should be pulled up longer than the width of the ridge when finished. Continue pulling each warp up into a loop with each double weft turn around the entire form. Once completely around the form, twine outward on the warp loops. This outward twining on the loops forms the ridge. The ridge will be twice the fabric thickness of the rest of the form because each warp element has doubled in thickness while being looped.

Twine outward until the desired width of the ridge has been reached. At this point the twined weft must be secured to prevent it from slipping off the ends of the loops. To secure the twined weft insert the two strands of the double weft through the loop hole of each looped warp. Pass the double weft through each warp loop around the ridge. The ridge is now made firm by pulling on the end of each warp element hanging free below the inner edge of the ridge. These warp elements are the ends which were not pulled through the double weft as each warp loop was being formed. Pulling on each warp end will draw a warp loop of the ridge tightly against the outer edge of the ridge. The tighter each warp end is pulled, the stiffer the ridge will become.

Regular twining resumes with each warp being pulled completely through the turns of the double weft. Each time a ridge is desired, the warp is pulled up in loops and the weft worked outward on the loops. When the entire form is completed, the warp ends are worked back up into the fabric with a needle or crochet hook. Each two side-by-side warp ends cross and are woven up into the fabric alongside their opposite warp. Another way to finish the warp ends is to use one of the border finishes described for baskets.

For Additional Reading

Christopher, F. J., **Basketry,** Dover, 1952.

Maynard, Barbara, **Modern Basketry from the Start,** Scribner, 1973.

Navajo School of Indian Basketry, **Indian Basket Weaving,** Dover, 1971.

Rossbach, Ed, **Baskets as Textile Art,** Van Nostrand Reinhold, 1973.

Tod, Osma Gallinger, **Earth Basketry,** Bonanza Books.

Whiteford, Andrew Hunter, **Indian Arts,** Golden Press, 1970.

The floral motif, one of the oldest design themes used by man, is still popular with the modern craftsman. The paper floral arrangement (opposite) brightens a corner window. (Courtesy, Dennison Co.) Delicate rose petals (right) were formed with bakers clay. A floral theme dominates the decorated tinware (below).

Leather Craft

The oldest craft of all is still one of the most popular.

It is very likely that as long as man has eaten meat, he has used leather. Leather ranks first among the many uses for wild and domestic animals. Obtaining food was the initial reason for slaughtering animals; the items that could be made from the hide were a close second. Prehistoric people used animal skins as clothing. Later, hides were used to provide shelter in the form of tents and lodges. Many other articles were made from leather: pouches and bags for storing grain and water; foot coverings; and eventually, weapons. Prehistoric people had nothing resembling rope or string. They relied entirely on the property of leather straps to expand when wet and contract when dry to secure stone arrowheads, drills, knives, axes, and spears to wooden shafts and handles. These wet straps were also used to tie together pieces of wood used for constructing tents, carts, and sleds.

Nomadic tribes used leather for harnesses and travoises, as well as for food and water containers. Until the development of weaving and rope making, leather provided the materials for all the clothing and strapping needs of early people.

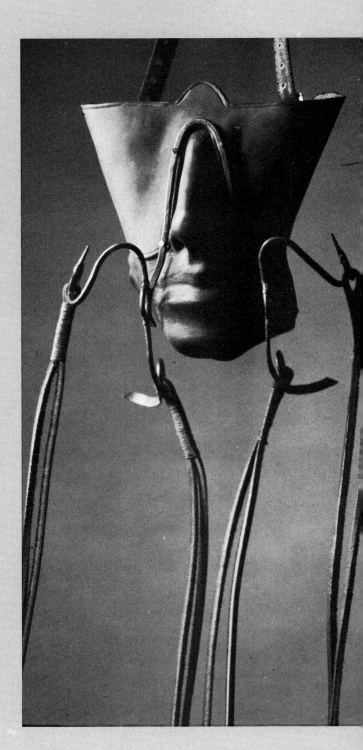

Figure 2. Note the decorative motif on the Blackfoot tipi (left). (Courtesy, Field Museum of Natural History, Chicago.) The chess set (above) was made by an eighteenth-century Spanish craftsman. (Courtesy, The Metropolitan Museum of Art, Gift of Gustavus A. Pheiffer, 1948.)

For centuries before brass and bronze were used, shields and armor were made of leather. There are accounts, during Julius Caesar's reign, of ships from Brittany with leather sails. Before the invention of paper, writing was done on parchment, which is very thin leather — similar to that used on drums. Leather has commonly been used for chair coverings and — exclusively to this day — for saddles and harnesses. Leather also has been used for jewelry, book coverings, floor tiles, window coverings, canoes, and picture frames. It has been stomped, stretched, shrunk, tooled, stitched, woven, compressed, knotted, knitted, molded, folded, polished, painted, embossed, and even gold-leafed. Even today new uses are being discovered.

The uses for leather expand as new ways of processing it are developed. Because early people did not tan their leather, it was hard, smelly, and perishable. Eventually salt came to be used as a preservative and eliminated the odor, but hides were still stiff and unsuitable for clothing. The people of some early cultures (as well as contemporary Eskimos) chewed hides to tan them. It was

Figure 1. This leather sculpture is the work of Lizbeth Wolf, who is also the author of the article on plastic crafts. Contemporary craftsmen have put leather to many imaginative uses.

discovered that tannin or tannic acid in tree bark could be used to make leather soft, pliable, strong, and odor-free. With few changes, this process was used for centuries and is still used. Known as oak tanning or vegetable tanning, it produces a leather with the right flexibility for stretching, tooling, and shaping.

It was not until the end of the nineteenth century that a process called chrome tanning was invented. This process uses chrome salts instead of tannin and was a boon to the leather industry. It not only shortens the time required to tan leather (from several weeks to several hours) but produces a leather of increased strength, resiliency, and durability. Goods such as shoes, luggage, and clothing last longer and resist scratching. Today, most leather is chrome tanned. However, such leather is not as suitable for craft projects as oak-tanned leather.

Leather craft in America (apart from the commercially manufactured leather goods) is traditionally of western style. The art of leather stamping and carving came to the west via Mexico and Spain where it is an old tradition. Leather craft has maintained its western tradition for 200 years with little change. Floral designs and mountain scenes are as popular today as they were years ago. How-

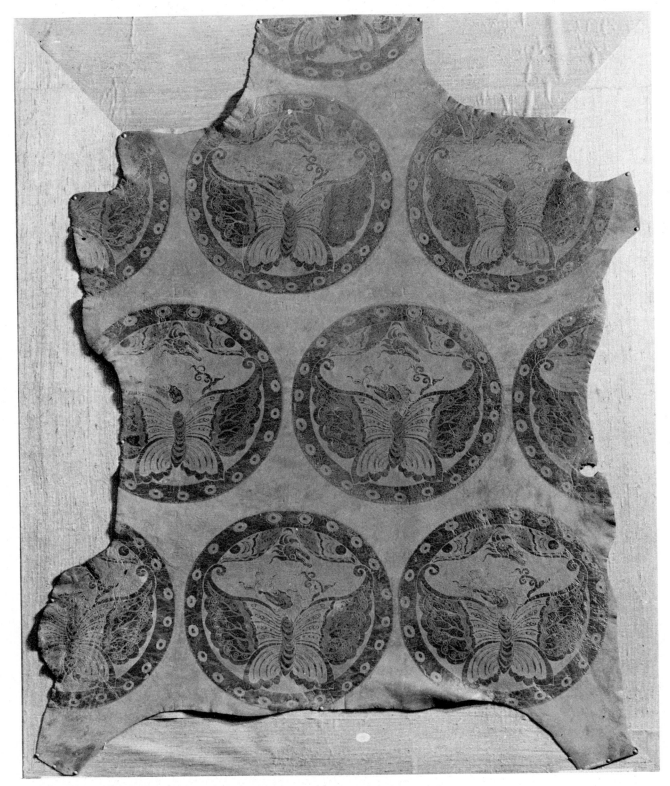

Figure 3. This Japanese leatherwork dates from the nineteenth century. The intricate design on this piece is a butterfly crest that was stenciled in black on brown leather. (Courtesy, The Metropolitan Museum of Art, Bequest of Mrs. H. O. Havemeyer, 1929. The H. O. Havemeyer Collection.)

ever, in the last few years artists and craftsmen, still excited by the texture and versatility of leather, have begun to experiment with and break away from the western tradition. The result has been a widespread rebirth of interest in leather as a creative medium.

Leather has traditionally been used for practical and functional articles such as belts, purses, and billfolds. Contemporary craftsmen still make these articles but also produce items of a more decorative or unusual nature: hanging pots, sculpture, room dividers, belt buckles, jewelry, macramé, and furniture. Contemporary craftsmen are beginning to discover that creativity with leather is limited only by the imagination.

Common Terms Used In Leather Craft

Anvil: the end of a snap-setting tool used to connect the socket and button of a snap.

Back: the leather taken from the back of a steer, including the shoulder.

Belly: the two sides of a hide which covered the belly of a steer.

Bend: the part of the hide taken from the back of a steer and not including the shoulder.

Bevel: a carving term describing the flattening of one edge of a cut line.

Button: the visible part of a snap.

Eyelet: the part of a snap which holds the stud in place; the bottom piece of the snap arrangement.

Finishing: the process of covering leather to protect and preserve it.

Oak Tanning: tanning process which uses oak bark.

Ounce: the thickness of leather; 1 ounce equals 1/64".

Oxalic Acid: a mild bleaching agent used to clean leather.

Rivet: a metal fastener which has the advantage of being easy to attach and very permanent.

Set: to attach one part of a snap or rivet firmly to another part.

Shoulder: the part of a hide taken from the shoulder of a steer.

Skive: to shave down the thickness of a piece of leather.

Socket: the part of a snap which attaches to the button.

Stud: the part of a snap which fits into the socket, metal-headed nail, or rivet used as ornamental trim.

Tannin: the chemical agent in bark which cures leather.

Tanning: the process of curing leather.

Vegetable Tanning: any tanning process using tree bark.

Figure 4. Leather has long been used to cover chairs. It can be used in its natural color, as on the chair shown, or dyed. The tanned leather used today is strong, resilient, and durable.

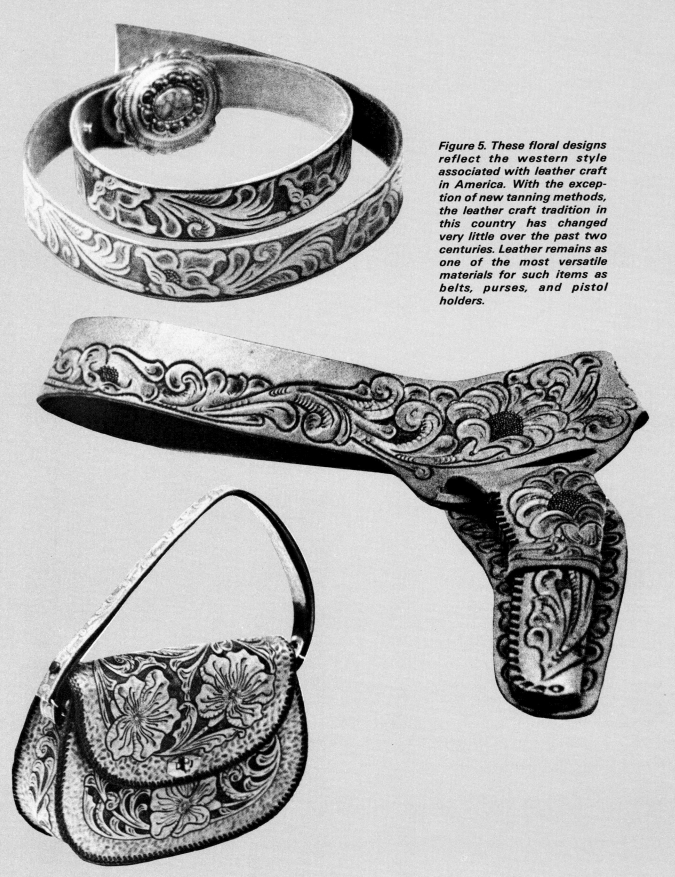

Figure 5. These floral designs reflect the western style associated with leather craft in America. With the exception of new tanning methods, the leather craft tradition in this country has changed very little over the past two centuries. Leather remains as one of the most versatile materials for such items as belts, purses, and pistol holders.

Figure 6. Stamping and tooling devices were used to create the various decorative patterns on the leather belt shown above.

Basic Equipment And Supplies

Before making any large initial investments in supplies, the beginner should be quite serious about pursuing this craft. If interested, the following tools and other materials are those that are necessary for the leather craftsman.

TOOLS

Tools needed include: (1) an awl for piercing and widening holes for lacing and stitching; (2) ball tracer for tracing designs from paper to dampened leather; (3) circle edge slicker, a round wooden tool used for smoothing leather fibers and making a smooth, lasting edge on leather; (4) common edger, a cutting tool used to round off an edge before using an edge slicker; (5) dividers for tracing circles, spacing stitching holes, and marking lines parallel to an edge; (6) edge creaser to crimp the edge of raw leather and to add a parallel groove along that edge; (7) lacing needle, a flat needle designed to be used with leather lacing; (8) leather shears — these have a slightly serrated edge which allows for clean cutting of leather; (9) mat knife; (10) modeler, a two-ended tool for modeling, lifting, and stippling leather in the carving process; (11) one-prong thonging chisel for cutting lacing slits around corners and curves; (12) rawhide mallet for setting snaps, rivets, and other permanent fasteners as well as for striking saddle stamps; (13) rotary punch, a hole punch with several sizes arranged on a revolving wheel; (14) round drive punch, a tool available in many sizes for punching holes; (15) saddle stamps, a general term encompassing over 100 various stamping tools used in leather carvings; (16) sewing awl, a kind of hand-held sewing machine used for stitching leather; (17) skife, a tool with replaceable blades used to reduce the thickness of leather in specific areas; (18) snap setter, a small set of tools used to fasten snaps; (19) square, such as a simple carpenter's square for laying out 90° angles; (20) swivel knife, a knife unique to leather craft which is used in the carving process; (21) thonging chisel, a chisel used to cut several lacing slits at a time; (22) V-gauge, a gauge used to cut halfway through the back of leather wherever a crease is needed; and (23) X-acto knife.

1. Dyes. There are several leather coloring agents on the market and most are available in craft stores. Felt-tip pens, acrylic paint, and oil paint can also be used.

2. Finishes. There are a variety of finishes on the market which protect the surface of leather. They are available in several colors and have varying characteristics. Some soften, some age, and some harden; some are shiny and others are dull.

3. Glue. White craft glue, rubber cement, or contact cement are equally acceptable.

4. Lacing. Made from goat or calf skins and available in 1/8" or 3/32" widths, lacing is available in colors or can be dyed.

5. Thread. Used for stitching, waxed and unwaxed thread is available in nylon and linen.

Other necessary materials include: (1) eyelets; (2) rivets; and (3) snaps.

LEATHER

Because there is a large variety of leather available, it is important to check the characteristics of each type before selecting a piece for a project. For general craft purposes, vegetable-tanned calf, steerhide, or cowhide is best. Calf is a fine-grained leather, ideal for carving and for small projects. Skins are about 2 1/2 ounces in weight and 8 to 10 square feet in size. Steerhide is a heavier, coarser-grained leather ideal for carving and molding. It averages about 4 ounces in weight and skins range to 28 square feet. Cowhide is the best craft leather. It has both the fineness of calf and the heaviness of steerhide. It weighs up to 10 ounces and sizes exceed 28 square feet.

When a smooth surface or a lining is desired, chrome-tanned leather is the best buy. Consult a dealer for what is available. Usually a variety of exotic leather such as alligator, lizard, suede, and ostrich can also be found. It is important to learn what is available in order to have the best and most appropriate material for a particular project.

Leather is sold in a variety of ways — usually by whole skins, half skins, full sides, backs, bends, and shoulders. As a rule, the larger the piece, the better the price. Leather is priced by the square foot and is often available at craft stores in small cuts. When buying, consider the weight or thickness of the leather. This is referred to in ounces. One ounce equals 1/64" in thickness.

Basic Procedures

Before actually beginning work with the leather itself, design the project on paper; then, cut out and construct the object with the paper patterns. The various parts of a purse, for example, should be laid out on paper, cut to actual size, labeled, and pinned together. The pieces should be altered or recut until they fit perfectly. Cutting paper patterns prevents costly mistakes in judgment and design. If the project is to be repeated, it is advisable to cut the shapes out of cardboard once the shape of the piece is decided.

A carved, or incised, design should first be done on paper. It is a simple matter to transfer an image from paper to leather, but a difficult one to actually draw on leather.

CUTTING LEATHER

Once the parts of a project have been cut into cardboard shapes, place them on the leather with as little waste as possible. Trace around the outline of the shapes lightly in pencil, and, with a mat knife or leather shears, cut out the leather shapes. It is important that the knife be sharp and that enough pressure be exerted to cut completely through the piece in one stroke. If a straight line is to be cut, place the knife along a straight edge.

CONDITIONING LEATHER

Conditioning leather for working and tooling requires that it be uniformly damp throughout. The leather should be soaked for several minutes in warm water and then wrapped in a plastic bag. This should then stand for several hours to allow the fibers to swell and reach a uniform density. Before carving or edging, remove the piece from the bag and allow it to dry until its natural color returns. If it becomes too dry, lightly dampen it with a sponge. These conditioning and dampening procedures will keep the leather supple and workable.

Figure 7. On paper draw a design which is to be carved; then, transfer it to the leather. Drawing directly on leather is difficult and does not allow for mistakes.

EDGING

Edging is the process of finishing off an edge so it is smooth and trim. This is done by first using a common edger to remove the surface corner of the edge. Then with an edge creaser, follow the edge with a firm, uniform pressure to crimp and groove the edge. To assure a neat, finished appearance, be certain the leather remains damp while edging is being done.

SKIVING

Skiving is the process of reducing the thickness of leather that is to be stitched, laced, or glued. The tool used is called a skife, which is like a potato peeler because only a narrow section of the blade is exposed. This helps prevent the removal of too much leather. The skife is drawn along the edge of the back, or fleshy, side of the leather several times until about half the thickness is removed. The purpose of skiving is to pare down the leather so that the thickness of two pieces together will equal the thickness of one piece.

FOLDING

Folding is the best method for creating a finished edge. Begin by skiving away half the thickness of the leather along an area twice as wide as the part to be folded under. With a straight edge and the small end of a modeler, make a crease on the fleshy side, where the fold is to be made. This crease should be made while the leather is still damp. (See *Conditioning Leather* above.) Using a straight edge, bend the leather, fleshy sides together, along the moist crease; remove the straight edge; and fold the leather. With a mallet, gently pound the edge flat, being careful not to mar the surface. Weight the fold with books and allow the leather to dry. Once the fold is dry, lift it and apply contact cement to both surfaces. When the cement is dry, press the fold together. If desired, the edge can then be stitched for added strength.

Figure 8. Skiving is an important step in leather working. A tool called a skife (below left) is used to reduce the thickness of the leather along an edge where a seam is planned. Two steps in the folding process are skiving an area twice as wide as the fold (above right) and using a modeler tool to make a crease at the fold (below right).

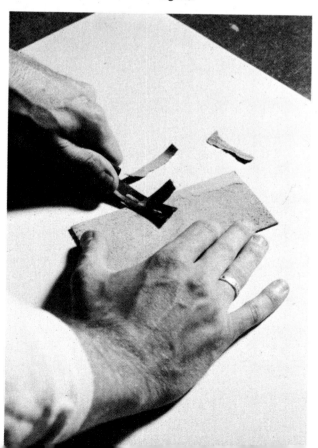

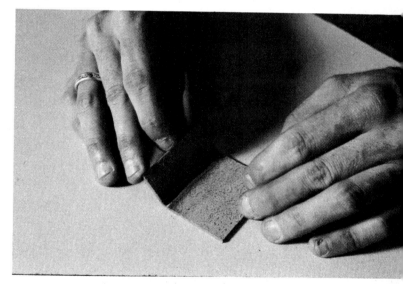

CREASING

Creasing is done when a piece is to bend in a particular spot. It is done simply by cutting a V-shaped groove on the fleshy side of the bend, halfway through the leather. The bend is made while the leather is still wet by folding over and lightly tapping the crease with a smooth mallet. The crease is then weighted with books and allowed to dry. When the leather is dry, the crease is permanent.

Figure 9. A hammer is used on wet leather during the creasing process. Prior to this step, a V-shaped groove was cut in the fleshy side of the bend, half way through the leather.

LACING

Lacing is the method of sewing or stitching pieces together with leather strips instead of with thread. Begin by laying the pieces together as they will be when the lacing is completed. Then, using a divider, work a line on the upper piece. The line should be parallel to and about 3/32" away from the edges to be laced. (Before the slits are stamped it may be necessary to glue the two leather pieces together to prevent slipping.) With the thonging

chisel, stamp slits along the line, going through both pieces of leather. To insure even spacing of slits, the first thong of the chisel should be placed in the last slit of the previously stamp slits.

There are three basic kinds of lacing techniques: the running stitch, the whipstitch, and the double buttonhole stitch.

Figure 10. When preparing to stitch leather with leather lace, a process called lacing, use a divider (below) to work a line 3/32" from the edge to be laced. Then, use a thonging chisel (right) to stamp slits along this line. Space the slits evenly by placing the first thong of the chisel in the last of the slits already stamped.

Skive the end of a piece of lacing, insert it into the flat needle, and tap the prongs to hold in the lace. Next, use an X-acto knife to cut a 1/8" slit at the other end of the lace, about 1/4" from the tip. To begin lacing, pass the needle through the first hole, from the back to the front, and then into the second hole, from the front to the back. Once through the second hole, the needle should be inserted through the slit in the end of the lace and pulled tight. This keeps the lace from coming undone. Continue passing the needle in and out of the holes. After passing through the last hole to the back, loop the lace twice around the previous stitch and pull tight.

The Whipstitch

Begin the whipstitch by inserting the needle through one piece of leather, from the fleshy side to the front. This means that as the lace comes out of the first hole, the tail end will be sandwiched between the two pieces of leather to be laced together. For the second stitch, the needle goes around the top of the seam, through the second hole (through both pieces of leather), and out the front again. Repeat the operation from back to front, going all the way around to the beginning.

Figure 12. Another basic lacing stitch is the whipstitch, which resembles a spiral binding. To finish the stitch, tie the lace off by running the needle through the back half of the first hole.

Figure 11. A basic lacing stitch, the running stitch, is similar to that used in sewing. Thread the needle through one end of the skived lacing, and cut a slit in the other end before beginning.

Tie off the lace by running the needle through the back half of the first hole so that the lace is again sandwiched between the two layers.

The Double Buttonhole Stitch

The double buttonhole stitch is begun by passing the needle from front to back through the first hole of both pieces to be laced, leaving out about 3" of the tail end. Make a full loop of lacing around the right hand side of the tail, front to back. Insert the needle through the second hole, and pull tight.

Figure 13. For the third lacing stitch, the double buttonhole stitch, pass the needle through the first hole; leave a tail of 3"; loop lace around tail; and insert through second hole. Pull tight.

Figure 14. For a double buttonhole stitch: insert needle under "X" created by the previous loop; pull tight; put needle through next hole; pull tight.

Next, insert the needle under the "X" created by the first loop, and pull tight. Insert the needle through the third hole, from front to back, and pull tight. Then, insert the needle under the "X" created by the previous stitch and pull tight. Continue the two-part procedure: first through the hole in front; and then through the "X." At the corners of an article it is necessary to go through two of the holes twice so that the lacing will fit smoothly.

After inserting the needle through the last hole and under the last "X," pull out part of the first stitch so that the tail end can be sandwiched between the two layers of leather. To end the lacing, insert the needle down through the first loop and halfway through the first hole. Pull tight and cut off the excess. Both ends of the lace are now sandwiched between the layers of leather (see illustration).

STITCHING

Another method of joining together parts of a project is by stitching or sewing with thread. To stitch together sections of a project, begin by using a divider to mark a line parallel to the edges. Also with the divider, mark off equal distances to designate where holes are to be punched. Holes should be made with an awl or a drill because making holes with a needle is very difficult.

Leather stitching is done with two needles, one at each end of the thread. The first needle is inserted through the first hole and pulled halfway through. Both needles are then inserted through the second hole from opposite directions and pulled tight. For the third hole, the needles are again inserted through the same hole from opposite directions. This method produces an extra strong double stitch which is a necessity for leather work.

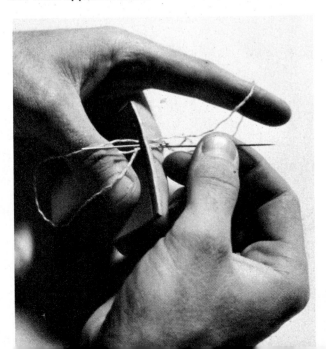

Figure 15. When stitching leather with thread, punch holes in the leather with an awl (above). Use two needles (below); insert both through the same hole but from opposite sides.

STRETCHING AND FORMING

Stretching is a process which alters the flatness of leather by stretching it over an existing form. The best forms are usually wooden, and it is often best to carve and shape the entire finished form. If, for instance, a pot is the project, it is necessary to make the entire form in wood first. To do this requires soft wood and common carpentry tools. When the wooden form is done, mark on the wood where the seams are to be located. Cut leather shapes large enough to cover the segments marked on the form, allowing enough for stretching and nailing. Immerse the leather in hot water for about 10 minutes until the leather is thoroughly wet. Begin stretching the leather and tacking it to the outside of the carved wood with small nails. Pull the leather tightly to avoid bumps, and allow it to dry for at least 48 hours. When it is dry, remove it and form each consecutive piece. Once all the pieces are formed, cut them to size according to the marks on the form and stitch them together.

Forming is a process similar to stretching, but two forms are used: one for a bottom and another slightly smaller matching shape to fit inside. Clamping the two together with wet leather between is known as forming. Forming is used for small and simple three-dimensional shapes, such as small boxes and bottles.

Begin by cutting the desired shape from a block of wood. This block is called the outside piece. The finished shape, called the inside piece, should not be any smaller than 2". Using a divider, mark a line around the top surface of the cut-out piece of wood to indicate the thickness of the leather. Cut away this margin all the way around the piece. This is done so that the leather and the wooden form will fit back into the hole left in the outside piece. If the article is to be a smoothly rounded shape, file the edge of the inside piece, for its shape will be the shape of the finished piece. Now soak the leather in water for 10 minutes. Next, place the leather over the inside piece and set the piece on plywood. Then take the outside piece and place it firmly over the inside piece. With three or four C-clamps, tighten the outer block until it is tight against the plywood. Allow the leather to dry for 48 hours; then remove and trim to size.

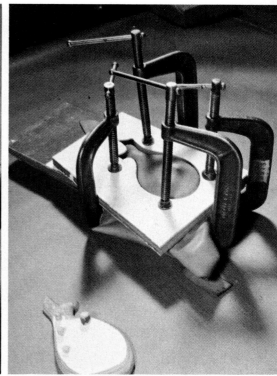

CARVING

Carving is the process of cutting and stamping a permanent design into the surface of leather. Once the leather has been conditioned (see *Conditioning* above) and the design has been traced, the next step is to cut the design into the leather. A swivel knife is used to cut a shallow groove into the surface. The first stamp used is the beveler, which slopes one side of the cut line to make some forms advance and others recede. This adds a three-dimensional quality to the design. The next stamp, a pear shader, makes gradual depressions which resemble shading. The next stamp is the background tool, available in a variety of sizes and textures. Background tools are used to give an overall even texture to the leather.

The beveler, the swivel knife, the pear shader, and the background tool are the basic tools that are almost always used in carving. In addition dozens of other stamps can be used to heighten the appearance of the carving. The choice is entirely individual. The stamps add surface texture to a design — the inventive use of stamps is always rewarding.

Figure 17. After leather is conditioned, it can be carved. The first step is to cut a groove from the surface with a swivel knife (above). Use a beveler to flatten one side of the cut line (below). Beveling produces a three-dimensional effect in the design. When a shaded effect is desired, use a pear shader (top right) to make slight depressions in the leather surface. When an even texture is desired, use a background tool (bottom right) on the background of the main design.

Figure 18. Two pieces of leather that are to be joined together must be cemented. Use a small piece of cardboard to spread the glue evenly on both pieces (left). When the glue is dry, press the pieces together slowly (right).

CEMENTING

Cementing is done to join two pieces of leather either for lining one piece with another, laminating, or cementing parts prior to stitching. Contact cement and rubber cement are the most effective glues, especially for lining. Do not use a glue which dries hard, as it will stiffen the leather. Begin the cementing process by cutting several small cardboard cards. These facilitate even spreading of the glue. Cut a piece of leather somewhat larger and slightly thinner than the area to be lined. Pour a small amount of glue onto the fleshy side of this piece of leather. Spread the glue evenly with one of the little cards, making sure all areas of the piece are covered. Repeat the operation on the piece to be lined. Allow both pieces to

dry. Beginning at one end, lay the thinner lining piece over the thicker main piece. Press the two pieces together gradually to avoid air pockets and wrinkles. When they are firmly together, trim off the excess lining.

For gluing pieces prior to stitching, white glue is often used in place of contact cement. It has the advantage of not dragging on the needle as it is pulled through the hole. Begin by applying a bead of white glue to one of the two sides to be joined — prior to punching any holes or slits. Join the two parts and slide them back and forth to distribute the glue evenly on both parts. Separate the two parts and let the glue dry slightly (1 to 3 minutes). Join the parts again and press them together with C-clamps for 45 minutes.

FASTENING

Snaps and rivets are handy and permanent for joining leather. They are particularly useful for straps and belts and for any item on which stitching or lacing is not practical.

Snaps

Snaps consist of four parts: the button and socket form the visible top half; the eyelet and stud form the invisible bottom half. Begin by punching a hole in the top piece of leather, making the hole large enough for the socket. Place the socket and leather on the anvil of the snap-setting tool (tool used to set in the snap). With the button over the socket and the concave end of the setting tool

Figure 19. Snaps used in leather work come in four parts. The button and socket are the visible parts, and the eyelet and the stud are the invisible components in the finished item.

over the button, strike with a mallet. One brisk blow is enough to set the snap top. For the bottom punch a hole the size of the eyelet. Insert the eyelet and place it over the opposite end of the set tool. Place the stud over the eyelet, the setting tool over the stud, and again strike with the mallet. The two halves are complete.

Figure 20. To set the snap top, use the mallet to strike the set tool one sharp blow (top). Place an anvil under the leather as shown. To set the bottom half of the snap, insert the eyelet, then the stud, and again strike the setting tool with the mallet (bottom).

Rivets

The easiest and most appropriate rivet for leather is known as a rapid rivet. It consists of two parts: the button and the base. Rivets come in several

lengths to accommodate various thicknesses. Begin by punching a hole through both pieces to be joined — the hole should be large enough to accommodate the button. Insert the base through

Figure 21. Rivets are a convenient way to join leather. The type most often used is the rapid rivet. It consists of a button and a base (right). Begin by punching a hole through the pieces to be joined (above).

the bottom of the hole, pat the surface, and, using the concave end of a snap set and a mallet, strike the button. The two parts are now permanently joined.

CLEANING

Once an article is constructed, it must be cleaned before dyeing or finishing. Dissolve 1 teaspoon of oxalic acid in 1 pint of water. Apply this solution to the leather with a clean rag and then allow the leather to dry. Oxalic acid is a mild bleaching agent and will dissolve grease and fingerprints — both of which will prevent an even dyeing.

DYEING

Dyeing is the process of coloring the leather. Dyes may be applied on small areas with a paint brush or over large areas with a sheep's-wool pad or a sponge. It is important to apply the dye evenly — this is done by applying the same amount with each stroke. Once the dye is dry, a second coat

Figure 22. Small areas of leather can be colored by applying dye with a small paint brush. Test the dye on a leather scrap before applying.

may be necessary for a uniform covering. It is often a good idea to test the dye on a leather scrap to get an idea of the result.

FINISHING

All leather should be finished to protect and preserve the surface. The best protection is leather lacquer, a clear coating which sinks deep into the leather and seals it against moisture and grease. The lacquer should be applied with a clean, lint-free rag and, if the leather is a natural color, the lacquer should be rubbed briskly into the surface. However, heavy rubbing on dyed surfaces may weaken some dyes. Once it is dry, the surface may be given a coat of paste wax or clear boot wax to heighten the shine.

Projects You Can Do

Three different items are suggested here as projects. Each involves a variety of skills, and it does not matter if a particular item is done first or last.

CARVED LEATHER BELT

1. Obtain a piece of 8-ounce cowhide which is long enough for a belt and at least 3" longer than the desired finished length.

2. Cut a straight edge through the selected piece, being careful to avoid waste. Use a mat knife and a metal straight edge.

Figure 23. When large areas of leather are to be dyed, use a wool pad or sponge to apply the dye evenly. A second coat may be necessary.

Figure 24. To begin a leather belt, cut the leather the desired length and width using a straight edge as a guide.

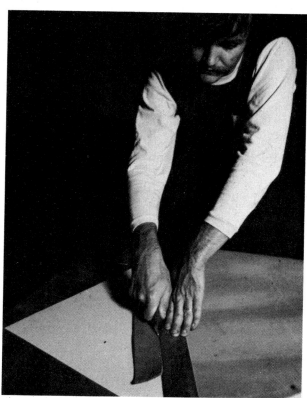

3. Measure the width of the belt and, with a knife and straight edge, cut the other side of the hide. Be certain to hold the straight edge firmly and to cut through the leather in one stroke.

4. Select the front of the belt and cut the point. Usually a curved point is best for the lead end of a thin belt and rounded corners best for the lead end of a wide belt.

Figure 25. Cut the point for the front of the belt. Make a curved point for a thin belt and rounded corners for a wide one. Then soak the leather in water for several hours, allow to dry, and remove the top corner edge of the belt.

5. Soak the leather in water and place it in a plastic bag for several hours.

6. Remove the belt from the bag and allow it to dry until the natural color returns.

7. With a common edger, remove the top edge of the belt all around.

8. With an edge creaser, firmly line and crease the edge all around.

9. Draw the design to be carved on a piece of paper, using the belt itself as a template to insure that the design will be the actual size of the belt.

10. Lay the finished design over the belt and, with a ball tracer, trace the image onto the belt. The pressure from the ball leaves a mark on the leather.

11. With a sharp swivel knife, cut the design into the surface of the leather.

12. With a beveler and a mallet, bevel the back-

ground side of the cuts made. This will make the foreground areas appear to protrude.

13. With a pear shader, stamp those areas which are to be shaded.

14. With any of the various other stamping tools, create patterns to be shaded on the surface of the design. Note: The marks of each tool vary depending on the angle from which the impression is made and the strength of the blow. When in doubt, test the stamp on a damp scrap of leather.

15. The final stamp is the background tool. It may be used over the solid areas or it may feather off away from the image. Again, experiment before beginning.

16. Once the stamping is done, many craftsmen use the swivel knife to add a few small, accenting cuts or details. Do this now, if desired.

17. Once the carving is finished, dampen the edge of the leather. With a circle edge slicker, smooth and polish the edge until it appears smooth. Just before finishing with lacquer, apply an edging compound and buff.

Figure 26. After a carving is finished, smooth and polish the edges of the leather. Use a circle edge slicker for this operation. Apply an edging compound and polish again.

18. Measure and decide upon the placement of the buckle. Skive the back of the belt at the point where the belt is to fold over.

19. If a buckle with a tongue is to be used, cut a slot for the tongue by punching a hole 3/8" on either side of the center of the fold and in the center of the belt. With a knife, cut two slits from hole to hole and remove the piece between holes.

20. With the buckle in place, punch the appropriate-size holes for the rivets or snaps to be used. Snaps are preferred if buckles are to be changed.

21. If a loop is needed to hold the tongue of the belt flat, it should be inserted between snaps or rivets.

22. Set rivets or snaps according to the directions in "Basic Procedures".

23. Put on the belt and mark the spot for the hole where the belt is most comfortable; punch the hole.

24. It is wise to punch two additional holes 1/2" on either side of the center hole to allow for adjustment.

25. If any coloring or dyeing is to be done, it should be done at this point. The leather should be dry. Follow the directions in "Basic Procedures."

26. Finish the belt with a coating of clear leather lacquer applied with a soft rag. Note: Burnishing the edge with a round slicker is possible while the lacquer is wet.

Figure 27. When using a buckle with a tongue, cut a slot for the tongue by punching a hole on either side of the center of the fold; then cut two slits from hole to hole (left). When using a buckle that requires a loop to hold the tongue of the belt flat, insert the loop between snaps or rivets and set them in place (above). Punch a hole at the point at which the belt is most comfortable; punch additional holes on either side to allow for adjustment.

FORMING A HANGING POT

1. From a square piece of 1" thick plywood, cut a form from the center. This form will be the mold for half of the finished pot — two halves will be shaped from leather and sewn together. The form should be cut out with a saber saw, which is a saw that will not destroy the outer piece of plywood.

2. From around the perimeter of the hole in the plywood, cut an amount equal to the thickness of the leather to be shaped. For example, if the leather is 8 ounces thick, remove 1/8" all around the hole.

3. Select an 8-ounce, vegetable-tanned leather and cut a shape large enough to completely cover the form, allowing at least 1/2" extra for error.

4. Soak the leather in hot water until completely saturated.

5. Lay the wet leather over the hole in the plywood and force the form into the hole and the leather with it.

6. It may be necessary to weight the form in place if it has a tendency to come out.

7. This should be allowed to dry for 48 hours.

8. Remove the first piece of shaped and repeat the operation for the other half of the pot. If the pot is to be exactly symmetrical, the operation will be the same. If the pot is not to be symmetrical, the reverse side of the wooden form will be used. Otherwise, the two shapes will not match when placed together.

9. After the second piece is dry, remove and trim both pieces allowing just enough room for stitching.

10. On the top of each half-section, carefully mark off the stitching holes with a divider. Be certain that each half has the same number of holes marked.

11. With an awl, punch the holes.

12. With white glue, spot glue the two halves together, using pins to make the holes coincide. Allow 45 minutes for drying.

13. Using a long piece of linen thread with needles at both ends, begin stitching the halves together. Remember each needle carries the thread through each hole from opposite directions.

14. Choose a place on each side to stitch on loops for hanging

15. Cut two long laces to attach to the loops for hanging.

16. Finish the pot with clear lacquer.

CHROME-TANNED WALLET

1. Write down the measurements for the pieces of a wallet. (The design of the wallet can be based on one you already have.) Draw outlines of the pieces on paper and cut them out so that they may be pinned together. If the paper pieces fit together properly, take the pieces apart and smooth them out.

2. Lay out the back of the wallet on 2-ounce chrome-tanned leather. Cut it out, adding a 1/4" allowance all around for folding.

3. Cut the lining from the same leather, making certain it is the size of the back template.

4. With a skife, skive away half the thickness of the back along a margin 3/8" from all edges.

5. Apply contact cement evenly over the fleshy side of both the back and the lining.

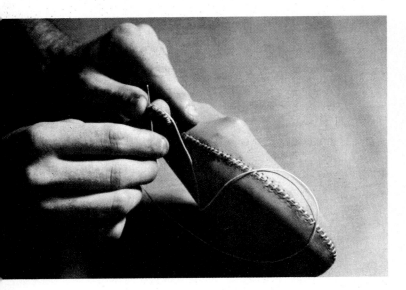

Figure 28. Linen thread is used to stitch together the two sides of a hanging pot. Remember that the thread is worked with two needles, inserted from opposite sides.

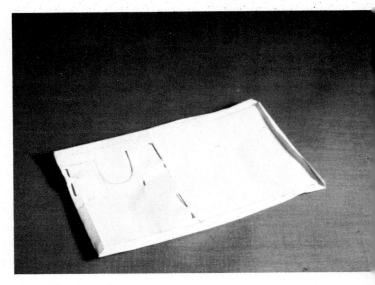

Figure 29. To begin a wallet, make a paper pattern of an old wallet. Draw and cut out a pattern for each part of the wallet, and pin the pieces together for fit.

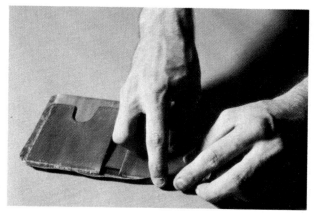

Figure 30. Steps in making a wallet include: applying the glue to the fleshy side of both the back and the lining after both pieces have been skived (above); cutting slits between the corners of the lining and those of the back to allow for folding (top right); folding the edges of the back (center right); and sewing around the edges using a sewing machine (bottom right).

6. Position the lining and lay it down slowly, removing air bubbles.

7. With a small, stiff paint brush, spread cement around the edge of the lining and allow it to dry.

8. At the four corners, cut a small slit from the corner of the lining to the corner of the back to allow for folding.

9. The divider should be cut from the same leather and be the same length as the liner, but 1/4″ less in width.

10. The divider should be cemented around the two side edges and the bottom edge and then glued to the edges of the liner.

11. The inside also has glued edges. This part should be made according to individual preference — some people like flaps, some like pockets, and others like plastic folders. Readymade insides can also be purchased.

12. The side edges and the bottom edge should be attached to the divider as in step 10.

13. With the liner, the divider, and the inside glued in place around the edges, apply glue to the

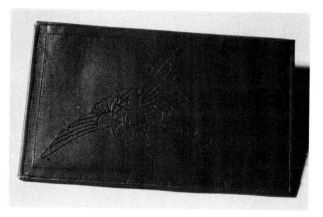

outer two side edges, to the bottom of the inside, and along the top edge of the liner. Allow the glue to dry.

14. Fold the edges of the back over to join the recently glued edges in step 13.

15. With the inside down, machine sew around the four sides about 3/32″ from the edge.

For Additional Reading

Cherry, Raymond, **General Leathercraft,** McKnight and McKnight.
Meilach, Dona Z., **Contemporary Leather,** Regnery.
10;hide

Early American Decorative Painting

Painted designs, authentically reproduced on tin and wood by early American craftsmen, is still a popular craft.

Country painting, one technique of Early American decoration, is a folk art which originated in the United States in the eighteenth century. It is not "tole" painting, which is the French word for sheet iron, nor is it "Pennsylvania Dutch," a kind of painting stemming from German folk art. The craftsmen of this early American era simply called it "japanned ware," the proper name of the truly American craft.

Figure 2. Leaves and flowers adorn this tin and brass box, made in the United States between 1825 and 1860. The origin of these pieces can be identified by the variations in their colors and patterns. (Courtesy, The Henry Francis du Pont Winterthur Museum.)

Edward Pattison, an immigrant from Ireland, is credited with the establishment of the tin industry in this country. He introduced the manufacture of tinware in Connecticut, trained many apprentices, and encouraged extensive peddling of tin products. He started making handmade, tin-plated kitchenware about 1750. The early pieces were left undecorated, but, near the turn of the century, the ware was japanned. This meant that the tin was given an asphaltum basecoat and dried by heat, an imitation of oriental lacquering. The pieces were then decorated or "flowered." Whole families were often involved in creating this tinware, with the women doing the decorating. Tin peddlers carried the japanned ware

Figure 1. A tin pot (opposite), suitable for coffee or tea, is dated between 1830 and 1860 and probably came from Pennsylvania. (Courtesy, The Henry Francis du Pont Winterthur Museum.)

from the northeast tin centers as far west as the Mississippi River and as far south as New Orleans.

Many shops and craftsmen clung to certain established styles in decoration so that the source of these can often be identified. One of these was Zachariah Stevens of Stevens Plains, Maine, who opened his shop in 1798; another Maine craftsman was Oliver Buckley. This tin center was, at one time, the headquarters for over a hundred peddlers. Maine designs were of a style similar to canvas painting and were on background colors of white, yellow, red, and black.

One of the best-known tin businesses was owned by Oliver Filley of Bloomfield, Connecticut. He opened branch shops in Elizabeth, New Jersey, Lansingburg, New York (near Troy), and Philadelphia, Pennsylvania; later his son opened a shop in St. Louis, Missouri. The decoration on the ja-

Figure 3. A bold floral pattern enlivens this tin coffeepot, dated between 1800 and 1850. Decorative painting of household objects was popular as early as colonial times in America. (Courtesy, The Henry Francis du Pont Winterthur Museum.)

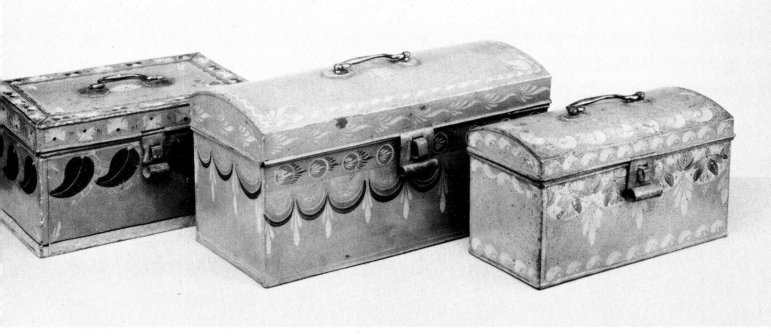

Figure 4. These three boxes, made of tin and brass, are decorated with painstakingly symmetrical designs. They date back to the period between 1825 and 1860. The largest is 6¼ " high; the smallest, 4¾ " high. (Courtesy, The Henry Francis du Pont Winterthur Museum.)

panned ware of the Filley shops was often symmetrical or characterized by white bands under designs of fruit or flowers with several fine, black brush strokes. Both types of painting often appeared on asphaltum backgrounds.

It seems logical that some of the Filley apprentice painters in Pennsylvania should have been natives of that state who adapted these Connecticut patterns to appeal to the local people. The Pennsylvania designs were more colorful and employed more blue.

Two New York tin centers were operated by men trained in Connecticut. One was Aaron Butler of Greenville whose daughters, especially Ann, are well known for their decorating. Their work can be recognized by profuse ornamentation: tulips; rosebuds; red stems; six- and eight-pointed stars;

and the design, often on a white band with many groups of tiny dots scattered throughout. The other tin center was at Fly Creek and was owned by Stephen North. Mercy North, his daughter, is known for her decorated pieces containing red and white bands with many combinations of beautifully executed brush strokes.

Much research on Early American decoration and its techniques has been done by Esther Stevens Brazer, a descendant of Zachariah Stevens of Maine. Her book, *Early American Decoration*, published in 1940, assembles the results of her research. After her death in 1945, a group of her students organized a guild in her memory. That guild is now The Historical Society of Early American Decoration, Inc., with headquarters at Cooperstown, New York.

Figure 5. This painted tray dates from the period between 1830 and 1860. (Courtesy, The Henry Francis du Pont Winterthur Museum.)

Common Terms Used In Early American Decorative Painting

Apple Tray: a square basket, originally created in 1840, with a 4″ floor and four 3″ curved sides.

Asphaltum: a solution of mineral asphalt mixed with varnish, which makes a dark brown varnish. When applied to bright tin, a brown finish results, the tone depending on the thickness of asphaltum applied.

Background Colors: colors applied to articles in flat enamel, giving an opaque finish.

Band: wide stripe used on boxes, trays, etc., and usually white or red.

Base Coats: the first color applied in a design, over which other colors, usually transparent, will be painted.

Border: the area within the boundary line or rim of the decorated piece.

Country Painting: brush-stroke patterns on wood and tinware.

Country Tin: tinware and utensils made by country tinsmiths of the eighteenth and early nineteenth centuries and often decorated with country painting.

Cut Corner Tray: an octagonal tray, sometimes called a coffin tray, with a 3/4″ flange and usually painted with country designs.

Flat Enamel: paint which dries to a soft, opaque, dull finish.

Hard Gloss Varnish: a finishing material of gum dissolved in linseed oil, used to give a hard, protective finish.

Japan: black asphaltum varnish for coating metal which produces lacquer-like results.

Japan Colors: pigment ground in japan for an opaque look.

Medium: a liquid used with paints to give fluency.

Oil Colors: pigments ground in oil which are slow drying; some colors are transparent, others semitransparent.

Quills: soft, pliant brushes made of camel hair.

Sanding Primer: an undercoat used to prepare a metal object for painting.

Satin Finish Varnish: varnish which dries to a soft, matte finish.

Supersee: common name for frosted acetate, used for painting patterns.

Tin: thin sheet of iron coated with tin; tinplate.

Wet/Dry Sandpaper: sandpaper which can be used dry or with water.

Basic Equipment And Supplies

It is most important to use only the equipment outlined in this section. Other kinds of brushes and paints will not produce the same effects. Local art supply stores and paint and hardware stores handle most of the items and will generally order the others if requested. There are also many mail order supply houses which carry supplies specifically for Early American decoration.

1. Brushes. 3/4" long, square-tipped quills, #3 and #4, and handles. These are used to paint base coats, and all sizes of brush strokes. Pointed, sable watercolor brush, #2; used for making very small brush strokes and thin, fine, short lines, dots, and curliques. 1" long liner quill, #1, with handle; used for long, fine lines and strokes as in veins, and also for striping. Oxhair one-stroke 1" brush: used for background colors and for varnish coats. 1" polybrush: sponge rather than a bristle brush, used for varnish coats.

2. Japan Paints. Striping white, chrome yellow medium, signcraft red. Available in cans and, when mixed with varnish, used for brush strokes and base coats.

3. Artists' Oil Colors. Alizarin crimson, prussian blue, raw umber, burnt umber, lampblack. Mixed with varnish and used for over strokes or mixed with other colors.

4. Background Paints. Flat enamel. Black is used most for backgrounds, but other flat subdued colors may be used such as mustard, antique red, or bayberry green; available at hardware stores and often in antiquing kits.

5. Varnishes. Clear gloss varnish. Used as a medium with japan and oil colors and also for finishing and protective coats; available at paint supply stores or hardware stores. Satin finish varnish: dull, matte finish used as a final coat. Sealer: thin liquid used to seal the grain of wood. Rust preventive. This stops the rust from developing under the paint; one type is naval jelly.

Other supplies include: (1) tracing paper; (2) tracing pen; (3) supersee; (4) black shiny paper for practicing brush strokes, experimenting with colors before putting them on a pattern, or for use in back of a pattern to show up colors; (5) palette; (6) palette knife; (7) practice board — a piece of cardboard covered with shiny black paper to practice brush strokes on and which can be cleaned with turpentine and used repeatedly; (8) board — a piece of masonite, or smooth, heavy cardboard about 14" by 18", necessary for fastening on tracings and patterns for painting; (9) pure gum turpentine; (10) lard oil or olive oil for dipping brushes after use and cleaning to keep them soft; (11) tack rag, a slightly sticky cheese-cloth, for dusting; (12) bottle caps, about 1" in diameter to hold varnish while painting; (13) small jar or deep bottle cap; (14) lava soap and Q-tips for removing unwanted marks; (15) wet/dry sandpaper, #600; (16) sponge; (17) masking tape; (18) white pencil for marking off measurements; and (19) lint-free rag.

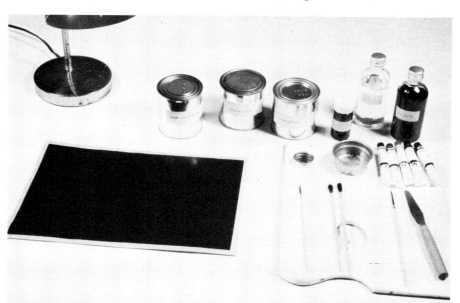

Figure 6. Special supplies and materials, such as Japan paints, are needed for decorative painting. Most of the items are available at art supply stores.

Basic Procedures

The basis of all Early American decorative painting is the brush stroke. Since country painting is essentially brush stroke painting, the importance of learning this technique is obvious. After some practice, a rhythm develops and with it much satisfaction in perfecting the strokes. By following the instructions carefully and by practicing, brush strokes will soon become lovely designs for decorative painting.

HOW TO PAINT BRUSH STROKES

Sitting in a good light, place the palette to the right, and the practice board in front of you. (Note: For left-handed persons, reverse the order, as well as the directions.) Keep the lint-free rag in the lap, handy for cleaning brushes.

Pour some varnish into a clean 1" bottle cap on the palette. Also pour some turpentine (for cleaning brushes) into a larger cap or small wide-mouthed bottle. Opening a can of chrome yellow medium, dip out about 1/8 teaspoonful with a palette knife and place on the palette.

Dip the #3 quill about halfway into the varnish, then into the edge of the paint. Stroke the brush back and forth on the palette many times to load or "dress" it. The consistency of the paint should be like heavy cream.

Figure 7. Mastering the brush stroke is a key procedure in decorative painting. Practice the strokes slowly and carefully until a slow, steady rhythm is developed.

Hold the brush like a pencil; put it down until about half of the brush is on the practice board and the tip is at this angle: / . Pulling down slightly and to the right, begin lifting the brush until just the narrow edge of the brush is on the paper, making the tail of the stroke. The stroke should look like an inverted eyebrow. Do the same stroke over and over until a rhythm is achieved: down, pull, up; down, pull, up. This is a slow steady rhythm; do not try to go too fast and do try to lift the brush gradually, beginning to lift it almost as soon as it is put down. Practice one or two pages and when comfortable with the brush, try a stroke going in the opposite direction, which will look like an upright eyebrow. Start the brush at this angle: \ . Pull up and to the right and follow through as with the first stroke. After learning this stroke, try making groups of strokes. Make the middle one first, then one on each side, bringing them to the same point as the first one.

The "S" Stroke

Having stroked the brush back and forth, notice that it has a wide side and a knife-thin side. The stroke above was begun with the wide side and ended with the edge. In making the "S" stroke, place the brush with just the tip on the practice board at the / angle; pull down slightly at this angle, then, putting more pressure on the brush, pull to the right and down, lifting and pulling to the left again for a fine line.

The Straight Stroke

For this stroke, reach out a little with the brush, put it down, and lift while drawing it straight toward you until there is a point.

Circles

Trace a circle on your practice board. Make two or even three strokes around the outer edge of the circle to give a firm outline. Fill this in with broad strokes, taking as few strokes as possible. Stroke out the paint on the palette, then with the tip of the brush, smooth out any ridges with a very light touch.

Leaves

For a heart-shaped leaf, paint the outer edges with brush strokes, as with the circle, but following the

#4 QUILL

#3 QUILL

#2 POINTED BRUSH

#1 QUILL LINER

Figure 8. These are samples of brush strokes made with quills of three different sizes and with a pointed brush. Note that each implement is designed for a specific type of stroke.

outlines; then, fill in with broad strokes, and smooth out any ridges. For leaves with rounded points, start at the top, making brush strokes toward the bottom. For pointed leaves, start at the bottom, bringing strokes to a point for the pointed tips.

Dots and Curliques

Use a #2 pointed watercolor brush for these. Make a soupy mixture with the paint; dip the end of the brush into the mixture. Hold the brush straight up, not at an angle as before, and very lightly touch the brush to the board. This should make a perfectly round dot. To make the curliques using the regular paint mixture, rest the right hand on the left and, again holding the brush straight up and down, move the tip into the circular motion of the pattern.

Helpful Tips in Brush Stroking

The size of a brush stroke depends on how much pressure is put on the brush. For a large stroke, press down all the way and let the brush spread out, then begin lifting. For a smaller stroke, use only the end of the brush. Practice the strokes listed on the chart, using the brush indicated.

If strokes seem runny or weak in color, add more paint to the mixture. If strokes have ridges or a ragged end, add more varnish to make the paint flow more freely. In both cases, be sure to stroke the brush back and forth on the palette to get a proper mixture. A stroke should be smooth and without streaks. Practice to learn the right consistency for the paint.

Hold the brush correctly.

Clean the brush occasionally — both paints and varnish dry out after exposure to air.

Make a *brush stroke* — do not draw or merely fill in the tracing.

If there are puddles on the side of the strokes, the brush is overloaded.

COPYING THE PATTERN

Place a sheet of tracing paper over the design, fastening securely with clips. Trace the pattern carefully with a fine-point pen. After tracing, place the pattern on the work board. Cut a piece of supersee the same size as the tracing and place it over the tracing, dull side up. Fasten both papers to the board with masking tape. Now it is time to paint the design, following these steps:

1. Set up the palette as for brush strokes, and dip a bit of red paint from the can onto the palette. If the brush has been kept in lard oil, clean it by dipping it in turpentine. Using the brush stroke technique and the #4 square-tipped quill, paint the base coats in the design. (In some designs, the base coats may be yellow or white. In such a case, follow directions for the pattern.) Try not to just fill in the spaces, but make every stroke a brush stroke. This is very important; it makes the difference between a stiff, unnatural look, and one

Figure 9. On tracing paper that has been clipped over the design, trace the pattern with a fine-point pen (left). Paint the base coat, in this case red, with a #4 square-tipped quill. Use the brush stroke technique carefully (right) to avoid filling in broad areas.

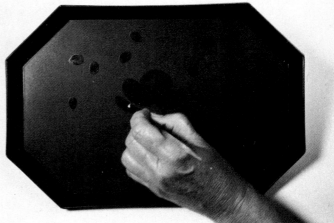

which has rhythm and feeling. *In all steps, let paint dry 24 hours.* After painting, clean brushes thoroughly in turpentine, dip in lard oil, and place in a position where they cannot be bent.

2. Squeeze out about 1/4" of paint from the tube of alizarin crimson, and about half that much of burnt umber. With a palette knife, add a touch of burnt umber to the alizarin crimson to tone it down. Mix the paint and varnish as for the first brush strokes, stroke out, and apply the strokes where shown. Since this is an oil color, the stroke will appear transparent. These strokes are the shadows and should be a medium tone — not too dark, not too light.

3. The white strokes create the highlights on the flower or fruit, and should be transparent and light. To get this mixture, add just a touch of white paint to a drop of the varnish on the palette and stroke it out many times, then test the color and texture on a piece of black paper. If the color is correct, but runny, stroke out more; if it is too white, add more varnish and stroke out. Apply white strokes where indicated. This stroke should not cover the alizarin stroke entirely; rather, it is usually half on the alizarin stroke and half on the red base coat.

4. Notice that green was not included in the list of paints. This is because the greens in country painting vary and must be matched to the pattern being copied. The most common color is a subdued green with a slight olive cast. To make

green: squeeze some prussian blue on the palette, then dip out some yellow and some red in separate places. Add a small amount of blue to the yellow until a medium shade of green is acquired. Then add red, a bit at a time, to tone down the color. Use the palette knife when mixing colors. To make the green darker, add more blue; to make it lighter, add more yellow; to tone it down, add red.

5. Put some chrome yellow medium and some burnt umber on the palette. Add a touch of burnt umber to the yellow and mix with the palette knife; this is to tone it down. Here again, the yellow must be matched to the pattern, as the shade varies. Paint all yellow strokes, dots, curliques, etc., except the thin yellow color which is used as overstrokes or veins on the leaves. For this thin color, add more varnish to the paint until it is thin and transparent. Stroke paint out on the palette so it will not be runny.

6. If black veins or strokes appear in the pattern, they are generally applied now. Mix lampblack with varnish and apply as directed. Use the brush which best fits the type of stroke desired.

7. When this part of the pattern is dry, do the striping. This is done by using the #1 quill liner and pulling it toward yourself in a straight line. The width of the line will depend on the pressure on the brush. If a fine, thin line is desired, use just the tip. For a heavier line, press more on the brush.

Figure 10. Next, mix some alizarin crimson with burnt umber, according to directions, and apply accent strokes on the red base coat (left). For the white touches on the flowers (right), add a little white paint to the varnish, and apply over the base coat and alizarin strokes.

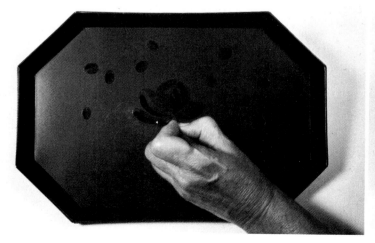

Figure 11. Because green shades in country painting vary widely, mix green paint as instructed to match the pattern being used. Apply green for leaves and other areas (left). Yellow is applied twice: once for the strokes and dots (right); the second time, for veins on the leaves after it is mixed with varnish.

8. When the pattern is completed and dry, varnish it with the polybrush. Pour a little varnish into a small paper cup or 3″ clean jar top; dip the polybrush in about 3/4″, then stroke it out on the pattern, smoothing out the varnish. Notice that the supersee turns clear as it is varnished. When the pattern is dry, fasten it to a piece of cardboard with Scotch tape. Fasten the tracing to the other side of the board. This becomes a permanent pattern which can be used many times on several different articles.

PREPARING AN ARTICLE FOR DECORATING

To paint a piece of tin which has a coat of paint on it, remove the old paint with paint remover and rinse thoroughly. If the tin has no paint on it, clean it with detergent and water to remove any oil or dirt and let dry thoroughly. If there is any rust at all, treat the tin with a rust preventive since rusting continues, even under paint. Rusticide or naval jelly can be used for this purpose. Again clean, then sand the whole piece, where necessary, until smooth. A damp sponge is useful for cleaning the article while preparing it. Clean the surface with a tack rag to remove all dust; now it is ready for the first coat of paint.

Sanding Primer

Apply one coat of sanding primer with the 1″ background brush. Use a light touch and just the end of the brush so that there will be no ridges when the paint dries. Allow to dry for 24 hours, then sand with wet/dry sandpaper.

Sanding

Using wet/dry sandpaper, rub down the primer coat. This is done by tearing off a piece of sandpaper about 1″ x 2″, folding it, and dipping it into water. Sand until smooth. Clean with a damp sponge.

Figure 12. To prepare a tin piece for painting, remove any old paint. However, if the piece is unpainted, clean it thoroughly with detergent. If there is still any trace of rust on the tin after the piece has been prepared, apply a coat of rust preventive. Use rusticide or naval jelly.

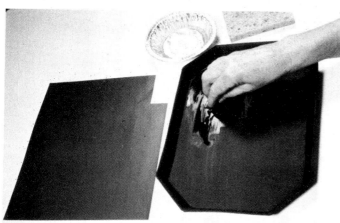

Figure 13. Apply background color (top), then sand carefully (bottom).

Background Color

Clean the surface with a tack rag. With background brush, apply one coat of black flat enamel, or another flat color, first thinning the paint until it flows from the brush like light cream. Use the tip of the brush to smooth out the paint and beware of ridges and drips. Apply a second coat of the flat enamel and, when this is dry, sand as with the sanding primer. When the coat is smooth, it is time to do the design. (Follow the same process for the reverse side if necessary.)

If working on a light-colored background, it is best to give the article a coat of varnish to protect it from marks and smudges. Sand before decorating.

Wood Background

Sand wood smooth with a medium-coarse sandpaper. Wipe clean with a damp sponge, and apply two coats of a wood sealer, 24 hours apart. Sand again with wet/dry #600 sandpaper. If the wood is going to remain the natural color, give it one coat of varnish and sand. To stain the wood, apply one coat of stain after the first sanding, then apply one coat of varnish and sand again. If painting wood, give it two coats of thinned flat paint, 24 hours apart, and sand lightly.

PAINTING THE ARTICLE

Now that the piece is prepared and has a smooth surface, it is time to decorate the article. Cut a piece of tracing paper the exact size of the piece to be decorated. Place the paper over the pen and ink tracing, and, after deciding exactly where and how the design is to appear on the article, center and place it correctly. Trace the design on the paper with a pencil.

For a dark background, rub a piece of chalk over the back of the new tracing, and then with the hand, rub off as much excess powder as possible. If working on a light background, rub a pencil over the back of the tracing and rub off excess with the hand. Place this tracing on the article, fastening it in one or two places with masking tape so it will not slip. Now trace the design with a sharp pencil and the design will appear on the painted surface. If tracing a design on a wooden piece, do not bear down too hard, as it will make an indentation in the wood which cannot be removed. Remove the tracing.

Figure 14. Trace the design to be used on the piece. First, make a tracing with pencil and paper. Then, use chalk for a light background and pencil for a dark background, as directed.

Follow directions for each pattern until it is time for striping and the brush stroke border. At this point, *before* proceeding with the striping and border, the article must be varnished so that corrections may be made more easily. Before varnishing, remove any unwanted smudges, fingerprints, or tracing marks with a sponge or Q-tip and lava soap. Clean with a damp sponge and when dry, clean surface with tack rag.

Varnishing

Use a 1" polybrush to varnish the surface. Varnish in a good light so that all areas are covered and there are no drips or dry spots. Varnish will go on more smoothly if it is at room temperature or warmed slightly (Place it in a cup of warm water a few minutes before using). It is a good idea to transfer the varnish from the can to small-topped bottles to keep it from being exposed to too much air. The article being varnished should also be at room temperature or warmed slightly. Clean polybrush in turpentine and detergent and water, or a household cleaner with grease-cutting solvents. Let dry before using again. A 1" background brush may also be used for varnishing.

Striping

Mix some burnt umber with the chome yellow medium, making a "dirty yellow." Use the liner quill for striping, and, holding it with the thumb and forefinger, place the outer fingers on the edge of the article and pull the liner toward you in a steady even line in the place to be striped. Striping is usually done along the edges of an article to accentuate the form and act as a frame for the painting.

Brush Stroke Border

Apply the brush stroke border when the striping is dry. This usually follows the line of striping and may be a line of single brush strokes, or a combination of strokes.

Finishing

When decorating is complete, and the article has been cleaned of any spots or smudges, give the article two coats of varnish, 24 hours apart, front and back. Allow it to dry for several days. When decorating a tray or another piece which will receive hard wear, rub it down with wet/dry sandpaper until smooth. Do not be alarmed if the piece appears to be gray — this will disappear when varnish or wax is applied. Give it another coat of varnish and let dry for several days. Rub this down in the same manner and, when smooth, apply a coat of spray wax, polish it, and repeat. This will give a hard, protective finish.

For an article such as a canister which will be used for decorative purposes, rub down with wet/dry sandpaper until smooth, and apply a coat of satin finish varnish. If the first coat does not cover completely, it may be necessary to apply a second coat.

Figure 15. Varnish the surface, using a 1" polybrush (left). Be sure to apply the varnish smoothly and evenly; leave no dry spots or bumps. A liner quill is used for striping (right). Striping is used to accent the edge, or border, of the piece.

Projects You Can Do

The following projects include all of the basic steps in Early American decorative painting and require a minimum of supplies. Other brushes and colors can be added later. However, these techniques are employed in all categories of decorative painting. The patterns are basic, and can be done by a beginner. Many pieces of old tin can be found in attics, flea markets, and antique shops, and there are many which lend themselves to decorating. Reproductions of early tin are also available, some with the background colors completed.

Most of these patterns are shown as they were used originally, but they can be adapted to other pieces. For instance, the cut corner tray pattern could be used on a canister, a box top, or a round tray. The coffee pot pattern could be used on a pitcher, a coal scuttle, a large canister, or even a tray. The border design on the canister could be used as a border on a box, around the bottom of a small canister, or a cut corner tray, which is where the design was used originally. The pattern on the bread board is a candle sconce pattern. Keep in mind the proportion of the piece and the pattern, and be sure it is appropriate to the piece being decorated.

Other objects which can be decorated are wastebaskets, wooden bowls, watering cans, letter holders or candle holders. Directions in "Basic Procedures" should be followed along with the step-by-step directions given with each pattern.

CUT CORNER TRAY

1. Prepare tray with black background according to directions.

Figure 16. *This is the pattern for a cut corner tray. For best results on the finished piece, follow the color key carefully.*

R — Red
AC— Alizarin Crimson
W — White
G — Green
Y — Yellow
TY— Thin Yellow
DY— Dirty Yellow

2. Trace design and transfer to tray.

3. Paint red base coats. If base coat does not appear to be quite solid looking, apply a second coat the next day. Always paint the entire base coat; green goes on top.

4. Paint alizarin crimson strokes.

5. Paint thin white strokes.

6. Paint all green leaves and strokes.

7. Add a touch of burnt umber to the yellow, and make yellow strokes, stems, and thin yellow veins in leaves.

8. Give tray a coat of varnish.

9. Do curliques and striping on the tray floor, and striping along edge of tray.

10. Do border brush strokes.

11. Finish as directed.

Figure 17. Apply border brush strokes to the tray (top) and finish as directed (bottom).

R — Red   W — White   G — Green
A — Alizarin Crimson   Y — Yellow

Figure 18. This is the pattern for a breadboard. Again, follow the color key exactly.

BREADBOARD

1. Prepare board according to directions for preparing wood.

2. Trace design and transfer it to board.

3. Paint red strokes.

4. Do alizarin strokes.

5. Do thin white strokes.

6. Paint the green strokes and do striping. (Piece was varnished in step 1 when the board was prepared.)

7. Paint yellow strokes and green border strokes.

Figure 19. The finished breadboard is a handsome object, and a functional one as well. A decorated breadboard would make an ideal gift for anyone interested in early American design.

COFFEE POT

1. Prepare coffee pot with black background.

2. Trace pattern and transfer to pot. Reverse pattern and trace on other side.

3. Paint red base coats. It will be easier on this piece to do the color on one side at a time, unless the artist is very careful not to smear the wet paint.

4. Paint alizarin strokes.

R — Red
AC— Alizarin Crimson
W — White
G — Green
Y — Yellow
TY— Thin Yellow
DY— Dirty Yellow
B — Black

Figure 20. This pattern for a coffeepot comes complete with color key. Note that the colors are coordinated to those used on the cut corner tray.

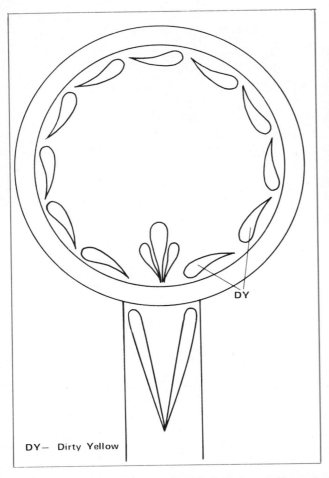

DY— Dirty Yellow

Figure 21. This is the pattern for the coffeepot lid. It is used in conjunction with the main pattern for the pot, shown on page 475. When painted a dirty yellow, this color provides a nice contrast with the black background.

Figure 22. The finished coffeepot is neat and professional looking. This project can be done easily and quickly by the inexperienced craftsman. The inspiration for this design came from nineteenth-century pots, which are now expensive antiques.

5. Paint thin white strokes.

6. Paint green strokes and leaves.

7. Paint yellow stems, strokes, and dots.

8. Paint black veins in leaves.

9. Paint thin yellow on green strokes and leaves.

10. Varnish.

11. Do striping around top, botton, and lid.

12. Do brush strokes around lid and on handle.

13. Finish as directed.

YELLOW WOODEN TRAY

1. Paint mustard yellow background on tray, preparing as directed; varnish and sand.

2. Trace design and transfer to tray.

Figure 23. Making a round wooden plate is easy and rewarding. Follow the basic procedures in the text for preparing a wood object. The background color is a mustard yellow. This plate can be mounted and hung on the wall, or it can be displayed on a plate hinge.

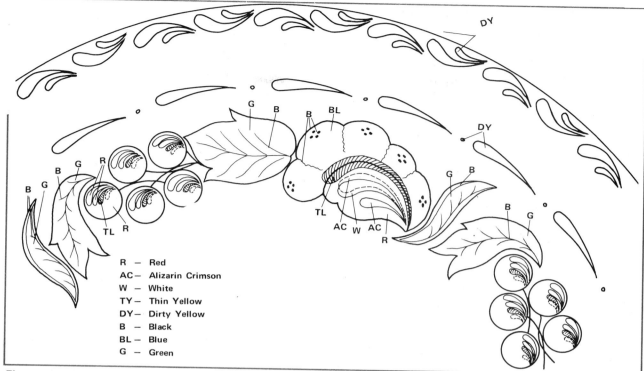

R — Red
AC— Alizarin Crimson
W — White
TY — Thin Yellow
DY— Dirty Yellow
B — Black
BL— Blue
G — Green

Figure 24. This is the basic pattern for the wooden plate shown on the opposite page. A color key is included for the artist's guidance. Note that the basic pattern is repeated four times to form a circle on the plate.

3. Paint all red, keeping cherries perfectly round.

4. Paint alizarin strokes.

5. Paint blue sections by mixing white and blue until a medium color is reached; add raw umber to tone it until there is a "dirty" blue on the palette.

6. Paint thin white strokes.

7. Paint in green leaves, making the paint a little thinner than on other patterns. This should also have just a touch more blue than used previously.

8. Add burnt umber to yellow. Do thin yellow strokes and striping. (Piece has been varnished.) Stripes may be marked around outside using a white pencil in a compass: make the pencil a little shorter than the pointed end of the compass, and hold the pointed end over the rim of the tray, the pencil in from the edge about 1/4 inch. Pull along toward you, turning the tray as you go. Cover the point with masking tape so it will not scratch. When you paint the stripe, pull the Liner Quill along the white pencil line.

9. Do black strokes and veins, using #2 brush and liner quill.

10. Do brush stroke borders.

11. Finish as directed.

SHAKER

1. Prepare tin with black background.

2. Trace pattern and transfer it to tin.

3. Paint red base coats; give second coat if necessary.

Figure 25. This shaker is another project for the ambitious craftsman. The background color is black and the flowers are mainly red.

R — Red
AC — Alizarin Crimson
W — White
G — Green
Y — Yellow
TY — Thin Yellow
B — Black

Figure 26. *Two final patterns are given for decorative painting projects. One is for a shaker (above), illustrated on page 477. The other is for a canister (below), illustrated on the facing page. Color keys are supplied, as is customary.*

Y = YELLOW
R = RED
BL = BLACK
G = GREEN
DY = DIRTY YELLOW

4. Paint alizarin crimson strokes.

5. Paint thin white strokes.

6. Paint green leaves and strokes.

7. Paint yellow strokes.

8. Paint black veins in leaves.

9. Paint thin yellow strokes and veins in leaves.

10. Varnish and stripe.

11. Do border strokes and strokes on handle in dirty yellow.

12. Finish as directed.

CANISTER

1. Prepare background by painting with antique red flat enamel and varnish.

2. Paint white band on as follows: Measure, and mark with white pencil, 1¾" strip to be painted. Place some white paint on the palette and mix in several drops of varnish until thinned out. Add a touch of burnt umber to make it off-white, then add a few drops of turpentine. The mixture should be quite runny. With the largest quill, test the color on black paper — it should be thin without being too transparent. Stroke out the brush and, starting on the outer line, pull it along one line as far as it will go, then along the other line, making a firm edge on either side. Fill in between with broad strokes. Do one section at a time, brushing as quickly as possible because the paint sets up quickly. Do not try to go back over it. Practice on black paper first.

3. Trace pattern on white band, rubbing pencil on back of tracing.

4. Paint yellow base coats (no burnt umber); this includes the entire large flower.

5. Paint red strokes on small yellow flower. Paint brush strokes across bottom of the flower following the bottom line exactly. With the end of the finger, pat out the upper part of red until the original line does not show. The dotted lines show where the red blended area should end.

6. Mix the green; thin it with varnish until it is transparent, but still a lively color. Paint in leaves with as few strokes as possible. This should be done quickly and left to even out.

Figure 27. The finished canister is an unusual and attractive object. The background color is red, and most of the accents are yellow.

7. Do all strokes and veins in black, using #1 quill and #2 brush.

8. Give canister a coat of varnish.

9. Add umber to yellow and do striping.

10. Do brush stroke borders.

11. Finish as directed.

For Additional Reading

Brazer, Esther Stevens, **Early American Decoration,** Pond-Ekberg Co., 1940.

Coffin, Margaret, **American Country Tinware 1700-1900,** Thomas Nelson & Sons, 1968.

Lipman, Jean, **American Folk Decoration,** Dover, 1972.

Murray, Maria, **The Art of Tray Painting,** Bramhall House, 1954.

Sabine, Ellen S., **Early American Decorative Patterns,** Van Nostrand, 1962.

Slayton, Mariette Paine, **Early American Decorating Techniques,** 1972.

Enameling

The art of enameling enables the craftsman to create precious and semiprecious metal objects with fused glass-like color forms.

Historians report that the first successful attempts at attaching brightly colored glass to a metal surface by using heat probably occurred in the thirteenth century B.C. Previously, craftsmen adorned metal objects with fragments of rich color by using precious and semiprecious stones, as well as bits of glass, in settings which were held either by adhesives or by bezels and prongs. With the ultimate establishment of enameling as an art form, a wider range of extraordinarily bright colors was available for direct application to metal surfaces. Eventually, the enamel was used to cover larger and more variously shaped forms, thus providing an artistic character that could not be duplicated in any other way.

Figure 2. This striking enameled medallion was created for a princess in ancient Egypt. Gold, carnelian, lapis lazuli, and green feldspar were used in the design. (Courtesy, The Metropolitan Museum of Art, Rogers Fund, and contributions from Henry Walters, 1916.)

The art of enameling had its most pervasive and sophisticated development in the Western world during the Middle Ages. The achievements of Medieval and Byzantine craftsmen were unparalleled. They exploited the inherent nature of the enamel, while at the same time, balancing it with the expressive needs of their cultural environment. Miniature scenes were rendered in styles corresponding to illuminated manuscripts. Concurrent with the development of Renaissance art and its expression of more earthbound cultural

Figure 1. Silver wire and foil were used in the design of this plaque (opposite page). It is an example of the enameling technique known as cloisonné.

attitudes, the techniques of enameling became increasingly devoted to naturalistic interpretations of worldly phenomena. By the sixteenth century, enamelists were creating works which nearly approached the character of oil painting.

During the succeeding centuries, enameling eventually evolved free of association with any distinctive style. It came to be exploited in any way possible which would add to an object's complexity and decorativeness. Enameling as an independent art form almost disappeared completely until the 1950s, when a kind of American Renaissance in crafts took place. At this time, the works of Kenneth F. Bates achieved national recognition and remain among the most important inspirations which influenced the new enameling movement.

Within the context of contemporary American art and its radical alterations of artistic attitudes and techniques, the art of enameling has been greatly misunderstood by both critics and artists alike. Consequently, it has often been rejected as an art form, especially on professional levels. However, in the last few years, there seems to have been a mild resurgence, a result of the interest in the unique qualities of a single craft form.

Enameling as an art form depends upon an understanding of its special aesthetic qualities. Its most extraordinary advantages are associated with small-scale works: the preciseness of technique, the jewel-like colors, the delicate as well as decorative nature of the glass material — all contribute to a tendency toward miniaturization. This provides an appropriate scale for promoting the most distinctive ingredients of the enamel medium.

Common Terms Used In Enameling

Abrasive: a coarse material used to clean or polish surfaces; for enameling, use only greaseless abrasives such as powdered pumice and Lea Compound (see below).

Alloy: a metal added in small amounts to another metal to strengthen it. (After being heated, alloyed metals form a fire scale coating.)

Annealing: the process of heating a metal piece to a temperature which will cause it to become pliable.

Bassetaille: an enameling technique in which the metal surface contains areas of stepped layers developed through the metal etching process.

Buffing: the process of cleaning or polishing a metal surface with an abrasive.

Burr: a fence-like form produced by filing the edge of a metal piece.

Champlevé: a technique in which the metal surface has been etched to create a single depression for holding enamel.

Cloisonné: a technique in which pure silver or gold wires are laid on a surface to enclose small walled-in areas of enamel.

Cloisons: the individual wires used in cloisonné.

Counterenamel: the process of applying a coat of enamel to the reverse side of a piece in order to equalize the expansion and contraction of the metal during the firing process.

Croquil Pen: an extra-fine ink pen which is flexible enough to be used with a thick liquid-like overglaze and still produce a fine line.

Enamel: a glass-like material with special oxides for coloring which form a smooth glass surface after being heated to a temperature of about 1500° F.

Etching: the process of creating lines or open areas in a metal surface through the use of acid.

Fire Scale: a thin black coating which appears on a metal surface after the metal has been heated to a high temperature.

Firing: the process of heating a piece that has been freshly enameled in order to fuse the enamel to the metal.

Firing Chamber: the oven-like area in a kiln which contains heating elements and in which the enamel piece is placed to be fired.

Foil: an extremely thin sheet of pure metal which can be placed on an enameled surface for the

Figure 3. Foil is used in enameling to provide a reflective background for transparent enamels.

purpose of providing a highly reflective ground for transparent enamels.

Force Dry: the process of drying freshly applied enamel without having to wait for the adhering liquid to evaporate naturally.

Fusion: the moment when the enamel turns molten and adheres to the metal surface in a kind of gripping action.

Gauge: the measured thickness of metal.

Gum Arabic: one of several kinds of adhering liquids for holding the powdered enamel in place until fusion.

Gum Tragacath: an adhering liquid for holding powdered enamel in place.

Kiln: a specially made oven for firing enamels and ceramic glazes at very high temperatures.

Klyr-Fire: an adhering liquid for holding enamels in place until fusion, at which time it dissipates.

Lea Compound: a special greaseless abrasive material for cleaning and polishing metal surfaces; available in special grades for copper and silver.

Marinite: a specially composed board-like material which holds heat well.

Mesh: a term which applies to the size of the enamel granules as they fit through the holes of a screen; also refers to the size of the screen holes themselves.

Nichrome: a special kind of synthetic metal used to create pliable, heatproof screens.

Nitric Acid: a liquid substance used for cleaning copper surfaces and for removing unwanted fire scale. An acid bath of one part acid and ten parts water is preferable — acid should always be added slowly to water, never the reverse.

Opalescent Enamel: a semitransparent enamel color which has a pearly luster quality.

Opaque Enamel: a solid enamel color which cannot be seen through.

Overglaze: a commercially manufactured liquid-enamel compound which allows enamel to be painted on.

Oxidation: a process in which the oxygen in the air affects a metal surface by causing a darkening (tarnish) or a thin black coating (fire scale).

Paint-On: a technique in which enamel is sifted into the adhering liquid, which is applied with a brush or pen.

Pyrometer: a temperature-measuring device which is connected to a kiln.

Rouge: an oil-based abrasive material for high polishing of metal surfaces not intended to be enameled.

Scalex: a commercially made liquid which prevents the formation of fire scale and is applied with a brush.

Scrap Enamel: a mixture of leftover enamel from the washing process and from various applications.

Sgraffito: a technique in which a line is inscribed through dried, powdered enamel before it is fired.

Sift and Spray: a technique of alternating steps in which enamel is applied with a sieve (screen) and then saturated by spraying on adhering liquid (Klyr-Fire).

Silica: a chemical substance used in the creation of glass, enamel, and ceramic glazes.

Squeegie Oil: a commercially produced suspension liquid for using the enamel in a paint-like medium.

Stenciling: a method of applying enamel shapes by sifting onto areas cut out of a stencil.

Synthetic Metal: a metal which is produced from combinations of other metals and materials; cannot be enameled successfully because the enamel will not fuse to impure metal.

Thermocouple: a combination of a durable heat-transferring wire and ceramic insulation which is inserted into the firing chamber. Connected to the pyrometer, it sends a signal of the amount of heat in the chamber to the measuring device.

Transite: a commercially manufactured fireproof slate which can be used to cover tabletops and shelves.

Transparent Enamel: an enamel color which can be seen through once it has been fired; resembles the character of clear glass.

Trivet: a support for a piece to be fired in a kiln; usually of a metal that will not collapse under extreme heat.

Wet Inlay: a technique in which the enamel is applied in a wet paste-like consistency.

Figure 4. These chalices are examples of enamel work involving the stencil, sgraffito, paint-on, and foil techniques.

Figure 5. This cloisonne plaque, "Rococo Monster," shows silver wire fired on an opaque black enamel surface.

Figure 6. A stencil was used to apply the enamel to the painted surface of this cup. The linear designs were created in the dried powdered enamel before it was fired. Then, a sheet of metal was placed on the enameled surface.

Basic Equipment And Supplies

Enameling supplies are usually available at ordinary retail outlets which sell a wide variety of craft materials. However, there are special items which are only available at retail outlets that specialize in professional metalworking tools. These outlets are the best sources for all enameling tools, but they are few in number and might require ordering by mail.

There are also a few beginner's kits on the market. The list that follows is meant to serve both as a "starter kit" and as one which contains enough basic material for several more extensive enameling projects. The only real distinction between the beginner and the experienced enamelist is in the application of artistry to the craft.

KILNS

A kiln is available in a number of different models and firing-chamber sizes. These range from very small hot-plate types which can fire only works the size of earrings to kilns which can fire pieces up to 17" square and 8" high. The best all-around kiln is one with a firing chamber that is 8" square and 8" high and is rated electrically at 115 volts — the normal household current. It is also important to purchase a kiln that provides as much safe insulation as is affordable. The inexpensive kilns have a tendency to leak heat and the lining disintegrates faster with continuous use. It is ideal to have a kiln with a device (pyrometer) for measuring the temperature of the firing chamber, as successful enameling requires control over the amount of heat used for fusing.

ENAMELS

In their prefired state, enamels are in a form of powdered glass — usually of 80 mesh. They can be purchased in four basic forms — transparent, opaque, opalescent, and overglaze — and are available in a wide range of colors. As enamels do not mix like paint, one should have the largest number of colors possible.

Containers for the enamels should be either clear plastic or glass jars. Most preferable are 4-ounce clear plastic jars because they have snap-caps and will not break. They should be labeled precisely.

TOOLS

Many of these items can be found or duplicated from other sources rather than purchased.

1. Standard-size shielded firing fork. This is used to insert the freshly enameled work into the kiln and contains a metal shield that protects the hand from extreme heat. If further protection is needed, purchase an asbestos glove.

2. A 10-inch, 4-point trivet.

3. A 6" x 6" 4-mesh nichrome screen. When bent slightly at each corner, the square screen becomes a handy firing rack for supporting trivets too small or oddly shaped to be inserted into the kiln by themselves.

4. A 6" x 6" piece of marinite board. When placed on the nichrome screen, this becomes an ideal support for flat pieces, holds heat very well, and is an important part of the force drying process. To prevent maximum warpage of flat pieces after their firing, it is important to support them on a flat bed rather than by the edges.

5. Pair of kitchen-type gripping tongs. These are handy for removing hot pieces from the trivet after firing.

6. A 4" x 3" wire screen (60 mesh). Once folded into a box, the screen can be used for sifting the powdered enamel onto the metal surface.

7. Wet inlay tools (spatula and spreader). These are special tools for applying wet paste-like enamel.

8. Brightboy handpiece. This is a rectangular block of abrasive material useful for removing fire scale from the edges of pieces, especially between firings.

9. A 6" flat, metal, hand file (medium cut). This is used for cleaning and shaping the edges of enameled pieces after the last firing.

10. Sheet of metal emery paper (fine grade) for removing file marks and burrs on metal edges.

11. DeVilbiss atomizer (No. 127). This is used to spray a fine mist of adhering liquid during the

sift-and-spray technique; may be purchased at any pharmacy.

12. Pair of fine-pointed tweezers.

13. A 6″ metal ruler with markings broken down into measurements smaller than 1/16″.

14. Metal scribe. This is necessary for making finely inscribed lines on a metal surface. Any metal point can be used, such as a large nail, as long as the point is very sharp and durable.

15. Paint brushes of various sizes.

16. Egg cup palette. This is used to separate the colors of wet, raw enamel.

17. Container for storing adhering liquid. Adhering liquids come in concentrated strength and have to be thinned for use in an atomizer. It is convenient to have some sort of easy dispenser in which to store the mixture of liquid and water. The ideal dispenser is one which can be used with one hand, such as a squeezable plastic bottle with a long snout.

18. Small double-sided (coarse/fine) carborundum stone. This is used for leveling enamel and wire (stoning) in the cloisonné technique. It is also used for smoothing fired enameled surfaces and for grinding small amounts of enamel off a metal surface. The stone is used only under running water and is not to be substituted by such items as oil

Figure 7. A carborundum stone is one of the items needed in enameling. The stone, handy for smoothing, is used only under running water.

stones and sharpening stones. The carborundum stone is available at any hardware store.

19. Pair of copper tongs. They are used in the nitric acid bath.

20. A 10″ to 12″ covered Pyrex bowl. This is for storing the acid bath or any other cleaning liquid. If nitric acid is used, the bowl must always remain covered as excessive breathing of vapors can be dangerous; **good ventilation is required when using the nitric acid bath.**

21. Miscellaneous items. These include a pair of good scissors, a medium-size bottle cork, a medium-size sewing needle, several lint-free cloths, large glass jars, a pad of tracing paper, and an eye dropper.

The following are items needed to complete the projects described in this article: 1-pound bottle of nitric acid, pint of Klyr-Fire, half-pint of Scalex, 8-inch copper saucer, 5″ x 8″ copper rectangle, one sheet each of pure gold and silver foil, 20 feet of pure silver cloisonné wire, and 1/4 pound of powdered pumice.

Basic Procedures

There are five basic steps in the production of an enameled work: preparation, application, drying, firing, and finishing. Any variations within these steps would depend upon the unique conditions of an individual technique and will be described as they occur in the projects. Most enamelists use copper in their work.

PREPARATION A

This preparation involves the cleaning of the metal surface for the best possible fusion. It includes methods for removing grease, dirt, and fire scale which interfere with enamel sticking to the metal.

1. Place the copper piece on a trivet composed of a nichrome screen stilt (*i.e.*, a screen with the four corners bent down to make a table-like base) and marinite board and insert it into the kiln, which should be at a temperature of 1500° F. The idea is to burn off the grease and, at the same time, anneal (soften) the metal to reduce the possibility of warpage.

Figure 8. To prepare copper for enameling, first place it on a trivet then, using a shielded firing fork, place the copper in the kiln.

2. The exposed copper piece is heated only until a discoloration appears (a kind of blue or purplish tarnish) — this does not take more than a matter of seconds. This can be seen while the piece is in the kiln. But if there is some doubt, the piece can be removed, at which time the air will oxidize the copper and make the discoloration more obvious. If the piece is left in the kiln too long, it will turn completely black, which is undesirable.

3. After removing the piece from the kiln, grab it with the hot tongs and quench it *immediately* under cold water. There will be a hissing sound as the cold water hits the hot surface — this is not dangerous. If fire scale has formed, quite often such a quick quenching will remove most of it. However, it will take a longer time to prepare the metal surface as it is difficult to remove all the fire scale, even with the acid bath. It may have to be ground off if a completely pure copper surface is desired.

4. Rinse the piece thoroughly under running water, removing with a cloth any silt that might be left on the surface.

5. Place the piece slowly in the nitric acid bath with the copper tongs. Replace the glass cover. The copper will immediately begin to turn pink. This represents the acid eating away everything except the copper, but eventually the acid will attack even the copper. A swab made of a wooden handle and wrapped sheeting can be used to rub areas for increased action and for removing silt which does not automatically come off while the piece is immersed in the acid. Be sure to hold the piece with the copper tongs. Do not lean directly over the acid bath and avoid inhaling the acid vapors. Always keep the acid bath covered when not swabbing.

6. Remove the piece from the acid when it appears that it is as clean as it is going to get. The clean copper has a kind of dull pink surface with no black spots or stains. Rinse *immediately* in running water and dry *immediately* without touching the piece with the hands — except on the edges. Be sure to rinse the tongs and the swab. If the piece is not dried as quickly as possible, brown stains will form from the oxidation of air on the copper. These stains are harmless to the fusion process, but will show under a transparent coating.

7. The piece is now ready for counterenameling. If not enameling immediately, wrap the piece in a lint-free cloth to protect the surface from dust particles.

PREPARATION B

Preparation B also involves cleaning the raw enamel itself. This is, of course, only done once for each newly purchased enamel and is called "washing the enamel." Its purpose is to remove foreign particles and dirt that are the result of the manufacturing process and ordinary exposure to air.

1. For opaque enamels, pour the powdered enamel into a large glass jar. Fill the jar with cold tap water. As the water goes into the jar, the enamel will swirl around and, after the jar is filled, it will begin to settle. Usually, the larger grains settle first, leaving the foreign particles and dirt, which are lighter in weight, floating on the surface. Count to 10 after the water is turned off — this is usually enough time for the enamel to settle. Carefully pour off the water, leaving only the wet enamel. (Because there will always be some enamel in the water which is poured off, pour the water into a large bucket. After all the enamels are washed, the poured-off enamel or scrap will have settled to the bottom of the bucket and can be used for the backs of pieces.) This washing and pouring off need only be done once, unless the water left after 10 seconds appears to be extremely dirty.

2. With the spatula, scrape all of the wet enamel out of the jar into an aluminum foil cup (or other fireproof container) for drying. This will return it to its original powdered condition.

3. Place the wet enamel (in aluminum foil cups) in a 400° kitchen oven. The more spread out the enamel is, the quicker it dries; but this requires larger containers. The more washed colors which can be put in the oven for collective drying, the better.

Be sure as much water as possible has been poured off by noting any remaining liquid in the drying container and then removing it. In collective drying, also be sure that the container walls are high; sometimes the heat of the oven will cause the wet enamel to form gas pockets that burst, spraying one color onto another.

4. Leave the enamel in the oven until it becomes a dry powder. It is sometimes necessary to bring the wet enamel from the bottom of the container to the top, as the top layer dries first.

5. After drying, put the enamel back into its storage jar. During this entire procedure, be sure to keep track of which enamels are which colors, so as to return the right color to the jar with the correct label.

6. Do all of the above for the poured-off scrap enamel in the large bucket.

7. For transparent and opalescent enamels, the overall process is the same except for the number of wash and pour cycles. As clarity is important, the transparent enamel should be washed at least 10 times or until the settled water is reasonably clear — whichever occurs first.

APPLICATION

The various techniques of applying the powdered enamel to the metal surface can be divided into two general approaches: dry condition and wet condition.

Dry Condition

This is a process of applying the enamel while it is still in its powdered state. The advantage of this approach is in the efficiency allowed in covering large areas.

1. To prevent excessive warping of the piece, it is necessary to enamel the reverse side (counter-enameling). The reason for this is that the metal will naturally expand while being fixed. Then, while the piece is cooling, a tension is created between the expanded side under the coat of enamel and the unexposed metal side, which tends to contract. The result of this tension is warpage. If, however, both sides are covered by enamel, the process of contraction is equalized and therefore greatly retarded.

2. After the copper has been thoroughly cleaned, paint a thin, even coat of water-thinned Scalex on the front or main design side of the piece. For best results, try not to go over a stroke once it has been applied. Use as large a brush as possible in order to cover the most area in one application. Be sure not to handle the other side while applying the Scalex. After it dries, look for uncovered spots; the Scalex should be thin enough to allow the copper surface to show through, while still covering that same surface. Allow to dry.

3. Turn the Scalexed side over onto a paper towel, holding both towel and piece in left hand. The towel will absorb most of the excess adhering liquid which, as it is sprayed, may loosen the Scalex. Now it is time to begin the sift-and-spray process.

4. Fill an atomizer three-quarters full with water, then add one-quarter of concentrated Klyr-Fire

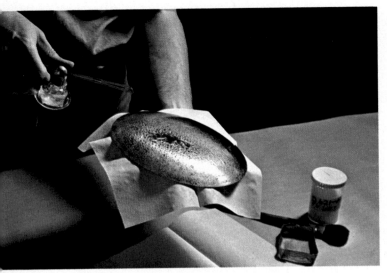

Figure 9. Turn the Scalex side of the copper over onto a paper towel. When adhesive is applied to the outside of the copper, the towel protects the Scalex side.

(always add the Klyr-Fire to the water to minimize bubbling). Squeezing the atomizer bulb firmly, to insure a fine spray, cover the copper surface lightly. With a clean brush, spread the Klyr-Fire so that it covers the surface as completely as possible. If the liquid crawls, it means there is still some grease on the surface. Either start the cleaning process all over or add a bit of saliva to the surface. This will act as a grease-cutting agent. When spraying, it is important to do so far enough from the surface to prevent too much liquid from forming at once, yet close enough to achieve efficient wetting. Experiment first.

5. Using a 60-mesh screen that has been formed into a box, sift a light, even coat of enamel over the entire surface. Use enough to cover the surface while still allowing the copper to show through. For smoother results, it is better to build up the enamel in a series of thin layers rather than one heavy application. Do all sifting over a large piece of paper which has been folded down the middle and then reopened. The paper will catch the excess enamel and the crease will act as a funnel for pouring the enamel back into its storage container. It may be necessary to occasionally shake the sifter itself away from the piece to dislodge large enamel granules that get stuck in the screen holes.

6. Spray Klyr-Fire onto the first coat of enamel. Do not spray so close that the force of the atom-

izer will displace the enamel which has not been wetted down. The idea is to completely saturate the enamel with the Klyr-Fire. This is done by spraying the Klyr-Fire until it forms a completely wet surface without being so wet that the enamel will run off. The purpose of the adhering agent is to form a binder when the enamel is dry. Klyr-Fire dries like a plastic and will hold the powdered enamel in place until it is fired; a well-saturated piece can be knocked slightly without displacing the enamel. At a certain temperature — just before the enamel begins to form — the Klyr-Fire burns away without leaving a trace.

7. Sift another light coat of enamel into the Klyr-Fire as quickly as possible after the spraying. If the atomizer runs out of liquid in the midst of spraying, you can refill it easily with your free hand.

8. Spray another coat of Klyr-Fire until saturation.

9. Sift another coat of enamel. When sifting, try to establish a pattern so as not to over-sift any one area. The edges of the piece should receive special attention as they have a tendency to burn out sooner.

10. Spray a final coat of Klyr-Fire, but this time only to make sure that all of the enamel has been wetted. Do not saturate. The sift-and-spray method is most successful when applied in a formula of three thin coats of powdered enamel: spray/sift/saturate; sift/saturate; sift/final spray.

Figure 10. Sift a light, even coat of enamel over the copper. Cover the surface, but be sure the layer of enamel is thin enough to allow the copper to show through.

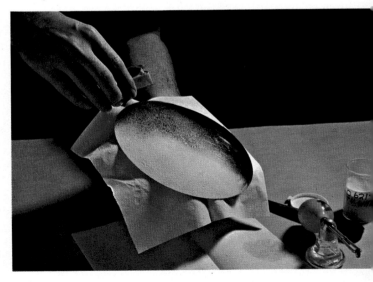

For very small surfaces, it may be necessary to apply only two thin coats. In any case, a layered build-up provides more control over the quality of the enameled surface.

11. The piece is now ready for firing.

12. After the piece has been fired, weighted, and the Scalex has flaked off, the front side or main design must be cleaned in case any fire scale has formed where there was not any Scalex or if there is grease on the surface from handling. Ordinarily, it is not necessary to clean this surface, but there will also be stains and discolorations which would show up under a transparent enamel. Immerse the entire piece in the acid bath for cleaning. Follow the same procedures as described under *Preparation A*. Most enamels are acid proof, but if the acid has become too strong, it quite often will affect the counterenameled surface by etching it. To correct this, another coat of enamel would have to be applied.

13. For a highly polished copper surface which allows maximum reflection, it is necessary to buff the surface with a material called Lea Compound. This is a greaseless agent which is best applied with a buffing motor and cotton buffing wheel. For hand buffing, however, a good agent is powdered pumice and water used in a paste form and applied with a clean cloth. Rubbing this abrasive by hand on the copper surface will produce a good luster.

14. Sift and spray a series of coats of enamel on the front side, fire, weight, and air cool.

Wet Condition

By applying the enamel in a wet paste, a surface can be covered with different colors simultaneously and without intervening firings. This technique is also practical for small areas on the metal formed by etching or metal wires. If the piece is small, it can be counterenameled in the wet condition approach. If large, the sift-and-spray method is preferred. The basic technique in this category is called wet inlay.

1. Place a small amount of powdered enamel in one of the cavities of the egg cup palette. With an eye dropper, squeeze a few drops of the thinned-out Klyr-Fire into the enamel. Squeeze just the right amount to make a paste which is wet enough

to be easily spread and dry enough not to be runny.

2. Using a spatula, scoop some enamel out of the palette. With the spreader, scrape the enamel off the spatula onto the surface to be wet inlaid. Using the spreader, flatten the enamel until it is almost as thick as three coats of sifted enamel. For transparent enamels, a thinner coat will be clearer when fired. However, coats of enamel which are too thin will burn out easily, leaving black areas in the surface or pin holes in the enamel coating.

Figure 11. For wet condition enameling, Klyr-Fire is added to the powdered enamel to make a mixture with a paste-like consistency. Use a spreader to remove the enamel from the spatula and to place it on the copper (top). Then, use the spreader to flatten the enamel on the copper (bottom).

3. Keep adding as much enamel as is needed to complete the covering of a single area with one color. If the enamel seems to be drying out, add a drop of water or Klyr-Fire to bring it back to a workable consistency. This is usually the case when applying a new batch of enamel to an area already laid in: the previously applied enamel acts as a blotter, absorbing the liquid of the freshly applied paste. It is a good technique to keep all of the previously inlayed enamel in a wet state by a gentle spraying of Klyr-Fire from time to time. This allows for a smoother and more even application of the enamel paste.

4. Be sure to join colors thoroughly with the spreader. Quite often colors will separate during the firing, especially if there is already an open space between them.

5. When all surfaces have been covered, allow the piece to dry. (To postpone the wet inlay in the midst of completion, cover the piece well to avoid dust settling on its surface. When returning to the piece, rewet the entire area of inlaid enamel.)

6. The piece is now ready to be fired.

FIRING

This process of using extreme heat to fuse the enamel to the metal surface is done in a kiln at a temperature of 1500° F. It is ideal for the kiln to have a pyrometer, although in small and inexpensive kilns this is not necessary because construction usually does not permit a heating of more than 1500° F.

Firing can be a dangerous process. Be cautious and remain at the kiln during the entire period. Have all the proper protection to prevent severe burns.

Be sure the kiln sits on a heatproof surface and that there is a fireproof surface for placing the fired piece during cooling. A large piece of transite makes a good fireproof material.

Triveting

The purpose of this procedure is to support the enameled piece while in the kiln in such a way as to minimize warpage and not leave marks in the molten enamel. Most commercial trivets are made from metal or fireproof ceramic material.

To fire the front side of a piece after completing the counterenameling, two basic kinds of supports are available. The safest is the kind which holds a piece by its edges (the four-cornered trivet, for example); the other is a star-shaped support with small prongs which is placed under the back side of the piece. The four-cornered trivet can be placed in the kiln by itself, while the star trivet should be on a piece of marinite. For drying the front side, follow the methods described below, but use the appropriate triveting.

Figure 12. The four-cornered trivet is one of the safest because it holds the copper by the edges. This trivet, like most trivets, is made of metal (left). In another type of trivet, small metal prongs are used to support the piece from underneath. This "star" trivet should be used with a piece of marinite (right).

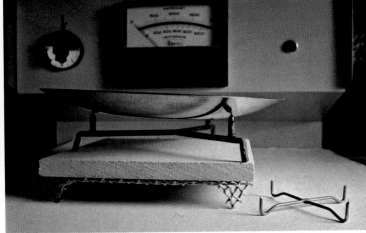

Drying

Before firing, it is necessary to dry the freshly enameled surface. Failure to do so will cause the enamel to form exploding gas pockets while in the kiln. This will blow the enamel off the copper and onto the kiln floor.

1. After completing the counterenameling process, and depending on the drying method used, place the piece with the Scalex side face down on a slab of marinite or on a screen stilt, the former being the better of the two. If placed on marinite, then place the whole unit on a low screen stilt or any other short-legged trivet.

2. The enamel can be dried by allowing it to stand in the open air for approximately 30 minutes. However, this is slow and dust can fall onto the enameled surface. It is better and more efficient to force dry the enamel, which can be done in two ways. The better of these is to place the trivet combination of marinite and metal support in the kiln before starting to apply the enamel. This allows the trivet to become red hot in advance of the drying process. The marinite holds the most heat for the longest time. Remove the trivet from the kiln and place the piece on the marinite with the Scalex side face down. Within seconds the enamel will begin to steam and, as it dries, it becomes lighter in tonality. Ordinarily, there is enough heat to dry the whole piece in one setting. However, if the steaming stops before all of the enamel is dry, place the entire unit with the piece

Figure 13. *One method of drying a counterenameled piece is to place the Scalex side down on marinite, using a short-legged trivet or low screen stilt beneath.*

in the kiln for a second or two without letting go of the firing fork. Merely close the door momentarily on the fork and then remove the unit. The steaming should begin once again. Repeat this process for as long as it takes to complete the drying.

3. The second force-drying method follows essentially the in-and-out procedure just described, except that the trivet is not heated in advance. The unit is placed in the kiln cold and, while maintaining hold of the firing fork, the kiln door is closed briefly. This is very tricky at first because the heat is meeting the liquid and, if the unit is left

Figure 14. *There are two force-drying methods used in enameling. One method uses a hot trivet; the other, a cold trivet. When either of these methods is employed, place the piece in the oven (left) and close the door while holding onto the firing fork (right).*

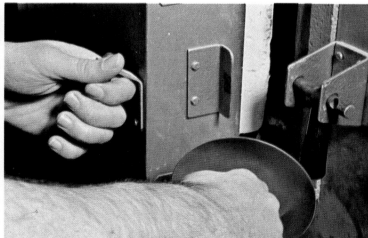

in the kiln a second too long, gas pockets will form. For the first insertion, approximately a half a second is enough. Subsequently, longer periods can be used. If the first insertion is too long and pockets do form, the enamel surface will have bumps in it. These can be gently pressed down with the finger, although when the piece is enameled, the surface will not be as smooth as it would have been without the mistake.

The same conditions of force drying apply to wet inlaid pieces.

Fusing

1. Allow the kiln to heat to approximately 1600° F, if possible. Rapidly place the completely dry piece in the kiln, closing the kiln door instantly so as to lose only a minimum of heat.

2. Once the piece is in the kiln, check its melting progress by opening the kiln door just enough to see the enameled surface. There are three identifiable stages: (1) the sandpaper stage, in which the enamel is just beginning to form and has a dull grainy appearance; (2) the orange peel stage, in which the enamel has progressed toward complete fusion and has a shiny but rippled surface; and (3) the final shiny and smooth stage.

Fusing usually takes place in a matter of several minutes or less, if all conditions are perfect. One indication that the piece has been fully fired (and perhaps overfired) is a slight red glow on the enamel itself. Overfiring a piece will cause the enamel to burn out and eventually puddle or run off the copper surface. Underfiring will cause the enamel to flake off after the piece is cool. When firing a piece which already has a fired enamel coat (which is standard procedure), the first coat will crack slightly. This is normal. However, if the kiln temperature is below 1500° F, requiring the piece to be left in the chamber for a longer period of time, the cracked enamel will eventually reform, but not perfectly. A properly heated chamber is essential to perfect fusion. Each time a previously fused coat of enamel is reheated to a molten state, it becomes thinner as the liquid enamel naturally turns to gas and burns off. This is important to keep in mind when determining the number of firings for the completion of a design.

WEIGHTING AND COOLING

Heating metal causes it to expand, while cooling causes it to contract to its original size. When covered by an enamel coating, the cooling metal does not contract so completely and, if there is also an exposed metal surface, the difference in contraction rates causes the piece to warp. Even in works which are totally covered with enamel, there is some warpage. After several firings, you will note that the piece has become somewhat larger due to the retarded contraction. It is possible to correct warpage which occurs when a piece is fired by a simple weighting method.

1. Remove the unit and place it on a fireproof surface. As the piece comes out of the kiln, the enamel is still molten, so before removing it from the trivet, wait approximately 30 seconds for the enamel to harden. Though this is difficult to measure — except by touching a metal tool to the enamel to see if it leaves a mark — it is important not to weight the piece too early or too late. Remove the piece from the trivet with the hot tongs and quickly turn it face down onto a clean, fireproof surface.

2. When the enamel hardens, the metal is still pliable. However, this lasts for only a matter of seconds, after which the metal is too hard to bend without cracking the enamel. At the moment of the greatest pliability, place a heavy metal weight

Figure 15. Because the copper is pliable only briefly during the cooling process, the timing of the placement of a heavy metal weight on top of the piece is crucial.

on the upside down piece — this will push the form back into its original shape. Most of the correction occurs at this time, but leave the weight on the piece until it is cool enough to be picked up by hand. This will reduce any further warpage as the piece cools. Old flat irons make very good weights as they are very heavy and have handles. Never cool a piece by placing it under water. This could shatter or crack the enamel. Cooling should be slow and achieved by merely allowing the piece to sit until cool enough to be held in your hand.

In the counterenameling process, the piece is weighted with the Scalex side down. Allow it to cool naturally, causing the Scalex to flake off completely and leaving a perfectly clean copper surface. After it is cool, the piece is ready for further application of enamel.

FINISHING

This method refers mainly to the treatment of exposed metal surfaces, such as edges, which are left after all enameling has been completed. Refined finishing is good craftsmanship and adds to the artistry of the work.

1. The edges should at least be cleaned of fire scale, if not polished. This is done by first rubbing the edges of the piece with the Brightboy handpiece. This will remove fire scale.

2. Using the metal file, shape the edge so that it forms a slightly reflective surface by filing it to an angle parallel to the enamel. Always file in a direction away from the center of the piece so as not to chip the enamel edge. Remove the file marks and any sharp burrs with emery paper. If possible, the edges can then be motor buffed with powdered pumice, water, and hard felt wheel or even with red rouge.

3. Coat the enamel surface with glass wax to reduce fingerprints.

Projects You Can Do

The enameling projects described below are designed not only to produce artistic enameled works, but also to provide experience in most of the major techniques in the enameling craft. It is important to remember that in these projects, the design approach is essentially two-dimensional, as in a painting or drawing. A complete sample of all enamel colors should be made prior to any project by firing the opaques on a piece of copper and the transparents on copper, opaque white, and silver and gold foil.

PROJECT I

This project involves the enameling of an 8" diameter copper saucer and contains technical introductions to the dry condition processes of sten-

Figure 16. Use a metal file to finish the edges of the project. Always file away from the center of the piece to avoid damaging the enamel near the edge.

Figure 17. The first project is an 8" saucer like the one shown, "Within My Soul," which was created by the author in 1959. Stenciling, sgraffito, paint-on, and foil techniques are used.

Figure 18. This 8" copper plate, entitled "Color and Variation," was made by using the enameling techniques described for the first project. It has been mounted for hanging on a wall.

ciling, sgraffito, and paint-on. As a two-dimensional approach, it may be more appropriate, in learning these new methods, to consider a simple and flat design.

1. For preparing the design, use the 8" saucer to trace a circle on tracing paper. Make the design as complete as possible, including color designations. Place another sheet of tracing paper, with the circle outlined, over the finished design. Redraw only those areas which will be the first shapes applied to the background color. Do a separate drawing for each layer of shapes. The number of layers depends upon the design. The steps listed below are based on one design layer per new method, so there will be four applications: background, stenciled shapes, sgraffito shapes, and paint-on forms. Though the actual shapes will be personal decisions, suggestions for specific colors will be made.

2. The first series of shapes should be in forms that can be cut out in a stencil. Transfer the first sepa-

Figure 19. Use an 8" saucer to trace a circle. Then, prepare the design. Make a separate drawing for each layer of shapes. The finished design (D) is a composite of the other three (A, B, and C).

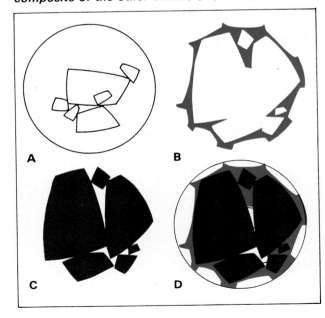

rate drawing of shapes onto a clean paper towel big enough to cover the saucer. This can be done by turning the drawing over and rubbing the design lines with graphite, which, when traced, will be reproduced on the towel. Also be sure to trace the circle outline onto the paper towel as well. Cut out the stencil areas with a single-edge razor blade or scissors.

3. Prepare and clean the copper saucer in the usual ways. Counterenamel it, fire, and weight upside down. (Sifting should always be done so that the enamel falls perpendicular to the metal surface. This may necessitate holding a piece in different ways so that the surface receiving the enamel is horizontal.) The color selected for the counterenamel should be chosen to compliment the design. Because the saucer has to be held by the edges during firing, use the four-cornered trivet for support. Although when firing the counterenamel, you can still use the marinite because the plate will sit on its edges in the upside down position. When firing the piece face up, using the four-cornered trivet, it will be necessary to use the second method of force drying because the trivet will not hold heat as long as the marinite (see *Drying,* step 3, under "Basic Procedures.")

Figure 20. Dry enamel should be sifted evenly onto a horizontal area. Turn the dish so that the enamel falls in a line perpendicular to the surface, as shown.

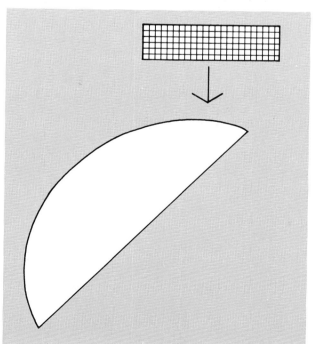

4. After the saucer has cooled and the Scalex has flaked off, prepare and clean the front surface for its first coat of background enamel. In this case, polish the copper with powdered pumice and water to attain a shiny surface. Sift and spray a background of clear flux (three thin layers), force dry, fire until golden in color, weight, and cool. (Note: If the saucer sticks slightly to the trivet, gently bang the trivet with the fork or tongs to loosen the piece.)

5. After cooling, scrape off any fire scale which has formed on the edges by rubbing them with the Brightboy handpiece. Fire scale which is not removed can continue to flake off, even while applying fresh enamel, and may fly into any unfired enamel.

6. Place the paper towel stencil on the saucer, lining up the edge of the saucer with the circle outline. Spray Klyr-Fire on the stencil, completely

Figure 21. Another step in the saucer project involves placing a paper towel stencil on the piece, then wetting the stencil with Klyr-Fire so that the paper clings to the saucer.

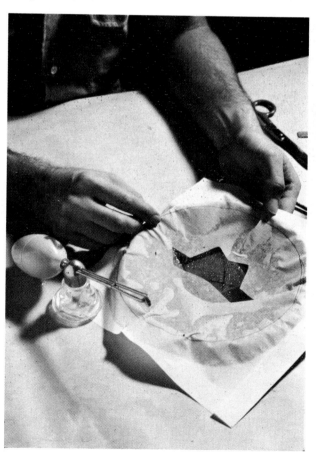

wetting it so that it will cling to the concave surface of the saucer. Depending on the depth of the saucer, it may be necessary to cut the stencil at certain points for it to set down completely on the surface. With another clean towel or lint-free cloth, dab away any puddles of liquid.

7. Sift and spray an opaque blue over the openings in the stencil. Because these areas may be small, it is advisable to build up only two layers of enamel.

8. Force dry by preheating and setting the piece directly on the marinite, but **do not fire.** As the enamel dries, so will the stencil, which will shrink and pull away from the stenciled shapes. Carefully lift the stencil away. Note that this method

Figure 22. A metal scribe is used to scratch a linear design, or sgraffito, on the dried enamel surface. Periodically, remove the excess enamel from the surface.

produces shapes with crisp edges. (The enamel left on the stencil may be added to the scrap enamel.)

9. Place the piece on the four-cornered trivet and fire. Remove it from the kiln, weight, and allow to air cool. Clean the edges with Brightboy.

10. Making sure not to get fingerprints on the design surface, sift and spray a coat of transparent red over the entire area. Keep this coat to three thin layers. Force dry the enamel on the marinite. **Do not fire.** Using the second separate drawing of linear shapes or patterns as a guide, gently scratch the line design (sgraffito) into the dried enamel. Occasionally blow the excess enamel away. If the enamel has been well saturated with Klyr-Fire, as required, the blowing off of the loose enamel will not displace any other enamel. The scratched lines can be varied in thickness and character by using such tools as a brush handle, scribe, toothpick, or pencil. In sgraffito it is important not to get the enamel coat so thick that scratching through it causes chipping at the edges of the line.

11. The piece is now ready for firing, weighting, and cooling. Clean the edges with Brightboy. The result of the sgraffito design is that the lines reveal parts of the blue shape and flux background, providing that the linear pattern extends beyond the stenciled shapes.

12. The paint-on method is always used as the last application, because it will not stand more than one good firing before burning away. This is a good way to achieve additional lines, shapes, shading, and other touch-ups. Paint a line, shape, or large area of Klyr-Fire on the enamel surface. Then, with a smaller screen box or the corner of the regular box, sift enamel into the Klyr-Fire. This can only be a single layered coat of a limited depth because the Klyr-Fire will absorb only so much enamel. Blow away all excess enamel and touch up the edges of the paint-on areas with a dry brush or any pointed tool, as though using the sgraffito technique. Use the mixed Klyr-Fire, but if it dries too fast, it may be necessary to use concentrated Klyr-Fire. There is also a commercial liquid called squeegie oil which does not evaporate while being painted on.

Lines can also be applied with overglaze, which is a special suspension liquid containing enamel.

It is painted on with a fine brush or croquil pen, which is cleaned in a special solvent that comes with the overglaze. This also requires drying and a very delicate firing.

13. Force dry, except for the squeegie oil (when fired, the squeegie oil will literally flame out). Be careful not to overfire because the enamel coat is thin. Since this is the last firing, be sure to do a good weighting. Allow to air cool.

14. Clean the edges with Brightboy and finish them as described under "Basic Procedures." It should be obvious that any variations of the stencil and sgraffito techniques can be made by applying additional layers of either process and by adding foils in between.

PROJECT II

Of the two projects, this one is the most complicated, both technically and aesthetically. However, it concerns one of the most unique art forms to be found — not only in enameling, but in all of art. This art form is called cloisonné. In a sense, cloisonné summarizes all that enameling is and embodies the "soul" of its artistic existence. Therefore, despite its highly sophisticated methods, this is a worthwhile project for the beginner to do.

In the cloisonné process, gold or silver wires (called cloisons) are formed into a linear design which is filled in with enamel. Cloisonné is most attractive when these wires dominate the surface, creating a variety of small areas of color. The design should be delicate and intricate, in keeping with the rich, precious quality of the gold and silver.

The final result of this project will be a cloisonné plaque that should be framed, but could be used as a jewelry-box top.

1. Prepare a line drawing of the design on tracing paper. While preparing the design, remember that the cloisonné wire is best shaped into a design which has firm looking curves and straight lines.

2. Clean and counterenamel a 5" x 8" copper rectangle. Fire it flat on marinite and weight it during cooling. Brush a heavy coat of concentrated Scalex (direct from the bottle) on the counterenamel. This keeps the counterenamel from sticking to the marinite during firing. After counterenameling, the piece is ready for the background color.

3. Choose the background color on the basis of whether or not subsequent layers of enamel, which will go between cloisons, will be transparents. It is preferable to choose a medium-fusing enamel to avoid burning out the silver wire during its first firing. If a transparent is used, be sure to polish the copper with pumice and water.

4. Sift and spray the background color. Force dry the piece, fire it, and weight it. Allow it to air cool.

Figure 23. Foils and silver wire stoned flush with the wet inlaid enamel have been added to the plaque, "Rococo Monster" (see Figure 5) to achieve a stark effect.

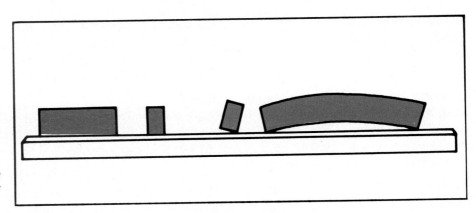

Figure 24. This diagram illustrates the correct (left) and incorrect (right) ways in which the cloisons should be placed on the enameled surface. The cloisons should be level and flat so that they will not detract from the finished piece.

5. Bend the silver wire into the pattern of the design. If the drawing is clear and precise, lay the wire along the drawn line to make an exact copy. Do not worry about touching the metal in this procedure — the metal wires are so small that the problem of greasy fingers will not be significant. To obtain firm bends and joins, the wires should be bent with tweezers and cut with very sharp scissors. Be sure the wires are free of bumps and ripples. While forming the cloisons, it is important to keep them level so that they will make firm contact with the enameled surface. Therefore, the bends have to be absolutely vertical. It is also advisable to avoid creating a wire line so long that it cannot be kept level. Break up the linear design into shorter lengths of wire. Straight wires will not stand up by themselves and either must have bent ends or be supported on both sides by other wires. When the end of one wire is to butt up against the side of another wire, a precise cut is required to achieve the effect of a continuous line.

6. Brush or spray Klyr-Fire on the enameled surface. The Klyr-Fire is critical because it will hold the wires in place. Place the wires on the surface.

(If the Klyr-Fire begins to dry after several wires have been laid down, more Klyr-Fire can be used. Be sure to spray the Klyr-Fire gently in order not to disturb the cloisons that are already set.) After all the wires are placed, check to see that they are level and that none of them are slanted or sticking up. Allow to dry.

7. This first firing is done at a temperature of 1490° F. **It is a critical firing.** The purpose is to adhere the cloisons to the molten enamel. Firing cloisonné wire requires more-than-usual care. It is difficult to see exactly when the fusion has been completed, but try to watch for molten enamel puddling slightly around the base of the wires. (If the puddling reflects light, it is easier to see.) To avoid overfiring, look for other tell-tale signs: if the temperature goes beyond 1500° F, the piece is probably too hot; if there is a red-hot glow to either the enamel or the metal trivet, it means that the cloisons will melt and probably burn away.

8. During the firing, most of the wires will settle down as they anneal, but occasionally there is one wire that does not. When the piece is re-

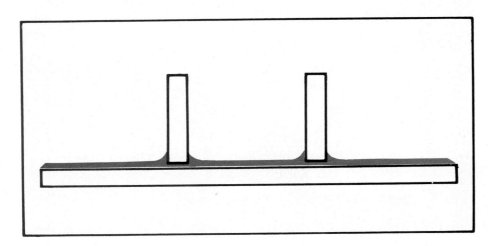

Figure 25. This cross-section shows how the fired enamel puddles at the base of the cloisonné wire. After the piece has cooled, the wire holds the cloisons in place.

moved, push any protruding wires down into the enamel with a metal tool just before the enamel hardens. Be prepared with tool in hand, however, as the enamel will harden in about 30 seconds.

Because the wires are soft, the piece cannot be weighted after this firing. Simply allow it to air cool. (At this stage, if the piece has not been counterenameled, it will warp drastically and the wires will pop off.)

9. At this point, silver or gold foil may be applied to the fired enamel background in order to provide a highly reflective surface beneath a transparent color. (Steps 9 through 12 are standard procedures for using silver and gold foils in enameling.) Because foils are extremely thin and fragile, they should be handled only with tweezers. By placing the foil between two sheets of tracing paper, it can be cut with a pair of sharp scissors without crumpling or leaving fingerprints.

If the foil shapes being used are larger than approximately 1/4", puncture them with a sewing needle while they are between the sheets of tracing paper. This creates small holes so that air can escape during the firing. (Trapped air causes pockets on the foil surface which, after cooling, will split open, thereby creating unwanted fissures.)

10. After preparing the foil shapes, lay them in place with tweezers on the fired enamel surface that has been coated with Klyr-Fire. The foil can be moved easily with a brush as long as the Klyr-Fire has not dried. Once in place, allow the Klyr-Fire to dry, which should not take very long.

11. Place the piece on the marinite trivet in preparation for firing the foils. This is a critical firing, as the foils are so thin that they will not survive the normal length of firing while not covered with enamel. To facilitate a delicate firing, it is necessary that the kiln be at a temperature of 1490° F after the door is closed. It is difficult to see when the foils have been fused to the enamel surface. Watch carefully. Usually the foil will appear to be flattening out and will look like it is stuck to the enamel. If in doubt, it is safer to remove the piece (as long as there are no cracks in the enamel) and test the foil with a metal tool. If not adhered, place the piece back into the kiln. Watch the pyrometer. If the temperature goes past 1500° F, the piece is probably too hot. Also look for other telltale signs: a red-hot glow to either the enamel or the metal trivet means the foil is starting to burn away.

12. Once fired, remove the foiled piece. This time, because of the delicate foil surfaces, it is not necessary to weight the piece. Allow to air cool. Whatever warpage occurs can be corrected in the next firing.

13. Wet inlay all of the areas between the cloisons. Lay in every color, as all of the colors will be fired together. Because wet enamel has liquid and air between the grains, it is important to place the enamel slightly above the height of the wires. When the piece is fired, the liquid and air dissipates and the enamel settles lower than when applied. The idea is to get the fired enamel as even with the wires as possible to minimize effort in the stoning process (step 16).

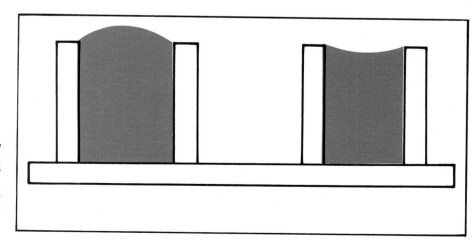

Figure 26. Wet enamel is used to fill the spaces between the cloisons. It must be applied to the top of the cloisons (left) because the wet enamel settles (right) during the firing process.

Figure 27. The openwork brooch (left) is an example of Ottonian art of the eleventh century. (Courtesy, Altertumsmuseum, Mainz.) "Broken Dreams" (right) by Ellamarie Woolley is a contemporary piece of enamelwork. (Courtesy, The Museum of Contemporary Crafts of the American Crafts Council.)

14. Force dry and fire the piece at 1500° F. Be especially careful not to overfire. This time the piece can be weighted upside down after removal from the kiln. Allow to air cool.

15. The surface can be finished in two ways, depending upon the desired artistic effect: the wires can be left higher than the fired enamel; or, the wires can be leveled to match the height of the enamel. If the wires are to be leveled, this is done by a technique called stoning, which produces a smooth, aesthetically pleasing surface.

16. To stone, place the piece under running water and rub the coarse side of a carborundum stone over the entire enameled surface. The stone grinds the wire and the enamel at the same time. The running water washes away the grindings so that they are not reground into the enamel. To avoid any further regrinding of debris, move the stone in a circular motion. Stone until the piece feels as smooth as possible, without grinding the enamel away altogether. Because of variations in the wet inlay application, some of the enamel may be too low to be leveled during one stoning.

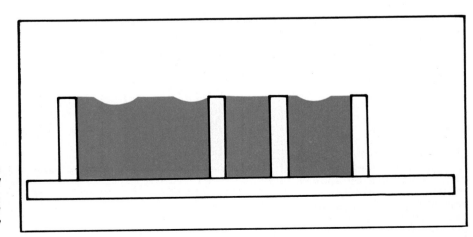

Figure 28. This cross-section shows pockets of unstoned enamel that must be filled, fired, and stoned to insure a completely smooth surface of enamel and cloisons.

This is to be expected. Another stoning will be done later on.

17. After the initial stoning, scrub the entire surface with a toothbrush under running water to dislodge any enamel particles and wire shavings that are stuck in crevices and pinholes. Dry the piece. The enamel now has a matte finish because of the stoning. Fill in the remaining shiny spots with matching enamel colors.

18. Allow the newly applied enamel to dry. Then fire the piece very *carefully,* as the enamel is now very thin from the stoning and is prone to burning out quickly. When the firing is completed, the finish will be shiny again. Weight the piece and allow to air cool.

19. Stone once more to level the new areas of enamel. This should not take as long as the first stoning. Scrub the surface as before, and allow the piece to dry. Then, fire it carefully, weight, and air cool. These procedures should be repeated as many times as necessary to assure a perfectly smooth surface. (Note: Too much stoning will eventually wear down the enamel to the original metal surface.) The final stoning should be done with the fine side of the carborundum stone to remove the marks left in the wire by the coarse side.

20. The final firing should be watched with great care. All that is necessary is that the matte surfaces become shiny — no more than that. Remove the piece from the kiln, gently weight it, and allow it to air cool.

21. The piece is ready for finishing and framing. A wooden frame is usually the most compatible with enamel. If the silver wires become dull after a few weeks, they can be polished by hand with pumice and water, which will not scratch the surface.

For Additional Reading

Ball, Fred, **Experimental Techniques in Enameling,** Van Nostrand Reinhold, 1972.

Bates, Kenneth F., **Enameling, Principles and Practice,** World, 1972.

Maryon, Herbert, **Metalwork and Enameling,** Dover, 1971.

Rothenberg, Polly, **Metal Enameling,** Crown, 1971.

Seeler, Margaret, **The Art of Enameling,** Van Nostrand Reinhold, 1969.

Untracht, Oppi, **Enameling on Metal,** Chilton, 1957.

Collage

Collage, the gluing together of small papers and articles into a design, is a rewarding, artistic, and practical form of self-expression.

The origin of collage is attributed to both Georges Braque and Pablo Picasso. Each artist utilized the method at the turn of the century. However, prior to this, Italian portrait painters had pasted small pieces of chain, gilded paper, and sometimes real stones and jewels onto their canvasses.

Figure 1. ''Musical Forms'' (above) is a collage by the French artist Georges Braque. This work was completed in 1918. (Courtesy, Philadelphia Museum of Art, Louis and Walter Arensberg Collection; photo, A.J. Wyatt, Staff Photographer.) The collage ''Eskimo Blue'' (opposite) is by Suzanne Peters, a Chicago artist. Crayons, ink, tissue, and watercolors were used to create the intriguing effect of overlapping contrasts and textures.

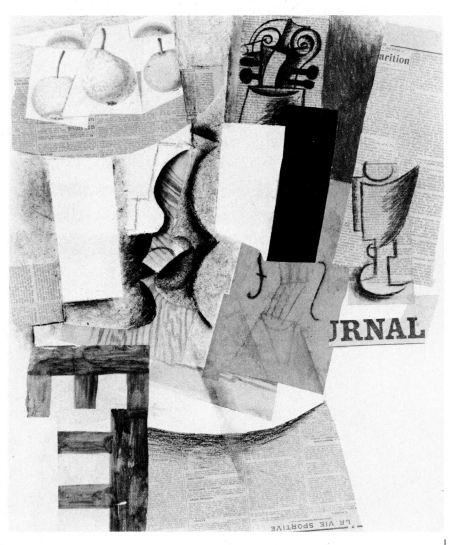

Figure 2. Artist Pablo Picasso completed this collage, "The Violin," in 1913. (Courtesy, Philadelphia Museum of Art, A.E. Gallatin Collection; photo, A.J. Wyatt, Staff Photographer.)

Both Picasso and Braque were influenced by the writings, theories, and paintings of Paul Cézanne. Along with another group, they began to paint in an abstract geometric style later referred to as analytic cubism.

In an effort to return to a more realistic form of painting, they retained the geometric format but began to incorporate such realistic materials into their work as sand, newspapers, and string. They built up areas and added texture in unorthodox ways by also including in their creations such items as hair, feathers, cloth, and even tickets and old matchbooks. Thus collage as a true art form was born as a result of the transition from analytic cubism to synthetic cubism.

However, collage did not stop at a two-dimensional level. The Dadaists used collage effectively to express their views of society by gluing together garbage and everyday items. One of their most famous works is "The Urinal" by Marcel Duchamp.

The word "collage" is taken from the French verb *caller*, which means to paste or glue. The beginning of a collage is the pasting or gluing of paper to paper, of paper to board, or of any of several materials to others.

Collage today is an accepted art form. It allows the artist the freedom to approach the medium in whatever manner is pleasing and does not restrict him to any format or material. This medium is a direct form of communication for an artist; that is, it allows the artist to work with whatever materials he chooses.

Collage is different from other art forms because it does not dictate a particular style. Style is often

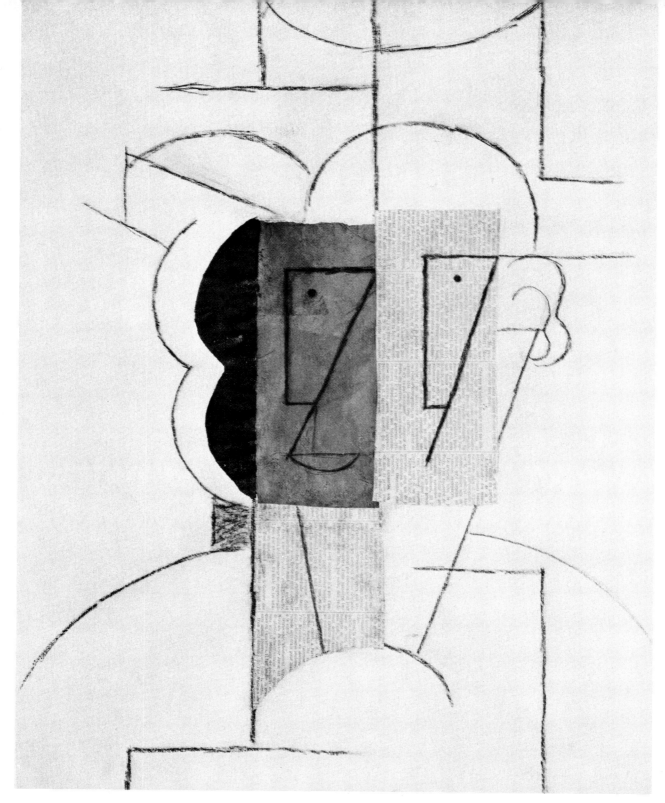

Figure 3. "Man With a Hat" is a collage by Pablo Picasso. The Cubist design, which was done in 1912, was created with charcoal, ink, and pasted paper. (Collection, The Museum of Modern Art, New York.)

controlled by materials and, because the materials are never the same for any two persons, the style of collage is always a variable. Collage is an excellent medium for both the beginner and the experienced artist. The inventiveness and creativity used in a collage usually do not result from experience but from a willingness to experiment with the basic procedures.

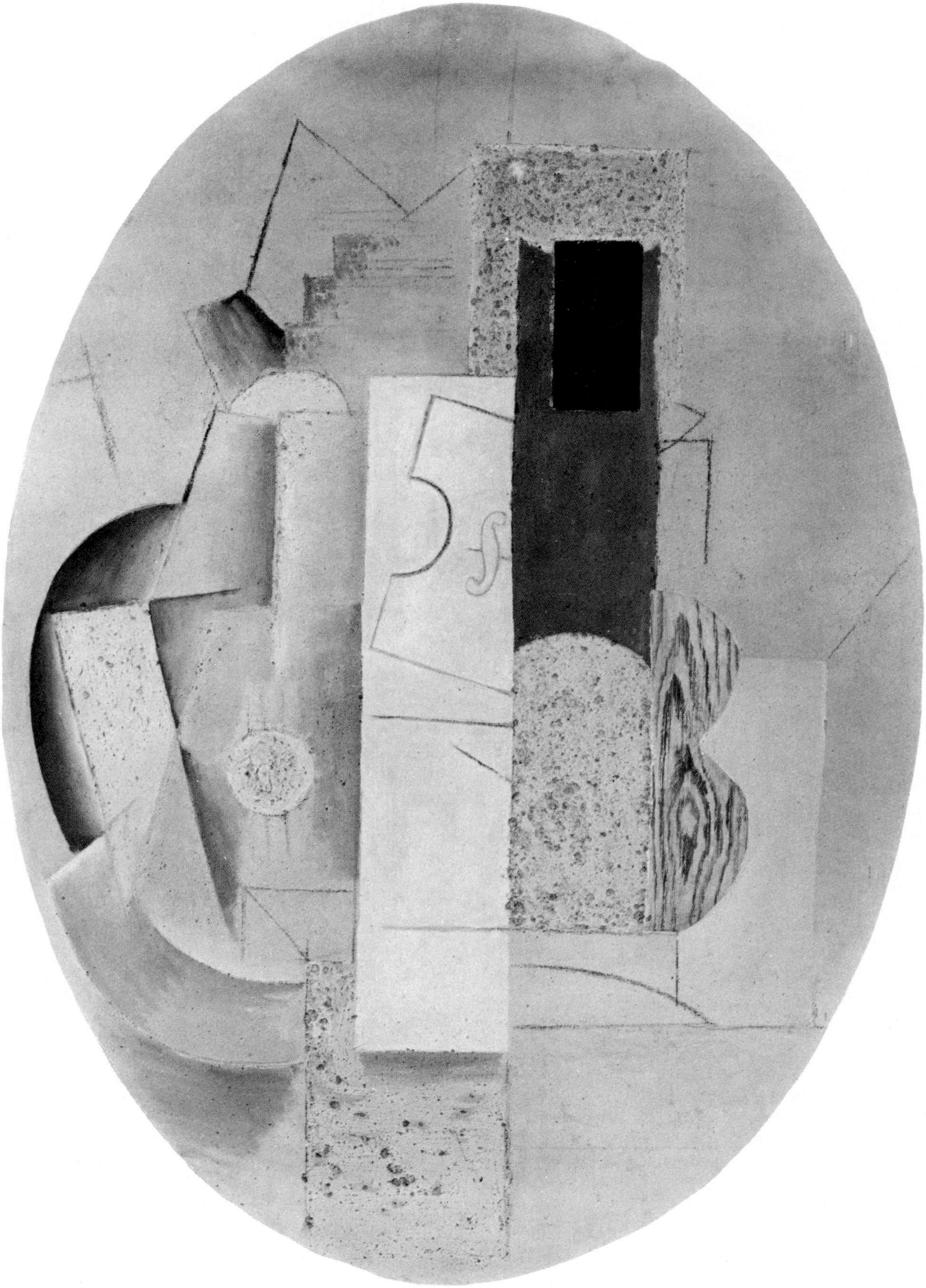

Common Terms Used In Collage

Assemblage: the grouping of found objects put on a three-dimensional level into a two-dimensional design.

Brayer: a roller, available in various sizes, used to press glued material flat.

Cover Stock: heavy paper used for glossy color photographs in magazines.

Dot Pattern: dots which result from the printing process for the photographs and illustrations in magazines and newspapers; used in collage for areas of texture.

Extender: an acrylic gel used either as an adhesive or to extend the amount of color or pigment.

Gesso: a mixture of lime, whiting, zinc white, and hide glue that is used as a water-based primer in preparing surfaces for collage.

Ground: the surface upon which a design is placed.

Priming: sealing the surface of a board with gesso or other sealers by the substance on the surface.

Printmaking Papers: paper especially suited to printing and excellent for collage; also called graphic papers.

Basic Equipment And Supplies

The materials listed here represent the tools needed for constructing collages. Particular papers and fabrics are discussed in detail in the "Basic Procedures" section which follows.

The essential items needed for almost any collage project are: (1) adhesives and glues; (2) background material (the board or paper to which the collage is pasted); (3) brushes for applying paint or glue (a variety of sizes is beneficial); (4) fabric and cloth; (5) found objects; (6) palette knife for applying glue and textures; (7) paper; (8) pins (plain straight pins are useful to organize or hold pieces of the collage down before gluing); (9) scissors or knife; and (10) a brayer.

Basic Procedures

Creating a collage is much like creating a painting or drawing, but collage permits more freedom for exploration. Before attempting a collage, experiment with various materials and tools to find desirable effects. Collage can be expensive or inexpensive. Several necessary materials — such as a scissors, crayons, pencil, heavy or light cardboard to use as a ground, colored papers, magazines, tissues, fabric scraps, paper tissues and napkins, string, old letters, white glue, and a small brush — are usually available in the home.

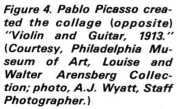

Figure 4. Pablo Picasso created the collage (opposite) "Violin and Guitar, 1913." (Courtesy, Philadelphia Museum of Art, Louise and Walter Arensberg Collection; photo, A.J. Wyatt, Staff Photographer.)

To create an original collage, scissors, paint brushes, pencils, a palette knife, and a sharp knife are needed (right).

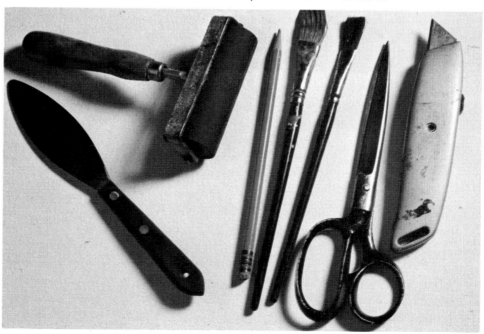

BACKGROUNDS

The first decision in collage is selecting a background. This may be anything from a piece of laundry cardboard to any of the boards described below, which can be purchased at an art store or lumber yard. The surface should be rigid because, without a strong background, there can be problems of warping, wrinkling, and cracking. All of the following papers and cardboards are different — each is best for its respective type of collage. Buy a sample of each and experiment with it.

Figure 5. The base of the collage should be a poster board, mat board, or illustration board strong enough to hold the materials pasted to it.

Bristol Board

Available in several thicknesses referred to as plys, this white board is often confused with tagboard.

Poster Board

Often called railroad board, this is a board available in several thicknesses as well as in a wide range of colors. Any collage created on this type of board may have a tendency to warp and should be mounted on something stronger when ready to frame. As the name suggests, this board is widely used for posters; it is also used for mounting photographs.

Mat Board

Very heavy board used for matting pictures and prints. It is available in a variety of colors and does not need to be backed when finished.

Illustration Board

This board, which is available in several grades of thickness and should be backed, has a drawing surface mounted onto regular cardboard. It can have either a rough or smooth finish and is particularly suitable for collage artists who combine watercolor with their work.

Watercolor or Rag Boards

These are often very expensive and only the heaviest ply will do for collage. They are high in rag content and must be backed.

Graphic Paper

Used by draftsmen, illustrators, and printmakers, graphic paper is available in a variety of types. It also must be backed.

Canvas Board

Excellent for use in collage, this is canvas which has been glued to heavy cardboard; it does not require mounting.

Hardboards

Hardboards, sometimes called particle boards, are available in a variety of thicknesses and sizes. They are made by pressing chips of wood together. Do not buy marine or tempered hardboard because it has been oiled to make it water repellent and collage materials will not adhere to it. Use the standard hardboard.

PREPARING THE SURFACE

Collage pieces adhere easily to a rough surface. Some surfaces which are either too rough or too smooth must be primed. A primer closes the pores of a surface so that the background material will not absorb too much glue or paint.

Hardwood boards, because they have been sanded, need a coat of primer to make the surface rougher. Canvas also needs a primer. Grounds which do not need priming include hard papers or cardboard which have been coated with a color, with any papers, or with a canvas board. Through experience, one quickly learns which type of background surface needs preparation and which does not. Rules to remember about priming are: (1) if the background absorbs too much water, glue, or color, it needs to be primed; and (2) if nothing will adhere to the surface properly, it is too slick and needs to be primed.

Primers

There are two types of primers: oil-based and water-based. Because water-based paints and emulsions are used in the projects described here, use a water-based primer. The most common water-based primer is *gesso*.

It is not advisable to use an oil-based paint since oil and water do not mix, nor should casein paint be used for priming because it often cracks.

Priming a Board

To prime a board, use an inexpensive 2″ wide brush or a small roller. Pour a small amount of gesso into a can or jar and add water until it is the consistency of cream. Because gesso in a can or jar will dry out quickly, keep the top tightly closed. Paint the board with the gesso — it is better to apply several thin coats of gesso rather than one or two very thick ones as they are likely to crack. Wait until each application is dry before applying another coat (usually about a half hour).

When working in collage, it is best to develop the habit of having a jar of water handy in which to keep brushes. This prevents ruining a brush with a buildup of gesso or glue and also makes cleaning the brush easier. However, never leave brushes overnight in water as they will deteriorate, become brittle, and lose bristles.

Gesso may be tinted with acrylic paints before it is applied to the ground. Simply mix the gesso with a small amount of pigment and water to make the proper color. Use pigment sparingly: the gesso serves as an extender for the pigment. To change the color, apply two coats of gesso to cover the color and then repaint.

Figure 6. To prime the background board, paint it with several thin coats of gesso. If a colored background is desired, the gesso can be tinted.

Figure 7. Tinting the gesso involves mixing it with a small amount of pigment and water until the desired color is attained.

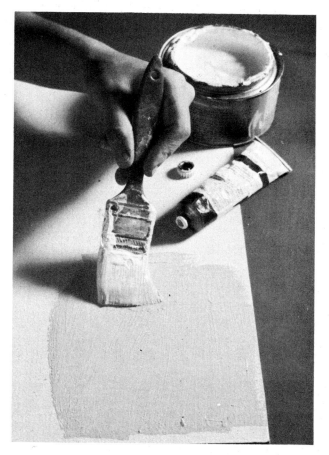

GLUES AND ADHESIVES

In some forms of art, many of the following are not categorized as glue or adhesive. However, for collage, they have particular properties which makes it advantageous to treat them as such. The following is a list of glues which are most reliable and give the best results in water-based work. It is not advisable to use children's paste or rubber cement because they are not durable enough.

White Glue

White glue is a plain adhesive which is available under many brand names. A good all-purpose craft adhesive, white glue is more economical when purchased in large quantities rather than in small bottles. The glue is thinned with water and the brush should be put in water between uses.

Polymer Mediums

In painting, polymer mediums are not referred to as adhesives. For collage, however, they are useful for both gluing and finishing a surface, especially paper or cloth. They have a plastic base, are water soluble, and dry to a clear, hard finish. Of the two types of polymer — gloss and matte — the gloss is preferable. Again, the brush should be put in water between uses.

Acrylic Gel

This is an extender which can be used as an adhesive. It gives the same effect as any polymer medium because it has a similar base. However, acrylic gel comes in a tube and is applied with a palette knife. It does not dry as hard as polymer mediums and requires more than one coat.

Modeling Paste

This acrylic product is thick, white, opaque, and dries quickly. It is used for building up layers of texture and also for adhering small objects (stones, coins, etc.) to a collage by embedding them in the paste. Modeling paste dries very quickly. The addition of gel will retard drying and allow some maneuvering, but not much. It is best to apply modeling paste, which may be sanded when dry, with a palette knife.

Epoxy

This glue is not water soluble and will bond together metal, wood, and most other substances. Available in various forms at both hardware stores and art stores, it sets up very fast. The tools used must be cleaned immediately by wiping them off because, if the epoxy dries, they will be ruined.

ASSEMBLING COLLAGE MATERIALS

After the ground and adhesive have been prepared, the collage can be assembled. The easiest way to work with the materials described here is to experiment with them. Learn to leave open spaces in a composition and do not use every material on hand.

Newspapers

Although they are flimsy, newspapers provide many types of textural and patterned materials which may be incorporated into collages. Look for large areas of light and dark grays, large dot patterns, graphs, charts of special interest, or photographs. Newspapers are generally used for textured effects on selected areas. When covered, these areas become gray tonal areas to be used as desired. Because newspaper deteriorates easily, the best adhesive is polymer medium — it will dry

Figure 8. Brush a coat of polymer over newspaper and magazine clippings that are used in a collage. Before applying the polymer, be sure that the pieces are completely flat or wrinkled, as desired.

very hard and is practically waterproof. Apply the newspaper to a collage as to any other paper, taking care to spread it over a layer of applied glue. Then work over it with a brush until the piece is completely flat or, if desired, leave some wrinkled areas in the composition. Be sure to coat the paper with polymer after it is in place to insure durability. This method can also be used for magazines, fabric, and other papers.

Magazines

Magazines are an endless source of collage materials. The quality of magazine paper is usually very high and it does not deteriorate quickly.

Figure 9. Newspapers and magazines are rich sources for collage materials. Keep a collection of interesting clippings; remember that magazine covers can also be used.

Moreover, the effects of the inks used in magazines are different from those of pigment colors. Look for differences and subtleties in both color and texture to provide a dynamic contrast in a collage.

Magazine covers, usually of heavier stock paper, often yeild interesting results. But whether using the magazine cover or the body stocks, check the other side of the page; it may bleed through when the paper is applied to the background. Also, the polymer medium will make the page so translucent that the reverse side will show up almost as well as the front side. However, this in itself can provide interesting effects.

Treated Magazines

Magazines may also be "treated" to alter the composition, color, and final appearance. One way of doing this is by "washing" a photo. Pick several photos from a magazine and experiment. Turn the water faucet on full force and run the water over one spot on the paper. The ink will run off in that area — how much ink will run is controlled by both the force of the running water and its temperature.

For a different effect, crumple the paper and then let water run into the crevices, weakening the color in those areas. Wet the paper, crumple it, run it under water again, and let it dry flat on a

Figure 10. "Treating" magazines can produce unusual appearances for collages (below). Wet the page, crumple it, and wet it again. Continued rubbing will partially remove the image (below right).

piece of newspaper. After a piece of paper is very wet, areas can be obliterated simply by rubbing the fingers over the unwanted areas. The harder the rub, the more color will be removed. Control the color by practicing with it first.

Work with the shape in addition to color. Pieces can be cut very neatly with scissors or ripped out of the magazine. Try both cutting and tearing all the edges. Also try using pinking shears. Experiment in several ways.

Printmaking, Drawing, and Drafting Paper

Although each of these papers is used for specific purposes, all can be used in collage. They are available in an almost endless variety. There are heavy white papers, thin papers, and some with rough or very smooth textures. Some of these papers absorb much water, some are shiny, and some are dull. There are also some specific papers which are available in colors. These include construction paper, charcoal paper (for charcoal drawings), and watercolor papers. There are even papers which simulate cloth, such as velour paper, which is available in a variety of colors.

Oriental Papers

These handmade papers, usually of Japanese origin, and used for a variety of drawings and prints. To the collage artist they are especially useful because they are very delicate in texture but quite strong when cut or torn. Some are actually collages in themselves, with inlaid leaves or pressed flowers.

Also available are *origami* papers — dull on one side, bright on the other. Some have flecks of gold or silver in them. These papers are traditionally used for origami — the art of paper folding — but they produce excellent effects in collage.

Figure 11. Artists' papers provide a variety of colors, textures, and weights for collages. The assorted colored papers (left) have flat or shiny finishes. The deckle-edged papers (right) have an interesting texture and a soft edge that blends well with other materials.

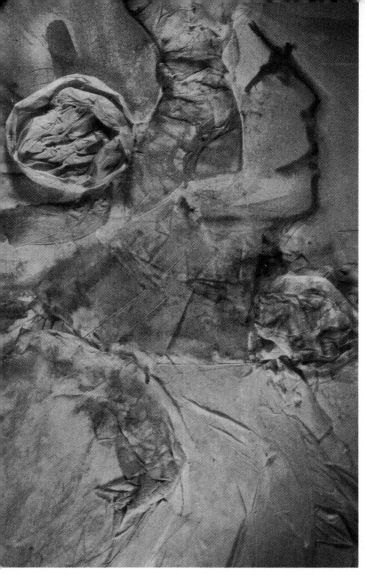

Tissue Paper

Tissue paper is the best paper for collage. It adds color and brilliance, is inexpensive, and is one of the most versatile collage mediums. It can be used directly or as a dye or stain, and it can be prepared in layers before assembling the collage. Tissue paper is easy to control and offers a wide range of colors.

By overlaying each of the three primary colors (red, yellow, and blue), the secondary colors (green, orange, and violet) are created. This is possible because of the transparency of tissue paper. Also by overlapping several strips of the same color, different shades of the color can be obtained.

A fine experiment to try when first working with tissue papers is to take all of the various paper samples on hand and cut or tear off a small piece (2" x 2") from each one. Then combine each of these pieces with a small square of tissue paper, overlapping the tissue paper onto the torn sample and adhering it with polymer medium. This will strengthen the tissue paper, just as it does newspaper. These small samples will demonstrate the possibilities which tissue paper allows.

Figure 12. In an untitled collage (top), the author used tissue paper effectively. Tissue paper is inexpensive and easily obtainable in a variety of colors (bottom). A stain can be made with wet tissue (right) by brushing the water from the paper to the surface that is to be tinted.

Also experiment by overlapping colors of tissue paper: try green on a white ground with a yellow over that; or glue the yellow down first and then the green; or, try different grounds, such as gray or foil, over doilies. The possibilities are endless.

After working with tissue paper, various sorts of odds and ends are frequently left. These should be saved and put to later use. They may be placed over areas as a color wash, for example, or used to color an area of newsprint. Pasting tissue paper over the newspaper with polymer enhances the newspaper but does not affect its readability. For scraps of tissue which seem too long or too small to be used as a wash, dampen a sheet of white paper with water and lay the pieces of tissues on the paper, arranging them in patterns. Let the paper dry and discard the tissues. The dye from the tissues will have transferred onto the paper. This can also be done with a polymer medium instead of water with one difference. If the tissue is left on the paper longer than a few minutes, it will be bound there by the polymer. When using polymer, try to find a compatible length of time for the tissue and paper being used. This will result in colors deeper than the diluted effect achieved with water.

There is one further simple experiment to try with tissue which demonstrates the versatility of collage. Glue a piece of fabric or paper onto a white background. Take a small piece of strong colored tissue and paint one side of it with polymer. Place it into position over the other object. Now, instead of brushing the top side of the tissue with polymer as before, either run water over the tissue and let it bleed, brush water over the tissue for watercolor effects, or dip the surface of the collage several times in water by holding the collage face down and passing it across the top of the water surface. (Do not plunge the collage into water or immerse it completely.) Each should yield a different effect. Let the collage dry and then proceed to finish it.

Fabric

All kinds of cloths — from sheer to loose woven — can be used in collage. One of the most widely used fabrics is cheesecloth.

Figure 13. An interesting effect is created when two colors of tissue paper are overlapped (below). The transparency of the tissue blends to make new colors. Water can be applied to the tissue for still another effect (below left).

Figure 14. Because of their colors and textures, fabrics are excellent materials for collages. Their use is limited only by the imagination of the artist.

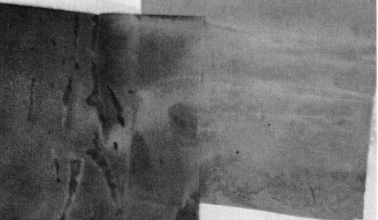

White glue works very well with cloth. Apply glue to the background area where the fabric is to be, then glue the wrong side of the fabric and press it into place. Roll over it with a brayer or by hand to keep it down. Of course, the fabric can be altered to suit individual taste. Paint on cloth with watercolor or acrylic, dye over it, tie dye areas of it, or batik the cloth. Often cloth is bleached to yield an old, faded look.

The fabric chosen does not have to be glued down flat — it can be gathered or pleated. Crumple or wrinkle parts of it. Once again, experiment — see how the cloth can be manipulated.

Figure 15. Wrinkled pages from magazines were used in the assembly of a collage (below) that has a multi-layered design. The details of the pictures — the bedding, the ceiling tiles, and the wood paneling — add depth to the overall design. Although a smaller number of individual pieces are used, an attractive collage (right) can still be created with an assortment of fabrics in coordinated colors. A collage that has a strong, bold design (below right) was produced by using only two different fabrics.

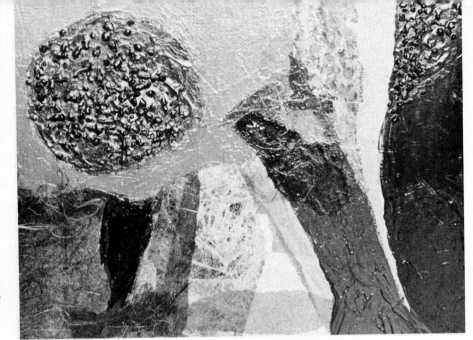

Figure 16. Acrylic paint, rice paper, tissue, and instant coffee were used to create this collage by Suzanne Peters. (Courtesy, Collection of Al Collins.)

Figure 17. Dried corn, peas, and rice (above) are but three examples of foods that can be utilized in a collage. White glue applied to the background (below) will hold textured objects. The layer of glue should be thick enough to hold the objects securely, but thin enough to be workable. Do not forget the pantry when looking for interesting objects to use for textures (right).

Materials to Provide Texture

Anything from sand, small stones, and glass to macaroni and dried grasses can be used to create texture. The best way to determine whether or not a particular material can be used is to experiment with it — often, for example, a material will dissolve in the glue. On a small piece of ground board, spread a medium layer of white glue. Sprinkle or place the materials onto the surface. Wait a few minutes and then tip the entire board sideways to allow the excess material to fall onto a sheet of newspaper. This residue may be reused or discarded.

The idea is to create a desired effect. Try the following experiments with sand:

1. Using glue as though it were a pen, write some letters or a name with the glue and sprinkle with sand.

2. Place a thin layer of white glue on a piece of ground, wait, then sprinkle with sand.

3. Glue down a texture material, such as macaroni shells or seeds, and allow to dry. Cover the material with glue and then sprinkle with sand. Or paint the glue only in certain areas of the texture material and then sprinkle with sand.

4. Glue a piece of fabric to a board, apply white glue, and lightly sprinkle with sand.

5. Spray the sand different colors with oil-based or water-based paint before gluing it down or paint the sand after gluing it down.

Modeling paste is a glue but also can be used as a textured material. Lay down a layer of modeling paste with a palette knife and run an old comb across the top of the layer, trying for deep and shallow effects. Add paint to color the mixture, paint it after it is dry, or glue sand to it.

Figure 18. Spreading a thin layer of glue on cardboard (above) and sprinkling sand or beads over it (below left) creates texture for a collage. Modeling paste can also be used as texture (below). Apply a layer to the background board with a palette knife; then, experiment with combs, toothpicks, or sponges to vary the design. There are unlimited possibilities for creating textures in collages.

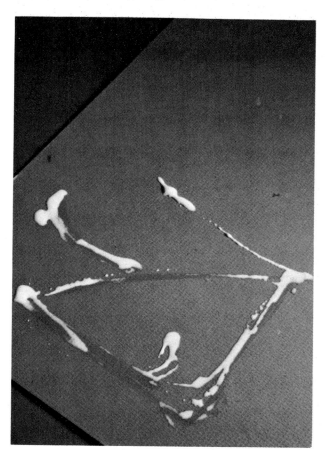

Figure 19. Paper, ink, rice paper, and watercolors were the materials used in "Moonshine," an original collage by Suzanne Peters. Its design is given an added dimension with the placement of words and pieces of type in an arrangement that appears random, but has been well thought out.

Figure 20. Fragments of words appear again in Suzanne Peter's "November Collage." This collage was created with crayons, rice paper, and acrylic paint.

Projects You Can Do

Working with collage is not only enjoyable but it can also become an increasingly rewarding pastime as ideas change. Following the techniques already described and trying such projects as those suggested below will help the reader to develop a sense of design and composition.

COLLAGE OF TEXTURES

Flip through magazines and find a seasonal picture of an outdoor panorama, such as snowcapped mountains in the winter. In this project the scene will be created in collage.

Transfer the picture to another sheet of paper by outlining around the major areas to indicate the boundaries of the collage. This is easily done by holding both the picture and the paper against a window, thus making them translucent. Feel free to change the size or to alter the picture in any way.

Now collect the materials which will give the textural effects desired. Possible materials for snowcaps are cracked marble, shredded styrofoam, or coconut flakes sealed with polymer. The blue of the sky can be blue paper; clouds can be made by

spraying light mists of white spray paint over the snowcaps or by using several sheets of white tissue, all glued together. Burlap or straw sprayed green are good for grasses. A dusty road could be

Figure 21. To begin the first project, find a photograph of a winter scene, then transfer the picture to a pattern. Assemble materials that can add texture, such as cotton balls.

made with sand and small pieces of crushed green glass for clumps of grass.

This type of collage may not be as satisfying as an original design, but the experience and practice of working only with textures is valuable. Be sure to evaluate each collage made and keep track of those which seem to generate ideas for other collages.

COLLAGE BASED ON A THEME

Many artistic collages have themes, and, although a theme is not always necessary, collage is a form of communication. Historically, collage has been used to illustrate an artist's particular thoughts and ideas on a subject. Often the materials in the collage were not only paper tissues and string but also found objects related to the subject matter.

This project will suggest four collages, each based on a different season, to illustrate how easily ideas can be generated as soon as a subject matter is decided upon.

Copy the design onto four separate boards. (Use either the design illustrated or an original one.) Decide which board is which season. For each season, rummage through available materials and choose those which seem to illustrate the feeling of a particular time of year. Decide which colors go with a season. There are, for example, many kinds of autumn: the bright, sunny yellow, gold, orange, and red autumn days of early October; the rainy, damp, dark brown, rust, and

black and gray skies of November; or the starkness of bare trees with their light brown branches and snow-flocked evergreens against threatening winter skies.

Each season need not be illustrated by weather. It can be represented by clothing, by special sports items, or by whatever else is appropriate. If mementos are collected, worked into a handsome design, and interspersed with the colors of the season, a portrait of an entire year can be created.

Figure 23. This collage project uses papers and fabrics suitable for a theme based on the four seasons.

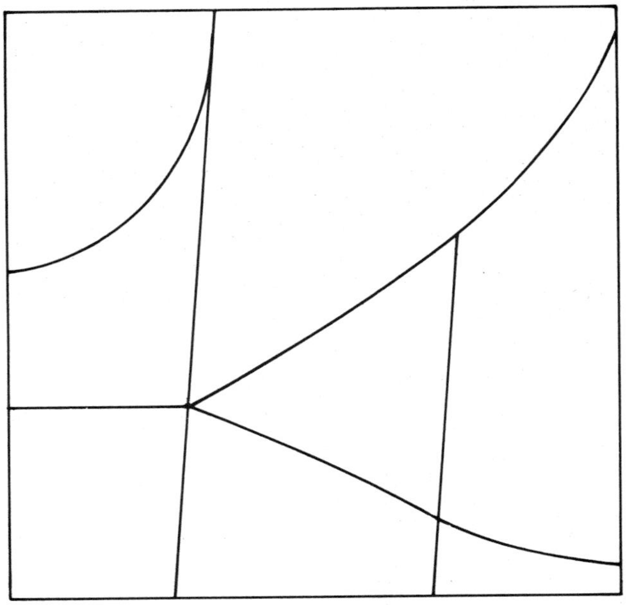

Figure 22. This diagram is a possible pattern for one of the seasons in the second collage project. Its design will be more effective if the materials overlap each other when pasted on the background.

Figure 24. For the costume doll project, mark a large piece of tissue to indicate which fabrics go where. Glue wads of tissue onto the background to add dimension. After the fabric is applied, add the face, hands, and shoes.

RELIEF AND THREE-DIMENSIONAL COLLAGES

Collage can be used three-dimensionally as well as two-dimensionally. Begin by finding objects which are three-dimensional but which can be viewed two-dimensionally if placed at a different angle. A good example of such an item is a costume doll. In addition to the usual collage materials, the following items are also needed for this project: (1) drawings or cutouts of a face, hands, and shoes; (2) buttons; (3) lace, ribbons, yarns, and threads; (4) fabrics; (5) tissue paper; and (6) a large sheet of cardboard.

Prime the large sheet of cardboard with gesso. Then, using either the accompanying diagram as a guide or an original design, pencil lightly the outline of the areas to be filled in. Now, use tissue paper to indicate the material being used for the dress — in this case, taffeta. With crumpled wads of tissue and polymer medium, pad areas where a three-dimensional effect is desired. Add laces and

yarns where shown in the illustration. Paint both the dress and the skin areas of the arms. Paste head, hands, and shoes into place. Glue buttons into place. Finally, mount the board to another board to prevent warping.

It is easy to experiment further with other free-form collages. However, they must be well thought out first: there should be a theme and attention must be given to individual objects. By working and arranging the items, one can successfully create a three-dimensional collage which is communicative as well as creative.

For Additional Reading

Beaney, Jan, **Adventures With Collage,** Warne, 1970.

Brow, Francis, **Collage,** Pitman, 1963.

Hutton, Helen, **The Technique of Collage,,** Watson-Guptill, 1968.

Vanderbilt, Gloria, **The Gloria Vanderbilt Book of Collage,** Van Nostrand, 1970.

Etching and Engraving

The art of cutting designs into hard surfaces as decorations is also a creative and versatile printing method.

Engraving, the process of cutting a V-shaped grooved line into a hard surface, began when ancient craftsmen decided to make their utensils decorative as well as functional. Because of the time and labor involved in engraving a design onto an article, it was practiced mostly on silver and gold pieces, as well as on armor. These were sold to wealthier customers who could afford to buy these exquisite pieces and who could appreciate the extra work and decoration involved. Thus, goldsmiths and silversmiths became the early masters of engraving.

Figure 2. "Tremendous Heroism With Dead Men" is an aquatint by Francisco de Goya (1746-1828) from his series, "The Disasters of War." Its tonal variations are evidence of the artistic expression possible in the aquatint process. (Courtesy, The Metropolitan Museum of Art, Rogers Fund, 1922.)

Engraving, however, was not limited simply to the embellishment of fine metal work. There are numerous examples of engraving on ivory, bone, and tusks. This craft was practiced very early in China, India, Africa, and Alaska; the first engraving practiced in America was known as *scrimshaw*. No one knows exactly what prompted the first printing of an engraved piece onto paper. It is known that a black substance was often rubbed into the lines to make them more visible (especially in scrimshaw), so the idea of

Figure 1. The name of this etching by Rembrandt (opposite) is "Rembrandt Leaning on a Stone-Sill." (Courtesy, The National Gallery of Art, Washington, D.C.)

using pressure to transfer the black substance onto paper seems a simple conclusion. Perhaps this was first practiced to preserve a particular design so it could be copied again later.

Regardless of the beginnings of *intaglio* printing, the practice of printing from lines cut into a surface, it has flourished ever since. Its first great practitioners were Martin Schongauer and Albrecht Dürer in the fifteenth century. They advanced the art to a point of excellence which has remained unmatched. Their works greatly increased the popularity of the technique and it was practiced throughout Europe by many artists who, for the most part, did their own engraving. However, some artists' engravings became so

Figure 3. In this large contemporary (1935) etching entitled "Minotauromachy," Picasso brought together various themes—a bull-headed man, a girl, and a philosopher—that he used in his first printmaking period. (Courtesy, The Museum of Modern Art, Purchase Fund.)

popular that the artist would hire engravers to help meet the demand. One of the most famous seventeenth-century artists to undertake this practice was Peter Paul Rubens, who hired engravers to copy his paintings.

The major drawback of engraving was the time involved. Every line had to be cut separately by hand, which involved several hours of hard labor. To speed the process of putting lines into metal, etching was developed. Etching involves scratching lines through a tar and wax coating onto a plate and then allowing strong acids to eat the lines into the metal plate. It evolved out of a need to put decoration on armor too hard to en-

grave. Eventually, artists began to use the technique and, through the influence of an Italian artist named Parmigianino, often referred to as the father of etching, the art became well established. However, it was used more to copy the character of engraving than for its own innate quality. It was Jacques Callot who carried etching as a substitute for engraving to its highest point. By twisting a flat needle, Callot could change a line from thick to thin, thereby matching the exact quality of an engraved line.

The first artist to exploit the natural characteristics of etching was Rembrandt. Because etching involves the scratching away of wax rather than the cutting away of copper, as does engraving, it is much looser and freer in quality. Taking advantage of this, Rembrandt used an etching needle as freely as a pen and produced prints which not only looked like pen-and-ink drawings but were much more natural and loose than engraving.

The first artist to use color in etchings was Hercules Seghers. He also experimented with both soft and hard grounds and found that textures could be etched into a plate with a soft ground, whereas before only lines could be etched into hard grounds.

After Seghers's experiments, a variety of techniques were developed to create tones. A crayon affect can be achieved by using a grained roller over a ground; a mezzatist produces an image similar to black velvet by completely covering the surface with tiny holes and scraping away light areas to create the image.

In 1778, Francisco Goya invented *aquatint,* which involves the sprinkling of small grains of rosin onto a plate and then melting them by heating the plate. This creates tiny acid-resistant dots. By controlling the depth of the acid bite, a complete range of gray can be created.

Today there are literally dozens of techniques for working on an intaglio plate, making it possible to produce almost any kind of image. Although intaglio can be tedious, it is practically the most versatile of all printmaking techniques.

Common Terms Used In Etching and Engraving

Aquatint: a method of creating a variety of gray tones or shades on a plate.

Bed: the platform or surface of an intaglio press which carries the plate through the rollers.

Bite: the process of making marks in a plate by using acid; often used instead of the word "etch."

Blocking Out: the technique of painting an acid-resistant material over areas of a plate which are not to be etched further or at all.

Brayer: a small rubber roller used to apply ink and hard and soft ground.

Dutch Mordant: a slow-biting corrosive used for etching copper.

Edition: the full body of finished prints made from a single print.

Engraving: the process of cutting lines into a plate.

Etch: the process of removing metal from a plate by using acid.

Ground: an acid-resistant layer on a plate.

Intaglio: any print made from lines cut below the surface of a plate; a term referring to all etching, engraving, and aquatint printing methods.

Resist: any material which prevents acid from attacking the plate.

Scrimshaw: engraved ivory or tusks with ink rubbed into the lines.

Tone: gradations in gray from black to white.

Basic Equipment And Supplies

Most of the items in the following list of supplies can be purchased at art supply stores and craft shops: (1) alcohol solvent to remove aquatint and shellac resists; (2) asphaltum, a tar-based resist; (3) brown water tape; (4) a burin, an engraving tool; (5) a burnisher to smooth over scratches on a plate; (6) a draw knife for cutting a plate in half; (7) etching ink, which is mixed to the proper thickness for intaglio printing; (8) etching needle, which is a scribe used to draw lines through a hard ground; (9) etching paper, a strong paper

Figure 4. Engraving on any surface requires only three tools. One of them, a burin, is used to cut lines on semi-soft surfaces. A large burin is used for heavy lines, a small one for fine lines.

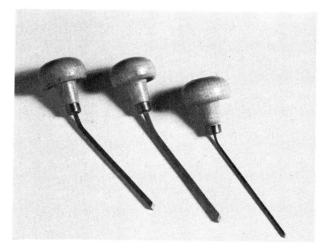

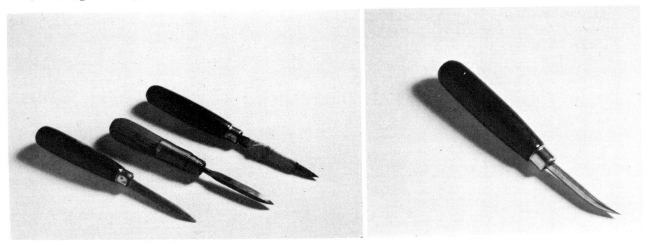

Figure 5. Another engraving tool, the scraper (left), is used on metal and on such other materials as plastics, bone, and ivory to remove mistakes and to make changes. The burnisher (right) requires a malleable surface and thus can be used only on metal. It is used to smooth out scratches after they have been scraped with the scraper.

capable of wet printing; (10) felt for use between the plate and the press rollers to allow uniform pressure; (11) fishing line; (12) hard ground, premixed resist used for line etching; (13) a hot plate to apply hard and soft grounds; (14) hydrochloric acid, an ingredient in Dutch mordant, a copper etch; (15) newspaper; (16) nitric acid, a universal etch; (17) nylon stockings to make an aquatint bag; (18) paint thinner; (19) plastic or glass trays; (20) a plate, the copper, zinc, or plastic surface used to print from; (21) potassium chlorate, an ingredient in Dutch mordant; (22) powdered rosin, a type of aquatint; (23) a press, such as a clothes wringer or some type of roller; (24) rubber rollers to apply hard and soft grounds; (25) sand-

paper (#400 grit emery paper is recommended); (26) a scraper to remove mistakes and make changes on a plate; (27) a sharpening stone to keep burin and scraper sharp; (28) shellac; (29) soft ground, a premixed etching ground; and (30) steel wool (use #000).

Basic Procedures

There are many many techniques used in intaglio printing, but the four discussed below — engraving, hard ground etching, soft ground etching, and aquatint — are the basic ones. They are enough to keep even the professional printmaker busy for some time.

Figure 6. This engraved brass tray, from a collection by the author, is a fine example of the beauty that can be achieved with a simple project.

ENGRAVING

Engraving on any surface — e.g., plastic, ivory, bone, copper, or zinc — is a very simple and direct process. It involves the use of three tools: a burin for engraving the line, a scraper for removing unwanted lines, and a burnisher for smoothing out removed areas. The uses of these tools, however, are limited. The burin can be used to cut the lines on all kinds of semisoft surfaces. The scraper works effectively on metal plates, plastics, and such organic materials as bone and ivory. The burnisher works well only on metal because it requires a malleable surface; it will not work on plastic or ivory.

Designing the Images

The first step in any engraving project is to decide what the finished product will be. Will it be an engraving on ivory, bone, or plastic; a piece of jewelry; or a print on paper made from a plate of copper, zinc, plexiglass or high-impact styrene? Once the surface has been determined, the design must be considered.

Developing the complete design or image on paper is always a wise procedure. Make all changes and corrections on paper because it is easier to correct an error at this stage than it is on copper or ivory. Make sure the design is exactly as desired before proceeding further.

Preparing the Plate

Before transferring the image for a print, make sure that the surface is completely smooth because every scratch and mark will be reproduced. This is usually not a problem if new copper, zinc, or plastic is used. If scratches are present on metal plates, they can be removed by scraping the scratch away and smoothing the area with a burnisher. If a scratch exists on plastic, scrape it away with a scraper, sand the plastic with #400 grit emery cloth, and then buff with jewelers' rouge. If scratches mar the surface of a piece of ivory, horn, or bone, sand them also with #400 grit emery cloth.

After the plate surface is clean and polished, it is necessary to file down the edges of the plate to assure smooth entry into the press. The angle should be about 30° and the bevel should extend

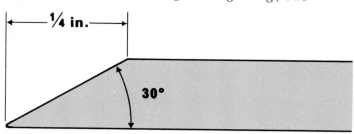

Figure 7. A plate must be beveled so that it will enter the press smoothly. The angle should be about 30°.

about 1/4" in from the edge of the plate. After the edge is filed, scrape and burnish to avoid printing the edge.

Transferring the Design

Once a suitable image has been decided upon and the surface has been prepared, transfer the drawing to the plate by tracing with carbon paper. If working on a curved surface, such as horn or a piece of jewelry, copy the drawing onto the surface in pencil. Once the image is transferred, the actual engraving can begin.

Engraving the Design

Engraving can be easy or it can be most frustrating; it all depends on how the burin is held. The burin should fit snugly into the palm of the hand with the fingers gripping the side of the blade. The angle of the burin above the surface should be from 5° to 15°, depending on the depth

Figure 8. The way in which the burin is held is important. Hold it snugly in the palm, which provides the forward thrust, and place thumb and forefinger, as shown, to guide the tool.

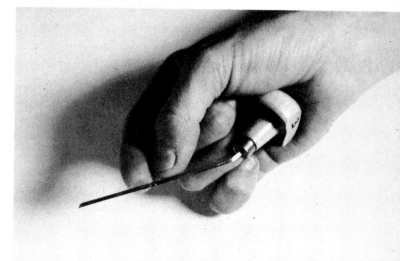

Figure 9. When starting a line with the burin, raise the handle to drive the point into the metal, then lower the burin almost to the plate. For safety, remove all burs and smooth out sharp areas.

and width of line required. The greater the angle, the deeper the cut. A very low angle is usually all that is necessary for a smooth cut. If the effort needed is excessive, the angle is too high or the burin is dull. If a heavy line is necessary, use a large burin. If a light line is needed, use a fine burin. Keep tools sharp at all times.

The one major difficulty in engraving is that the burin tends to slip, causing an unwanted line. To avoid this, keep pressure uniform, keep angle of burin to surface above 5°, and, when coming to a stop, increase the angle rather than decreasing it. After the image is engraved, scrape off all unwanted lines and burnish.

If the project is simply to engrave a decoration rather than to make a print, the job is done. If a darker line is needed, rub printers' ink into the lines and wipe the surface clean. Let dry. If, however, the engraving is to be printed on paper, several other steps are required.

The Press

Printing a plate requires a small printing press consisting of two hard rollers. There are many varieties on the market with a wide range of prices. For small plates, an old clothes wringer or mangle can be used. If a wringer is used, cut a bed out of masonite and insert it between the rollers. This will serve as a platform on which to arrange the plate, paper, and belts.

Inking the Plate

To ink the plate, rub intaglio ink the consistency of honey into all the lines. The consistency can be altered by adding linseed oil or burnt plate oil to the ink. Once all the lines are filled, rub the surface of the plate with newspaper to absorb the excess ink. After several wipings with the paper, most of the surface ink will be gone. The final cleaning is done by wiping the palm of the hand quickly across the surface with as little pressure as possible. Talcum powder on the palm will also help to remove final traces of ink. The image should be completely visible and clear on the plate.

Figure 10. Rub intaglio ink, thick as honey, into all lines on the plate (top). Wipe the plate first with newspaper and finally with the palm of your hand, using a slight pressure (bottom).

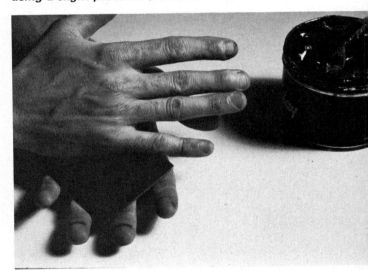

Figure 11. To print the plate, soak a piece of etching paper in water and blot. Lay the paper on the plate, which has been placed on the bed of the press.

Figure 12. The balls shown are hard ground, a mixture of tar and wax. Hard ground is applied to a zinc or copper plate that is heated. The ground melts and forms a thin layer over the plate.

Printing the Plate

To print the plate, place it on the bed of the press. Soak a piece of etching paper in water, blot out excess water, and lay it onto the plate. Over the paper place a fine piece of felt and then a heavier piece. This stack of plate, paper, and felt is then fed into the rollers of the press while turning. Run through the press once and remove felt pieces and paper. The impression has been made.

HARD GROUND ETCHING

Etching is a method of creating images on a metal plate by using acids and acid-resistant materials or grounds. The acid does the work and the grounds limit the areas which the acid attacks. There are three basic etching techniques: hard ground etching, soft ground etching, and aquatint.

Applying Hard Ground

A hard ground is a mixture of tar and wax. Purchased as a ball, it is applied by placing the ball on a copper or zinc plate, which is then placed on a hot plate or stove. Once the ball begins to melt ever so slightly, small amounts of the ground are rubbed onto the plate. Then, using a brayer, the ground is rolled smoothly into a thin layer, covering the entire plate. Let the plate cook for about five minutes over a low flame, then remove and let cool. Once the plate is cool, the ground should feel hard and dry. If it is tacky, reheat and cool it again.

Figure 13. Scratch away the hard ground with an etching needle, a roulette, a scraper, or a razor blade to draw the image. The resulting bare metal will print black after the plate is treated with acid.

Drawing the Image

Drawing the image requires nothing more than scratching away the hard ground, leaving bare metal for the acid to attack. The most common tool for this process is an etching needle; however, any tool, such as a roulette, a scraper, or a razor blade, will work for various effects. Remember that what is removed will print black.

Acids

The acids used to etch a plate depend on the kind of metal in the plate. A good etch for either a zinc or copper plate is a mixture of nitric acid and water. Depending on the strength desired, the ratio of the mixture may be six to ten parts water to one part acid. If a mixture is used for copper, the same batch cannot be used for zinc. Another good etch for copper is Dutch mordant, which consists of 10 percent hydrochloric acid, 2 percent potassium chlorate, and 88 percent water. This etch is used where extra fine detail is needed. These etches should always be mixed by adding the acid to water. Adding water to acid causes dangerous spattering. Place the etch in either a glass or plastic tray.

Etching the Plate

Before immersing the plate into the acid, cover the back and edges of the plate with shellac to avoid etching of those surfaces. With the plate cradled between two pieces of heavy fishing line, immerse it into the acid for two to three minutes. Remove the plate, rinse it in water, and examine the depth. Each line should be about half as deep as the diameter of a pin. If necessary, etch the plate again until this depth is achieved. Lighter areas are obtained by blocking them out with

Figure 14. To etch a plate, cradle it between two pieces of heavy fishing line and immerse it in an acid bath. Remove the plate, rinse it with water, and examine the depth of each line.

shellac to avoid further biting. If the ground lifts or bubbles up, the etch is too strong. Weaken the solution and repair the ground with shellac if possible. If not, begin all over again.

Removing the Ground

After the plate is etched, remove the ground with paint thinner and the shellac with alcohol solvent. The plate is now ready to be inked and printed.

Printing the Plate

The etched plate is inked and printed in the same manner as described above for an engraving.

Correcting the Plate

After a proof or trial print is made, corrections can be made by scraping away lines, burnishing the surface, applying a new ground, and etching in new lines. This procedure is repeated until the desired image is achieved.

Figure 15. When it is necessary to correct a plate, use the scraper (left). Hold the scraper as close as possible to the surface of the plate and carefully shave away the unwanted lines. Smooth the surface with the burnisher (right).

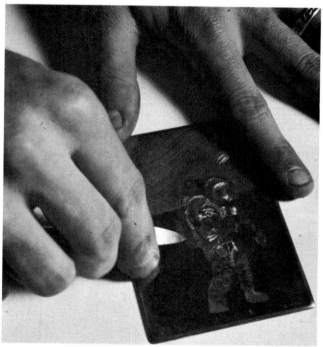

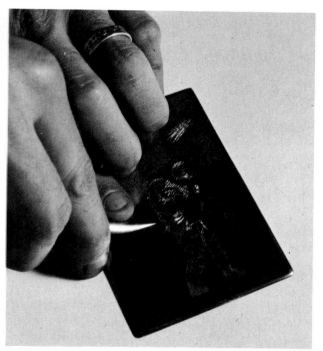

SOFT GROUND ETCHING

Soft ground etching is similar in all respects to hard ground etching except for the procedures used to place the image onto the plate. As the name implies, the difference between a soft and a hard ground etching is that the former is literally soft. Because it is soft, the image can be achieved by pressing objects or textures into the ground and lifting the ground away in those areas.

The procedure is very simple. Apply the soft ground in exactly the same way as a hard ground.

Figure 16. When soft ground is used, a material such as lace is placed on the ground, covered with paper, subjected to pressure, and removed. An image of the lace remains on the ground.

However, because the soft ground is more delicate, be careful not to mar the surface. One method of creating the image is to place a sheet of paper over the ground and draw the image with a ball-point pen. The pressure of the pen causes the ground to stick to the underside of the page, thus exposing bare metal on the plate. Likewise, any kind of texture — e.g., lace, burlap, sandpaper, cloth, leaves, feathers — can be reproduced by laying the object on the plate, covering it with paper, and applying uniform pressure, usually by running it through the press. When the object is removed, it lifts off the ground, leaving on the plate a mirrored image of the object.

Etching on a soft ground should be done with a somewhat weaker etch than a hard ground. Other than this, the processes of etching, inking, and printing are identical.

AQUATINT

Aquatint is different from either of the ground methods. It involves taking powdered rosin and placing it in a bag made from a nylon stocking. The bag is then held about 12 inches above a clean plate and carefully shaken. Fine particles of rosin fall through the bag and land on the plate. This is continued until the plate has a fine, even covering of rosin dust. The plate is then moved very gently to a hot plate and heated. The heat causes the rosin to melt, creating a multitude of acid-resistant dots. By etching and blocking out with shellac at intervals of between 10 seconds and 15 minutes, a variety of gray tones can be achieved. Before removing the aquatint resist with alcohol solvent, be certain that areas have been etched to satisfaction, because the same aquatint can never be repeated the same way. Aquatints are inked, printed, and corrected in the same manner as described for engraving and etching.

RUNNING THE EDITION

Running the edition refers to printing the number of desired prints once the plate has been finished. This is done by first taking what is to be a perfect proof of the plate. It might require several inkings and wiping variations to achieve a proof that is satisfactory. Once the proof has been made, it is used as the standard of quality for the edition.

Each print must then match exactly the quality of that proof, no matter how many are printed.

DRYING THE PRINTS

The final step is the drying of the prints. Because a print is wet when printed, the paper will curl up when dry and the print will not be flat. To avoid this, use brown water tape to tape each print while damp on all four sides to a board. Thus, the paper is kept flat while drying and, as it shrinks, it pulls itself tight against the restraints of the tape. Care should be taken to adhere the tape properly because the pull exerted by the paper while drying often is enough to tear improperly applied tape. Once the prints are dry, they are cut off the board and trimmed to the desired size.

Figure 17. After a print has been made, it must be dried. To keep the paper flat and to avoid curling, tape the print carefully to a board with brown water tape and allow it to dry.

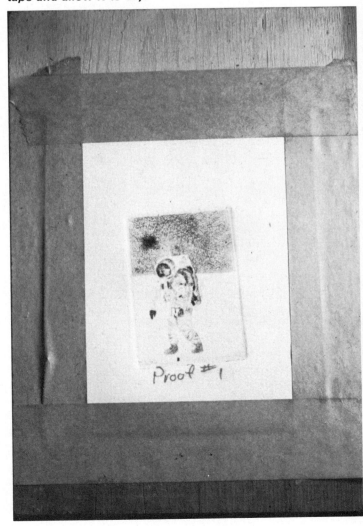

Projects You Can Do

The projects described here represent each of the techniques discussed above. One should read through each project before deciding which one to undertake first.

ENGRAVING AN ELK CALL HORN

Finding whale teeth or walrus tusks for scrimshaw is extremely difficult because the hunting of these mammals is restricted by law. Therefore, the craftsman desiring to work with scrimshaw must expect some problems. The best source is through antique dealers and flea markets with persistence usually paying off in the end. Another source is to inquire at companies which deal in jewelry supplies and materials. They often carry quantities of ivory. A more realistic and less expensive approach is to accept substitutes, such as bone, horn, and plastic. The steer horn used in the project was discovered with many others behind a livestock auction center where the animals had been dehorned before shipping.

Figure 18. Some of the steps involved in engraving a steer horn are: using a burin to engrave a design on the clean smooth horn (top left); rubbing oil paint or printers' ink into the lines; and wiping the surface clean (right). The completed horn is shown at the bottom.

Procedures

1. Before beginning any work, the horn should be thoroughly washed in soap and water and then allowed to dry.

2. After drying, examine the surface and wet sand any and all scratches with #400 grit emery paper. Finish the surface by buffing with #000 steel wool.

3. Now sketch the desired image on the horn with a soft pencil (a white colored pencil if a dark horn is used).

4. Before starting to engrave the horn, practice engraving on a piece of copper or, better yet, a piece of semisoft plastic. Try engraving circles and straight, curved, thick, and thin lines. When feeling confident in the use of the burin, begin on the horn.

5. Grip the horn firmly and start on the most insignificant area of the horn. Because the horn is curved, be careful to follow that curve or else the burin will slip. Work slowly and carefully until becoming accustomed to the shape and quality of the horn.

6. If a slip occurs, causing an unwanted line, carefully scrape the line out with a scraper and sand the area smooth.

7. Once the engraving is finished, the lines can be made to stand out by rubbing oil paint or printers' ink into the lines and wiping the surface clean. If the horn is white, use a dark-colored ink; if the horn is dark, use a light-colored ink.

8. Allow horn to dry for three days, then polish with paste wax to add a final luster.

The above procedures would be the same on ivory, bone, tusks, teeth, or plastic. Plastics, however, probably would not require the first three steps.

ENGRAVING A COPPER PLATE

Obtain a copper plate of a relatively small size, approximately 5" x 7". Because engraving is a very time-consuming process, begin with a small plate. A plate which is too large can be cut to size with a draw knife as follows. Using a straight edge as a guide, draw the knife across the plate several times until a deep groove is created. When the groove is about one-third as deep as the plate is

Figure 19. Because engraving is time-consuming, choose a small plate; if a piece of copper is too large, cut it to the desired size (left). Bevel the edges, and burnish and polish the surface so that it is perfectly smooth. Trace the design on the plate; it will help avoid unnecessary changes. Practice using the burin on a piece of scrap copper before beginning to cut the design. Stop before proceeding very far and make a proof (right).

thick, place the plate on the edge of a table and break it apart by bending it along the groove.

Procedures

1. After the plate has been cut to size, the edges must be filed down so that the plate will be able to go into the press easily. This is done by using a standard mill bastard file (a tool for filing metals of commerical coarse grade) until the angle at the edge is about 30°, almost eliminating the vertical edge of the plate. Once the proper angle has been achieved, scrape the filing marks away with a scraper and burnish smooth.

2. The surface of the plate should be checked for scratches and tarnish. If scratches exist, scrape them away and burnish. It is a good idea to buff the entire surface with extra fine steel wool until it is shiny, and then polish it. There are a number of polishing compounds available at art stores and graphic arts companies, but any standard copper or brass polish will do. It is important to begin engraving with a flawless plate because it is easier to remove blemishes.

3. It is always a good idea to trace the desired image onto the plate with carbon paper or to draw the image on the plate first with a felt-tip pen be-

fore engraving. This helps to avoid unnecessary mistakes and changes.

3. Engrave the plate, following the procedures and rules described previously.

5. As unwanted areas occur through accident or bad judgment, scrape them away with a scraper and burnish smooth. Do not be afraid to change an area and to reengrave — remember that many changes and alterations can be made in engraving.

6. Throughout the engraving, stop occasionally and make a proof as described under "Basic Procedures." This will make it possible to see both the image being produced and the corrections.

7. Once the plate is satisfactory, make as many prints as desired. An engraving is capable of several hundred impressions before it begins to show signs of deterioration.

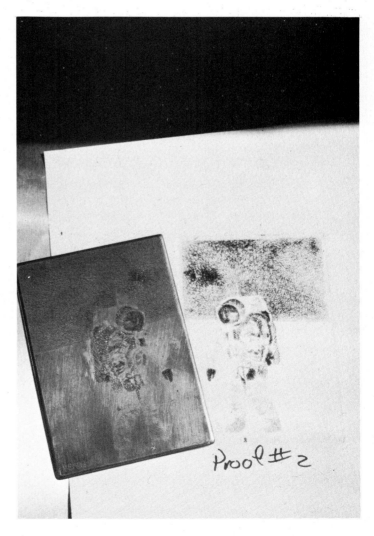

Figure 20. The plate can be corrected as engraving progresses: unwanted lines are removed with the scraper (left), and the area is smoothed with the burnisher. Continue making proofs (right) to check the image. Make corrections as necessary until the plate is satisfactory. The finished plate can be used to print hundreds of impressions.

LINE ETCHING (HARD GROUND)

Preparing the plate for a hard ground etching is exactly the same as the first three steps for the previous engraving project. It is essential that these steps be followed.

Procedures

1. After the copper or zinc plate has been prepared, place it on a hot plate until warm. Rub the hard ground ball across the warm plate until the ground forms globs. With a soft rubber roller begin to roll the ground evenly over the plate, adding more ground as needed. An even layer is important. If areas are too thin, they will break

Figure 21. Apply hard ground to a warm plate. Rub the ball on the plate until small globs of the substance form. Then roll the ground with a soft roller until a uniform layer covers the plate. Bake the plate a few minutes and allow it to cool.

down in the acid bath; if too thick, they will chip when drawing with the etching needle. Once the ground layer is even, allow the plate to bake for several minutes, then remove and let cool.

2. After the ground is cool, begin drawing the image. The advantage of etching is that the image can be created as easily as drawing with pen and ink. To correct a line, paint over it with asphaltum and draw the line again through the asphaltum when dry. Be careful to keep lines distinct and separate from each other. If too large an area is exposed to the acid, flat biting will occur, and that area will not print properly.

3. After the image has been drawn, block out all areas which are not to be attacked by the acid. This includes not only the beveled edge but also the back of the plate if it does not already have a commercial coating.

4. Before beginning to etch, decide which areas are to be etched longer for darker lines and shorter for lighter lines. It is important to plan ahead so the etching procedure will progress smoothly.

5. Using plastic netting or plastic fishing line as a cradle, lower the plate into the etching bath. (Use the etching mixture described under "Basic Procedures." Make sure the tray used for the etching bath is plastic or glass — a metal tray will be attacked by the acid.) Remove, rinse, and examine the plate periodically — the lightest lines may need as little as 1 minute of immersion and the darkest as long as 15 minutes. Using a pin and a magnifying glass, examine the lines. A dark line should be about as deep as it is wide; a light line should just begin to show a wall. Once the bite appears, correct for the lightest lines desired and block out with asphaltum or shellac those areas which should be light. Lower the plate again after the block-out is dry and continue etching. As bubbles appear, push them away occasionally with a feather. This allows a better bite. If the bubbles appear quickly and rise by themselves, chances are the bath is too strong; add water to dilute. Continue etching, examining, and blocking out until the darkest lines are properly etched. Remove and rinse.

6. After etching is completed, remove the ground with paint thinner. If shellac was used, alcohol solvent must also be used. Remove the ground

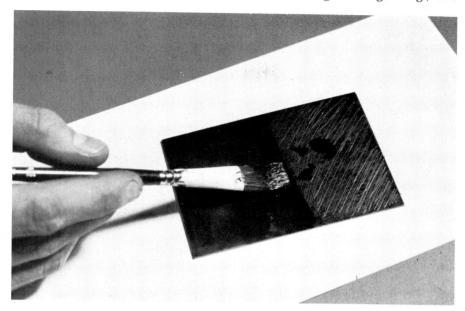

Figure 22. Remove an un-wanted line drawn on ground by painting over it with as-phaltum. The line can be redrawn over the dry as-phaltum.

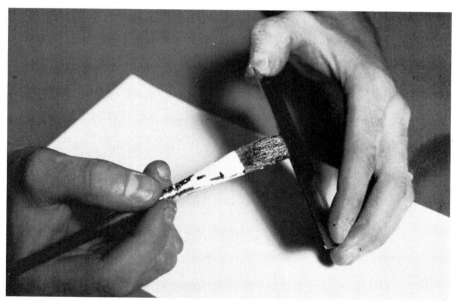

Figure 23. Before etching is begun, block out all areas that are not to be attacked by the acid.

Figure 24. During etching, examine the plate with a magnifying glass and a pin. A dark line should be as deep as it is wide (top). A light line should show only a slight bite (bottom).

only after being certain that the lines have been etched properly. Once the ground is removed, the lines cannot be made any deeper.

7. Ink the plate and take a proof as described under "Basic Procedures." At this point, any corrections may be made by scraping out, bur-nishing, applying a new ground, and etching again. This correcting process can be repeated until the desired image is achieved.

8. When the plate is complete, run the edition as described under "Basic Procedures."

SOFT GROUND ETCHING

The soft ground method relies on the fact that a soft acid-resistant material can be manipulated differently and with more versatility than hard ground. A soft ground etching is identical to a hard ground etching in all respects except for the nature of the ground itself and for the methods used to create the image within the ground. Application of the ground, preparation of the plate, etching and blocking out, inking and proofing, and running the edition are done in the same manner as described for the preceding project. Therefore, only the information relating to the creation of an image on a soft ground will be discussed here.

The soft ground method is very similar in principle to the function of carbon paper. After the ground has been applied to the plate and cooled, a piece of smooth drawing paper is placed on the plate. The artist creates the image by drawing on the paper with a ball-point pen or a hard pencil. As one draws, the pressure of the pen point causes the soft ground to adhere to the paper and pull away from the plate, thus leaving exposed metal exactly as the line on the paper was drawn. The difference between this approach and line engraving is that the hard ground line is like a pen-and-ink line, while a soft ground line is more like that of a pencil.

Figure 25. To draw an image on soft ground, cover the ground with a piece of drawing paper, and draw on the paper with a ball-point pen or a hard pencil. The ground adheres to the paper.

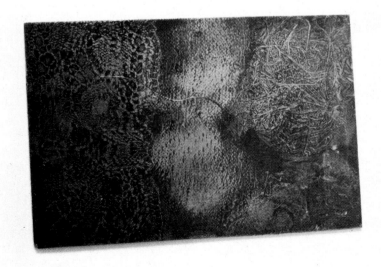

Figure 26. Various textures have been reproduced on this copper plate by placing fabrics and other items on soft ground and running the plate through a press.

The true value of a soft ground is that any texture can be reproduced. The procedure is the same as in the pencil and paper method described above. Begin by laying some semiflat texture onto the grounded plate. The texture can be burlap, lace, leaves, fishbones, crumpled plastic or tinfoil, string, ribbon, textured paper, or screen — anything which can be run through the press without being damaging. Place a sheet of wax paper over the texture and plate to keep the ground from soiling the felts. After positioning the felt pieces, run the plate through the press several times, using somewhat less pressure than that used for printing. Next, the felts, wax paper, and texture are slowly lifted to avoid damage to the sensitive ground. By using this method with various textures on the same plate, and by etching for various time periods, several different effects can be achieved.

AQUATINT

Aquatint is a very different process from the two ground techniques already described. It involves the use of rosin dust which, when heated, creates small acid-resistant dots. When etched for various periods of time, these dot-studded areas create different shades of gray.

Procedures

1. Prepare the plate in the same manner for a hard ground etching.

2. Fill a piece of nylon stocking with dry rosin which has been pulverized with a mortar and pestle.

3. Keeping the plate level, place it on a piece of cardboard near a warm hot plate. The cardboard serves as a carrying device so as not to tilt the

Figure 27. Rosin powder and acid are necessary for aquatint. Dry rosin is pulverized using a mortar and pestle, and the resulting powder is placed in a nylon stocking (left). Place the plate on a piece of cardboard so that it is level and easy to carry. Gently shake an even layer of rosin powder on the plate, covering about 50 percent of it (right). Move the plate onto a hot plate, and slide out the cardboard.

plate and disturb the rosin particles. Holding the bag or rosin, gently shake an even layer of dust onto the plate.

4. Gently move the plate to the hot plate and slide out the cardboard. Extreme care should be taken not to disturb the deposit of rosin.

Figure 28. The rosin powder melts as it warms (below). After all of the rosin has melted, allow the plate to cool. With carbon paper, transfer a design to the plate, and, using a fine brush and shellac, paint out the areas that are to be white (right). After the shellac is dry, etch the plate. It is important not to over-etch when doing aquatint.

5. Once on the hot plate, the rosin will quickly begin to melt. After the entire area is melted, remove the plate and allow it to cool.

6. While the plate is cooling, decide which areas are to be white, gray, and black. Once dry, carbon paper can be used to transfer the design to the plate.

7. With a fine brush and shellac, paint out those areas which are to be white, allow to dry, and etch. A light-gray value will often take as little as 10 seconds in the acid; a medium gray, about 30 seconds; a dark gray, 2 minutes; and a black as long as 10 minutes. If the values are critical, do a small test plate to determine the times required in the particular acid bath being used.

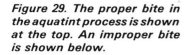

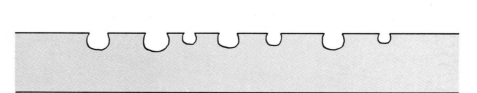

Figure 29. The proper bite in the aquatint process is shown at the top. An improper bite is shown below.

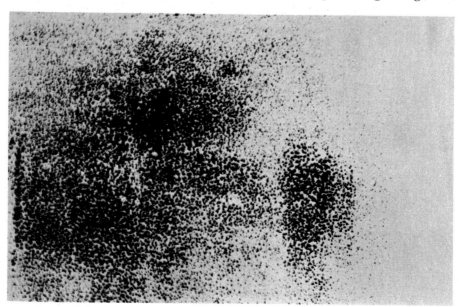

Figure 30. The etching shown is a piece that was done by the author.

8. After each degree of gray has been etched, remove the plate, rinse, dry, and block out those areas which are to remain the value of gray that was just etched. Once the block-out is dry, re-etch for the next darker value of gray. With practice, as many as 15 different and distinct values of gray can be achieved. (It is very important, however, not to overetch the plate. If allowed to etch too long, the acid will etch away under the dot of resist. This destroys the value of the aquatint as a reservoir for the ink. Also, if the aquatint is etched too long, but not long enough to be completely destroyed in the acid, it is weakened to such a degree that it will not hold up long under the extreme pressure of the press.)

9. Once etched, areas can be lightened by scraping away various degrees of the aquatint with a scraper. This allows the aquatint to print gradual gradations of gray. As always, color can be scraped away and burnished back to white.

10. Upon completion, the aquatint plate can be printed the same as any other plate.

For Additional Reading

Heller, Jules, **Printmaking Today,** Univ. of Southern California Press, 1965; Rev., 1971.

Peterdi, Gabor, **Printmaking,** Macmillan, 1971.

Ross, John, and Romano, Clare, **The Complete Printmaker,** The Free Press, 1972.

Jewelry Making

Metal casting—one of the simplest and most basic of techniques in jewelry making—has been used by almost all ancient and modern cultures.

The ancient cultures which did metal casting developed it spontaneously from the knowledge that metal became liquid and flowed when heated. Once this was discovered, the logical next step was to allow the molten metal to flow into a cavity and then cool. When the cold metal was removed, the early craftsmen found that it had taken on a cast, the texture and shape of the original cavity.

Figure 2. This bracelet was cast in bronze, using the lost wax process. It is probably the work of Benin craftsmen in Africa. (Courtesy, American Museum of Natural History.)

Among the artifacts of ancient cultures are found many intricate and beautiful cast metal pieces which indicate varied casting techniques. About 700 years ago in Africa, in what is now Nigeria, a tribe of superb craftsmen from the ancient city of Ifé cast life-sized hollow bronze portrait heads of their kings. These were first molded in wax over earthen cores. The walls of the heads were amazingly thin and uniform, indicating great skill in both modeling and casting techniques.

The craftsmen of Ifé taught casting to the people of Benin, a powerful tribe from the same area. These Benin craftsmen made many fine bronze castings (c. 1300-1700 A. D.) in a style which was more expressionistic in character than that of the Ifé, but certainly influenced by them.

Figure 1. This bronze ceremonial vessel (opposite) was metal cast during the Chou dynasty in China. (Courtesy, Collection of William Rockhill Nelson Gallery of Art, Kansas City, Missouri.)

Today, Yemi Bisiri, a Yoruba tribesman from Nigeria, still uses the ancient casting methods of his ancestors. He carves his models from beeswax over a core of hard red earth from a termite hill, and covers it with horse dung, which he packs into a ball and allows to dry and harden. Holes are made in the top and bottom of the mold with a metal tube, and a pan of water is placed under the mold. Metal is then heated, and when it becomes liquid, it is poured into the hole at the top of the mold. The molten metal melts the wax model inside. As the metal fills the cavity inside the mold, the melting wax drips out the bottom hole. The wax is caught for reuse in the pan beneath.

Other cultures which created exceptional cast metal work were the Pre-Columbian Indians of South and Central America (c. 1200 B. C. to 1500 A. D.). These people cast magnificent pieces in gold long before the discovery of the New World. Unfortunately, most of this work was stolen by the

Figure 3. This ceremonial wine vessel, cast in bronze, was made in China during the Chou dynasty. (Courtesy, Museum of Fine Arts, Boston, Anne Mitchell Richards Fund.)

Spanish Conquistadors in the 1500s, and shipped back to Europe where it was melted down for use by the Renaissance goldsmiths. The few examples which remain show exquisite detail and fine craftsmanship, such as the delicate cast wire work of the Mixtecs.

Other craftsmen in ancient India, Egypt, China, Greece, and Rome, as well as Celtic metalsmiths and American Indians, have given us rich and exciting examples of the art of casting metal. From the large bronze vessels of the Chinese to the small pieces of gold jewelry of the Pre-Columbians, one can see the tremendous range of objects, styles, and techniques used historically by man in metal casting.

The modern jewelry maker benefits from studying these examples and adapting many of the ancient methods to his own work. In this article, two different ways of casting metal will be discussed: steam casting and sand casting.

Figure 4. This silver wrist guard was designed by a Navajo craftsman to protect the wrist from the impact of the drawstring of a bow. (Courtesy, Museum of the American Indian, Heye Foundation.)

Common Terms Used In Jewelry Making

Alloy: a metal made up of two or more metals, usually to improve the strength and durability of the original metal.

Asbestos: a mineral unaffected by fire which is ground up and used to make fireproof board, cloth, and paper.

Binding Wire: in steam casting, iron binding wire (about 20 gauge) is wrapped around a tin can flask to keep it from springing out of shape.

Burnout: in steam casting, the process of melting or burning out the wax model from the investment mold.

Casting: the pouring of molten metal into a mold cavity where it cools and hardens.

Casting Sand: in sand casting, a specially treated sand which is packed into the open frames and surrounds the model to form a mold.

Cope: the horizontally placed upper part of the frame in sand casting.

Crucible: a container made of graphite or any other refractory material, in which metal is heated until it is molten.

Drag: the horizontally placed lower part of the frame in sand casting.

Flask: in steam casting, an open-ended tube of metal, usually stainless steel, in which the model is to be placed. In sand casting it is also called the frame (q.v.).

Flux: borax powder that is sprinkled on the melting metal to prevent oxidation.

Frame (also Flask): in sand casting, two parts resembling two open frames that fit together, one on top of another (the cope and the drag). The parts are usually made of cast iron, and often have one or more openings at one end for the sprue (see below). Casting sand is packed into the frame to make a mold.

Gauge: a measure of the thickness of sheet metal or the diameter of wire; also applicable to wax sheet and wire.

Figure 5. These stunning pins were fashioned from 14-karat gold. Note the stark contemporary designs employed by the craftsman. A turquoise was set into one of the brooches (below), which—though basically abstract—suggests the figure of a bird. Either pin can be made with a loop on the back, for hanging on a neck chain.

Investment: in steam casting, a specially formulated plaster-like substance designed to withstand high temperatures. It is mixed with water and poured into a flask that contains a model.

Karat: a unit of measure indicating the amount of pure gold in an alloy. Unalloyed gold has 24 karats; most commercial jewelry is made of 14-karat gold.

Liver Of Sulphur: a chemical compound (potassium sulfide) which, when mixed in a water solution, darkens metal, especially silver (see Oxidation).

Model: the pattern or piece to be cast. In steam casting, the model must be made of a material that will burn out easily, such as wax or styrofoam. In sand casting, it has to be of a material that can retain its own shape under pressure, such as wood or metal.

Mold: a solid form containing the cavity into which the molten metal flows to produce a casting. In steam casting, the mold is a steel tube filled with investment plaster. In sand casting, the mold is a double frame of metal packed with casting sand.

Oxidation: the natural process of metal combining with oxygen, causing impurities to form that can inhibit the flow of molten metal into the mold. In a finished piece, surface oxidation is often desired. This is achieved by using a chemical solution to darken the metal. Then, when areas are polished, there is a dramatic contrast between clean and oxidized surfaces.

Parting Powder: in sand casting, the finely ground powder that is dusted on the inside surfaces of the mold making it easier to separate the mold parts after casting.

Pickle: a 10% acid solution used to remove carbon or oxidation from the metal piece after casting.

Pumice Powder: a powder made from pumice stone, used as an abrasive to remove oxidation from metal.

Rammer: in sand casting, a wooden mallet or a piece of dowel rod used to pack casting sand into a mold frame.

Rouge: an abrasive compound used for final polishing of metal.

Sprue: the vertical channel that connects the model to the outside of the flask. Molten metal flows through this channel to the mold cavity.

Sprue Base: in steam casting, a wooden or rubber bottom that fits securely over one end of the flask, allowing the flask to be filled with investment.

Sprue Former: in steam casting, a dome-shaped piece attached to the center of the sprue base. When removed from the bottom of the finished mold, the sprue former creates a basin in the mold in which to melt the metal.

Tripoli: a coarse abrasive compound used to remove sandpaper scratches from a metal piece.

Vent: a narrow channel made in the mold that allows gases formed in casting to escape. The vents lead from the model cavity to the outside of the mold.

Basic Equipment And Supplies

Many of the supplies and equipment needed for casting can be easily made or purchased at a pharmacy or hardware store. If a local jeweler's supply house can be located, it will have everything needed for casting, including metal. Another good source of supplies is a dental supply house. One's dentist might prove helpful in giving advice on where to find needed items. Art supply stores, particularly the larger ones, or those which cater to universities where jewelry making is taught are also a possible source. Finally, there are many mail order jewelry supply houses all over the country which stock everything one could possibly need to make jewelry. These houses will send catalogues upon request. For a complete listing of these places see the book *Metal Techniques for Craftsmen* by Oppi Untracht (Doubleday, 1968, pages 467-80.)

STEAM CASTING

The first method to be considered is steam casting, a technique which uses the pressure of steam to force molten metal into a mold.

Tools and Supplies for Model Making

In order to cast, one must first make a model. For steam casting the most workable material for

Figure 6. This startlingly original ring (above) was designed and created by co-author Naomi Peck; she made the ring of silver and entitled it "Foot and Mouth Only." Co-author Lee Peck fashioned a 14-karat gold ring (below) and incorporated a jade stone in the design. Rings are especially popular with jewelry craftsmen.

model making is wax. Buy beeswax and paraffin at a pharmacy and melt them together in equal parts in a double boiler. Beeswax is soft and sticky and paraffin is hard and brittle, so a wax mixture different from the half and half combination may be achieved by varying the amounts of beeswax and paraffin. When the wax is liquid and thoroughly mixed, pour it out as evenly as possibly on a flat smooth rubber pad that has been spread with vegetable oil or sprayed with a silicone spray. When cooled, the wax can be lifted easily from the rubber pad. In this way one can make sheet wax that may be cut into shapes or narrow strips with a knife and straight edge.

Special wax for dentists and jewelers is made and sold in sheet, block, or wire form at jewelry and dental supply houses. It comes in colors which denote the softness, brittleness, or melting temperature of the particular wax.

Figure 7. The necessary tools for making a wax model for casting include a wax spatula, homemade spatula, half-round file, jeweler's saw, an alcohol lamp, and needle files.

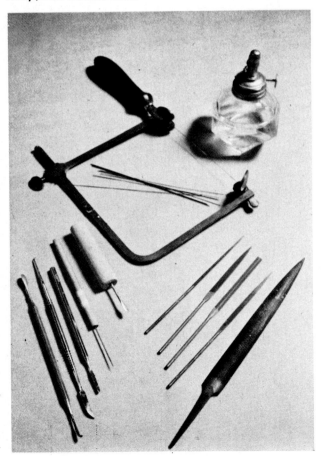

Tools are necessary to work the wax. Dental spatulas are excellent. However, wax modeling tools are easily made. Drive a nail into the end of a piece of wooden dowel rod. After the nail is firmly in place, snip off the nail head and hammer the tip of the remaining piece flat. Then, with a file, round off the edges of the flattened nail to get a small spatula-shaped tip.

Another good tool for wax modeling is a dissecting needle from a school biology kit, often sold separately from the kit. These can be made simply by gluing a heavy sewing needle eye first into the end of a piece of dowel rod. Small paring knives may also be used to work the wax.

For working on the harder File-Wax, it is a good idea to have a set of inexpensive hand files: a number 2 cut half-round file, and an assortment of different shaped needle files. Also needed are a jeweler's saw and some wax-cutting blades.

Because most waxes must be heated in order to carve or shape them, one needs an alcohol lamp and a can of denatured alcohol. The alcohol burns cleanly, and carbon does not get on the wax tools the way it does from a candle flame. Carbon should be avoided because it can work itself into the wax of a model and create a rough or porous surface on the metal casting. The lamp and denatured alcohol can usually be purchased at a hardware store.

Tools and Supplies for Mold Making

First, a flask is essential. This should be seamless and made of stainless steel which can be reused indefinitely. A good standard size is 3 inches tall by 2½ inches in diameter. Enterprising craftsmen might try to find an automobile tailpipe and cut it into sections. However, flasks can be purchased at a supply house. As an alternate, a tin can, open at both ends, may be used; but the heat from the burnout will make the tin can unusable after one casting. A good size can to use as a flask is the standard frozen orange juice can — just be sure it is metal and not cardboard. Other taller cans may be cut down in height with metal shears. It is a good idea to bind the tin can with 20-gauge iron wire to prevent the can from springing out of shape and causing the investment mold to crack during the burnout. Binding wire is not necessary with a steel flask.

Next, one must have a sprue base and a dome-shaped sprue former. These can be purchased commercially, but one can also make do with a small square of plywood or masonite board, one bar of plasticene clay, and a ping-pong ball sawed in half. The board should be two inches wider all around than the diameter of the flask.

Figure 8. A sprue former can be made by sawing a ping-pong ball in half. A sprue base can be made from a piece of plywood. The dome shape is then glued to the wood square.

Glue the ping-pong ball firmly to the center of the board, domed side up. A few pieces of specially made jeweler's wax wire, 14-gauge, will be needed for the main sprue and auxiliary sprues.

The investment plaster must be purchased. It is a special plaster mixture that is made to withstand high temperatures when ordinary plaster would break down and become powdery. This can be bought at a jewelry or dental supply store. The investment is mixed in a clean mixing bowl, preferably rubber, which is flexible and easy to clean out afterwards.

Equipment for Burning Out

Most jewelers use a kiln, a small oven which is electrically or gas powered, to burn the wax out of the investment mold. Purchasing a kiln can be an expensive undertaking, so until one decides it is worth the cost, the wax can be burned out of the flask with only a few inexpensive items.

The first item needed is an ordinary electric hot plate. Then get a large metal jar lid (larger in di-

ameter than the flask) that will rest on the coils of the hot plate and a trivet which will fit inside the jar lid. Finally, find a clay flowerpot that is wide enough and tall enough to completely cover the flask as it rests on the trivet inside the jar lid. The flowerpot must have a drain in the bottom of it and should be lined with aluminum foil with the

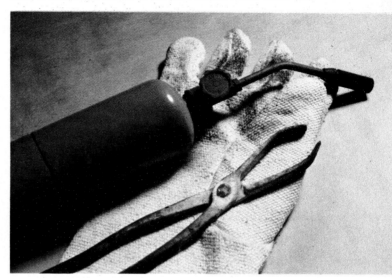

Figure 9. A propane canister-type torch can be used to burn the wax out of the flask. A pair of thongs and an asbestos glove should be used for safety reasons.

hole left open. For safety's sake, have a pair of tongs with which to grasp the flask after burnout, and an asbestos glove for lifting the flowerpot. The entire burning out process must take place in a well-ventilated room, as the wax fumes are strong and unpleasant to inhale.

Supplies and Equipment for Casting

One must have metal to begin. When buying precious metals from a supplier or a refinery, be sure to specify clean casting metal. This saves the time of cleaning the pieces before casting them, and it also saves money since sheet metal is more expensive.

If buying silver, specify sterling silver because it is harder and more durable than pure silver. If buying gold, keep in mind that most commercial jewelry is made of 14-karat gold, which is more precious than 10-karat, and less expensive and harder than 18-karat.

It is best to stay away from casting bronze or brass, as both metals give off harmful fumes when melting, and one must have a good exhaust system for cleaning the air when casting with either of these.

In order to melt the metal one needs a torch. The most inexpensive and readily available kind of torch is the propane canister type usually found in the hardware store. This type of torch is good for melting small amounts of metal, or metals that have low melting temperatures (such as pewter) because the flame is not very hot. For repeated use and a hotter, more efficient flame, an acetylene or oxygen-acetylene torch is best. (Sears, Roebuck and Co. sells a fairly inexpensive unit.)

When using the torch, always remember to keep it away from anything flammable. Be sure to have a piece of asbestos board behind and underneath the flask while the metal is being heated. Good ventilation is also necessary during the melting of any metal, as fumes are given off that are harmful if inhaled.

Figure 10. A plunging device can be made by attaching a dowel rod to a screw-type jar lid. The lid is lined with layers of wet asbestos paper and should easily fit over the top of the flask.

While melting the metal, you will need to flux it. Borax powder, found in the grocery store, is an excellent flux for casting metals like gold and silver. Pour some into a clean salt shaker and it is ready for use.

The very last item needed is the "plunger," which will create the steam needed to force the molten metal into the mold. This item must be made. Have a screw-top jar lid ready, one that fits loosely over the top of the flask (usually the lid from a large mayonnaise jar is a good size). Then a piece of wooden dowel rod, about 3/4-inch in diameter, is needed for the handle. This should be screwed to the top center of the jar lid. Finally, the inside of the lid is lined with four or five layers of wet asbestos paper (to a thickness of about 3/16-inch) and the whole device allowed to soak in a bowl of warm water until ready for use.

Have a bucket of water handy in which to quench the entire flask after casting. A plastic gallon bucket is good for this purpose.

SAND CASTING

The other method being covered here is sand casting, a process that is very direct. There is no burnout, and the metal is poured straight into the mold cavity.

Supplies and Equipment for Model Making

There are two considerations in making a model for sand casting: (1) there is no burnout because the model is removed from the frame (flask) by hand before the metal is poured into the mold, and (2) the sand is packed tightly around the model with light blows from a rammer. Therefore, the model can be made from a permanent material, and one that is strong enough to withstand the pressure exerted on it by the rammer. Models can be made from such items as wood, metal, plastic, stone, and hard File-Wax. The tools needed depend on the medium chosen. It is wise to select a medium with which one has had experience — this improves the chances for a successful model on the first try.

Supplies and Equipment for Mold Making

It is best to buy a complete sand casting kit from a jeweler's supply house. This kit should cost approximately $17.00 and usually contains the flask from, but does lend itself well to the making of pendants, brooches, and small sculpture. Of course, sterling silver or any of the gold alloys may also be used in sand casting.

The necessary crucible, tongs, and flux are in the kit. A torch to melt the metal (see supplies and equipment for casting under Steam Casting) and some asbestos board to put underneath and behind the flask and crucible to protect the casting area are the only other items needed.

FINISHING

When the metal has cooled and the cast piece is removed from the mold, there are still several things that must be done before it is considered a finished piece of jewelry. The metal must be cleaned, extraneous sprue wires must be removed, and areas should be smoothed and sanded. Then it is time to decide whether to give the piece a matte or shiny surface.

Supplies and Equipment for finishing the Cast Piece

When the metal casting is removed from the mold, there may be a black or brown carbon residue on it. This is normal, especially in steam casting. To eliminate this dark film from the surface of a sterling silver piece, one will need pickle — an acid sold in powder form at a jeweler's supply store. Do not pickle gold or pewter. Pickle may be made from one part sulfuric acid added to ten parts cold water. Sulfuric acid may be bought at a pharmacy. **CAUTION: always add acid to water and not vice versa**, otherwise an explosion may result. To mix the solution a glass rod and a Pyrex dish are needed. Also have ready some 18-gauge copper wire or copper tongs to lift the piece from the solution. Whenever acid is used, it is wise to have a box of baking soda handy to neutralize the acid in case it spills. Never pour acid down a drain.

The carbon residue may also be removed from gold pewter, or sterling silver by scrubbing the piece with pumice powder on a dampened toothbrush. Pumice powder is a standard hardware store item.

For removing sprue and vent wires, a jeweler's saw frame and number 2 saw blades are needed. Buy at least a dozen number 2 blades because

Figure 11. Equipment needed for sand casting includes a flask (frames), casting sand, parting powder, borax flux, a crucible, and tongs. These items can be purchased in a kit.

(cope and drag), casting sand, parting powder, borax flux, a crucible, and tongs. Everything in it except the flux and the parting powder can be reused indefinitely.

In addition to the kit, the following items are needed: (1) two pieces of plywood cut to the outside dimensions of the flask; (2) two C-clamps; (3) a piece of ordinary screening to sift the sand through; (4) a wood or metal straight edge (used to level off the sand after it is packed into the flask); (5) a small spatula to cut the sprue channel and vents into the sand; and (6) a wooden mallet or piece of one-inch diameter dowel rod to use as a rammer.

Supplies and Equipment for Casting

Again, metal is needed to begin. Sand casting presents an excellent chance to use pewter, which has a low melting point of about 500° F and is quite soft. In fact, it is too soft to make rings they break easily. To hold the piece steady while sawing, use a small bench vise.

To smooth over the saw marks and remove rough edges from the piece, have ready a large half-round hand file, number 2 cut, and a small inexpensive set of needle files in assorted shapes. Finally, to remove the file marks from the piece, use emery or sand paper. Usually three grades of paper — coarse, medium, and fine — are enough to remove most file marks and give the piece a smooth surface.

To have a contrast of light and dark areas on the piece of jewelry, use a liver of sulphur solution to darken the metal. Liver of sulphur is a chemical compound that comes in dry lump form. (See the section on *Finishing* under "Basic Procedures.") It works best on pewter and silver; on gold with limited success. Most jewelry supply houses sell a specially prepared bottled gold oxidizer as well as liver of sulphur. Store the liver of sulphur in a dark airtight bottle to keep it from deteriorating.

To achieve a matte finish on a piece, rub it with fine steel wool, any grade from number 1 to number 000. Steel wool, hand files, and emery paper may be found at the hardware store.

To achieve a shiny finish, buff the casting with a felt buffing stick which has been rubbed with special abrasives. Buffing sticks are available at a jeweler's supply house, or can be made by glueing two or three layers of white felt to a flat, narrow stick.

Most supply houses sell the abrasives in solid form, either blocks or sticks. One should have a stick of the more coarse abrasive called tripoli, and a stick or red rouge for final polishing. It is important to remember not to use more than one kind of abrasive per buffing stick, so have at least two buffing sticks — one for tripoli and one for rouge. A rouge cloth is excellent for keeping jewelry shiny after it has been worn for a while.

Figure 12: These three jewelry pieces were designed and made by co-author Lee Peck. A pin, or brooch, was fashioned from 14-karat gold (above). Sterling silver is the basic material for the cast ring called "Heart-On #3" (right). Another 14-karat gold ring in the same series is called "Heart-On #4" (above right). Note that "Heart-On #4" is decorated with pearls—usually associated with more traditional jewelry design, but here used effectively with a contemporary style.

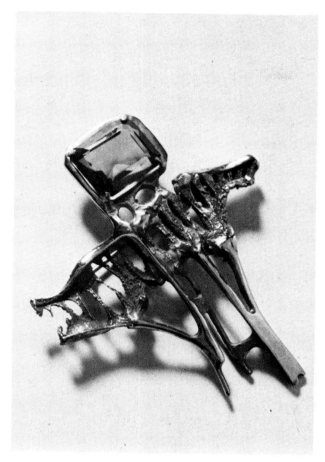

Figure 13. A 14-karat gold cast pin by co-author Lee Peck incorporates a striking stone of smoky topaz (left). The 14-karat gold ring (below) was entitled "Clasped Hands" by Naomi Peck. Metal casting is an ancient art, known in many countries and in many periods. Some of the most striking pieces ever cast in gold were created in Mexico in Pre-Columbian times.

Basic Procedures

The casting processes explained here are relatively simple ones. Once all the tools and equipment are assembled, the only major concern is the creation of the model. Then, by following these instructions, step by step, make as many different kinds of jewelry pieces as time and ideas allow.

STEAM CASTING

As mentioned earlier, steam casting requires the making of a wax model. Since there are several different kinds of waxes, and as many wax modeling techniques, the discussion will be limited to the basics. And after working with the wax for a while, one begins to develop his or her own personal technique.

Wax Modeling

One manner of wax working is done with the soft beeswax/paraffin mixture, or the more pliable dental wax sheet and wire (pink or green sheet and green or blue wire). Bear in mind that it will take a little while to learn how to work with the wax. The more experience one has with the nature of wax, the better the model will be. So experiment with the wax first. Here are some suggestions:

1. Heat the tip of the wax tool over the flame of the alcohol lamp. Press the tool into a piece of wax and watch how the wax melts, puddles, then cools.

2. Take a thin strip of wax and hold it near the flame. When a droplet of wax forms on the tip, move the strip and let the droplet fall onto another piece of wax.

3. Take a small spatula and scoop up some wax. Hold the tool over the flame and allow the wax to melt. Pour the wax onto a second piece, as with the wax droplet, and build up a mound of wax.

4. With the wax tool, carve into the mound. For a sharp cut, use the tool cold. For a smoother, rounded edge, heat the tool before cutting.

5. Try pressing small shapes like nail heads, needle points, or anything else that is handy into the wax for a texture.

6. Take thin strips of wax sheet or wax wires and experiment with ways of joining them — side by side, at angles, etc.

7. Bend wax wires around such items as dowel rods or pencils to make coils.

8. Put two wax shapes together, heat the wax tool, and insert it briefly between the two edges, causing them to fuse together.

9. Roll sheet wax back and forth on itself, creating folds or wrinkles.

11. Poke the wax tool all the way through a piece of wax, making a hole. Make odd-shaped holes and holes of different diameters.

Note: If soft wax breaks while being bent, it needs to be warmed. It may be warmed in the hands, in hot water, or by passing it several times quickly over the lamp flame.

To experiment with the harder File-Wax, do the following:

1. Saw off a block of wax to the desired thickness.

2. Incise it with knives and saw blade.

3. File away parts of the block with different shaped needle files.

4. Bore a hole all the way through the block of wax with the sharp tip of a file. Change the shape of the hole by filing into it at different angles.

5. Use sand paper to smooth sharp or rough edges.

This experimentation will demonstrate that the softer wax lends itself to the making of organic shapes, while the harder File-Wax works better with more geometric designs. Remember, with any wax, the model should be kept as light as possible. Otherwise, the finished piece of jewelry will be too heavy and difficult to wear comfortably. Also keep in mind that the cast piece will look exactly like the finished model, so be certain that rough edges have been smoothed out and that the model is completely satisfactory. It is much easier to make changes in wax than it is when the piece is cast in metal. It is wise to make a small sketch before beginning work on a model.

Spruing the Model

Once the model is completed, it is time to set it up in the flask.

1. Gather together the model, some 14-gauge wax wires, and the ping-pong ball sprue former and wooden base.

2. With the wax tool, firmly attach the sprue (a 14-gauge wax wire) to the heaviest part of the model. In the case of a wax ring, attach the sprue to the ring shank opposite the ring top. If the model is large and flat, tilt the piece to allow the metal to flow easier later on. Broaden the sprue where it attaches to the model. Auxiliary sprues, also of 14-gauge wax wire, may be added to help the metal flow to the extremities of a large model.

Figure 14. Sprues are made from a 14-gauge wax wire and attached with a wax tool to the model. A single sprue is attached to the wax ring at the shank opposite the ring top.

3. Now measure out the amount of metal needed to cast the model. Take two small glasses and fill them half full of water, with exactly the same amount in each glass. In one glass submerge the model and sprues until the main sprue is one-half inch under water. In the other glass add metal until the water level is the same in both glasses. Add about a fourth more metal to allow for a complete fill of the mold.

Figure 15. The water displacement method is used to measure the metal needed to cast a model (above). Using a large, flat model (above right), attach the main sprue to the heaviest part and auxiliary sprues to the extremities. The model is attached to the sprue former and positioned inside a flask (below right). Place tape around the edges of the flask top, and use plasticene clay as a filler between the flask bottom and the sprue base.

4. Attach the sprued model to the sprue former (ping-pong ball), allowing the main sprue to be one-half inch long.

5. If casting a big piece which will need a large volume of metal, the auxiliary sprues can touch the ping-pong ball dome, but none should be closer together than 1/8 inch.

6. Paint the model and sprues with a solution of one-half liquid detergent and one-half water. This will help prevent bubbles from forming on the model during investing.

7. Place the flask over the model so that the model is centered in the flask. The model should never be more than one-half inch from the top of the flask so that gases formed during casting can escape. The model should never be less than one-quarter inch from the top or sides of the flask, or the investment may crack from the force of the metal entering the flask and break out of the mold.

8. Roll a coil of plasticene clay and use it to make a fillet between the base of the flask and the wooden sprue base.

Once the model is sprued up and the flask is in place, it is time to invest.

Investing the Model

1. Fill the prepared flask two-thirds full of luke-warm water.

2. Pour the water into a rubber mixing bowl.

3. Add investment and begin mixing it by hand. Be sure to mix the investment thoroughly, dissolving all the lumps. When the investment is the consistency of pancake batter, not watery or stiff, it is ready to be poured.

4. Tape a strip of masking tape around the top edge of the flask, allowing it to project about an inch above the top of the flask. This will allow for filling the flask entirely without having to worry about overflow.

5. Pour the investment into the flask, making certain to pour down the side of the flask and never directly on the model. In this way the investment surrounds the model without trapping large air bubbles on the underside of it. Fill the flask completely.

6. Gently agitate and/or tap the flask to release air bubbles that may be trapped around the model. Be very careful not to dislodge the model from the sprue former. (If this occurs, remove the model immediately and rinse it thoroughly. Pour investment out of the flask into a water-filled bucket, and clean the flask. When model and flask are dry, resprue and reinvest.) Note: Do not pour investment down the drain, because it will clog the pipes. Rather, pour the excess into the garbage.

7. Set the mold aside, allowing it to harden and dry for at least one hour.

8. When the investment is firm, remove the tape from the top, and the sprue former and the base from the bottom.

9. Be sure the top of the mold is flat. If not, file or sand it flat.

10. Scrape off any plasticene clay still stuck to the flask.

Burning Out the Wax

1. Place a metal jar lid on the coils of the hot plate, so that the lid will trap any melting wax.

2. Put a trivet inside the metal lid, and place the flask on the trivet, with the sprue hole at the

Figure 16. A hot plate is used to heat the flask during the investment process. A trivet holds the flask inside a metal lid resting on coils. Then, a flower pot is placed over the flask and coils.

bottom. This will allow the melting wax to drip out freely.

3. Line the flowerpot with aluminum foil, leaving the hole at the bottom open.

4. Invert the flowerpot and place it over the flask and coils of the hot plate.

5. In a well-ventilated room, plug in the hot plate and allow the wax to melt out of the mold. This should take approximately two to three hours.

6. When the flask is glowing a dull red, the mold is ready for casting. Check the color of the flask by lifting the flowerpot slightly with an asbestos glove. The interior of the pot is supposed to reach 1100° F, so if the flask is not glowing, close the hole in the pot with foil only after there is no longer any smoke coming from the hole.

Casting the Mold

1. Assemble the metal, flux, torch, asbestos board, tongs, "plunger," and water-filled bucket. If metal appears dirty or greasy, clean it according to the instruction in the later section on Finishing, steps 1-4. **CAUTION: Never use casting metal pieces that are small enough to fall into the sprue hole and clog it.**

2. Remove the flask from the hot plate using tongs.

3. Holding the flask with the sprue hole facing down, clean the sprue hole rim with small spatula. Make sure that any residue or loose investment does not fall back into mold.

4. Place the flask, sprue hole up, on the asbestos board and fill the basin with metal.

5. Sprinkle metal lightly with flux.

6. Light torch and begin melting metal. When metal is completely molten, it begins to "spin" on the surface.

7. Remove plunger from the bowl of water. *Do not remove the torch from the metal until the plunger is poised above the flask, or the metal will freeze and not flow.*

8. As one hand removes the torch, the other hand presses the plunger down *immediately* and *squarely* on the flask top. Hold the plunger in place for about 45 seconds. It is a good idea to practice placing the plunger on an uninvested flask top, just to get the feel of it.

9. Allow the flask to cool for about five minutes. With tongs, lift the flask and plunge it into the water-filled bucket. The investment will bubble and disintegrate, leaving the cast piece, which can be removed from the water by hand.

Figure 17. After removing the flask from the hot plate, place it on an asbestos board (below left). Add the metal to the basin, and sprinkle it with flux. Then, light the torch and begin the melting process. It is important that the plunger be placed over the flask (below) immediately after the torch has been removed from the metal. Hold the plunger in position for about 45 seconds.

SAND CASTING

In sand casting the most important thing to remember is that the model must be smooth and have no undercuts. Otherwise, it would be impossible to remove it from the sand without destroying the impression it made there. As in wax modeling, always keep the model as light and thin as possible, so that the finished piece is not too heavy to wear comfortably.

Procedures

1. Carve a design in wood, bone, stone, clay, metal, plastic, or hard wax. Sand and polish the model until it is smooth. (If using wood, sand it and apply three coats of shellac to the finished model to seal the grain.)

2. Place the drag, the frame without the pins, face down on the plywood molding (sprue hole facing down).

3. Center the model inside the drag, but slightly toward the lower end away from the sprue opening.

4. Sift parting powder lightly over the model and surface of the molding board.

5. Check the sand to see if it is well tempered: when broken in half by hand, it should break cleanly and not crumble. If the sand is crumbly, sprinkle some glycerine (available at a pharmacy)

Figure 18. After the model has been made, check to be sure that the surface areas are smooth. Then, position the model inside the drag, centering it at the lower end opposite the sprue.

on the sand and knead it in as one would clay or dough. New sand will not usually require this treatment.

6. Through a piece of screening, sift enough sand over the model to cover it with about one inch of sand.

7. Pack the sand firmly around the model with the fingers.

8. Sift enough sand into the drag to fill it to the top. Take the rammer and pack the sand down around the model and along the sides of the drag.

Figure 19. When using this casting technique, it is important to examine the sand to determine if it has the correct consistency. New sand is usually well tempered and should break in half without crumbling (top). Use a piece of screening to sift about an inch of sand over the model (bottom).

9. Sift more sand into the drag until it is overfilled. Again pack the sand down firmly with the rammer, and remove the excess by scraping a straight edge diagonally across the surface of the drag.

10. Place the second molding board on top of the drag and turn the entire works over. Remove the first molding board and expose the model.

11. Place cope over the drag and secure it in position with the locking pins. Dust the model and surface of the sand with parting powder.

12. Repeat steps 6 through 9.

13. Clean away excess sand from work area.

14. Carefully separate the cope from the drag and set it aside, mold cavity up.

15. Gently remove the model from the drag, taking care not to upset the surrounding sand. (Press a piece of sticky modeling wax or a wad of chewing gum to the model to help remove it from the sand.) Blow away all loose sand from the mold cavity.

16. Using a small spatula, carve a sprue channel from the model to the sprue opening in the end of

Figure 20. Continue to sift sand into the drag until it is overflowing (top left). Then, use a rammer to pack the sand firmly inside the mold (top right). Next, place the cope over the drag and scrape off excess sand (bottom left). Repeat sifting and packing processes. Separate the cope from the drag, and set aside the drag from the excess sand before attempting to remove the model (bottom right).

the drag. Cut a few short channels as vents radiating part way out from the model. Always cut away from the model cavity.

17. Blow away all excess sand and replace the cope on top of the drag.

18. Secure the molding boards to either side of the assembled flask (cope and drag) with two C-clamps.

19. Stand the flask on end with the sprue hole facing up.

Figure 21. Use a spatula to carve a sprue chanel from the model to the sprue opening. Carve several sprue chanels radiating out from the model (top). Use tongs to pick up the crucible containing the molten metal and pour it through the sprue hole. After the mold has cooled, separate the frame (bottom).

Figure 22. After separating the cope from the drag, remove the button and store the sand for future castings. The finished piece should be thoroughly cleaned, and any rough edges should be smoothed.

20. If using a new crucible, prepare it before filling it with metal. This is done by shaking some flux into the crucible (both halves) and heating the flux with the torch. Make about four applications of flux, heating it after each application, until a glassy surface builds up.

21. Put the metal into the crucible and sprinkle it with flux. (See measuring metal under "Basic Procedures," Steam Casting, *Spruing the Model.* Melt the metal with the torch.

22. Pick up the crucible with the tongs, keeping the torch on the metal all the time.

23. When the metal is molten (it moves easily when rocked), pour it steadily into the sprue hole. Keep the torch on the metal while pouring.

24. Allow the mold to cool (ten minutes). Separate the cope from the drag. Remove the piece. Knock the sand out of the frames with a rammer and save it for another casting.

FINISHING

Just as the term implies, "finishing" is all the things done to a casting to make it a completed piece of jewelry: sawing, filing, sanding, and so on. Finishing techniques are used on all metal castings, no matter what method was used to cast them.

Procedures.

1. Remove all investment, oxidation, and dirt by pickling the cast piece. (See *Finishing* under "Basic Equipment and Supplies.") Use pickle only with sterling silver work.

2. Place one quart of water in a Pyrex dish and add one-half cup of pickle. Or use ten parts water and add one part sulfuric acid. **REMEMBER: Add acid to water.**

3. Heat the pickle on the stove or hot plate, but do not boil.

4. Drop the piece into the solution and allow it to remain there until it is free of oxidation (about a half hour).

5. Remove the piece and rinse it. It is important never to allow anything made of iron to touch the pickle solution, or it will cause all pieces in the solution to be coated with copper. It is also possible to skip steps 1 through 4 and simply scrub the piece with a damp toothbrush that has been loaded with pumice powder. The cleaning will not be as thorough as with pickling, but it will be adequate. Use the pumice powder technique for cleaning gold and pewter pieces.

6. Brace the piece in a small bench vise. Pad the jaws of the vise with paper toweling so that the jaws do not mar the surface of the piece.

Figure 23. A bench vise and jeweler's saw are used in the finishing process. The piece of jewelry is placed between the padded jaws of the vise, and all extraneous pieces are cut off with the saw.

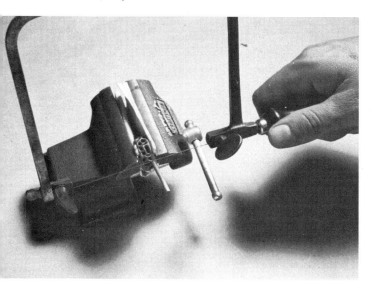

7. Insert a blade into the jeweler's saw frame so that the teeth angle down toward the handle. Tighten the top nut. Press the frame against a table edge to compress it. While it is compressed, insert the bottom of the blade into the bottom clamp and tighten it. Release the compressed frame slowly. The blade should be rigid and under tension, or it will not saw. Because these thin blades break easily, do not apply great pressure during sawing. Apply a little beeswax to lubricate the blade if it is sticking. Remember, the cutting action takes place on the downward stroke.

8. Saw off all sprues, vents, and extraneous metal pieces.

9. Take a half-round file and smooth over blade marks. For hard-to-reach areas use needle files. The correct way to file is from the tip of the file to the handle, in a forward motion. At the same time, file away all unwanted bubbles and rough surfaces from the cast piece.

10. Fold a small piece of coarse emery paper and sand away file marks from the piece. Rub in several directions so as not to make deep parallel scratches.

11. When sanded areas are smooth, change to medium and then fine grain emery paper and repeat the process.

12. Thoroughly wash and rinse the piece.

13. If planning to oxidize areas of the piece, take a small lump of liver of sulphur and dissolve it in a Pyrex dish with a few cups of water. The solution works best when heated, so place it on the stove or hot plate and heat it almost to boiling.

14. Attach a copper wire to the piece and immerse the entire piece in the solution.

15. Remove the piece to check the progress. Reimmerse it until the desired darkness is achieved. Never leave the piece in the solution too long, as a thick black coat that chips easily may result. (To darken gold it is best to use the specially prepared gold oxidizer from a supply house and follow the directions on the bottle.)

16. Rinse the piece thoroughly and dry it.

17. Dip thumb in water and then in the dry pumice powder. Rub it on the piece, removing oxidation from the raised areas and leaving the hard-to-reach areas alone.

18. To give the piece a matte finish, rub it in one direction only with fine steel wool.

19. To achieve a shiny surface, omit the steel wool and rub the piece rapidly with a buffing stick to which tripoli has been applied.

20. Clean off the tripoli residue by scrubbing the piece with a toothbrush and some liquid detergent. Rinse and dry the piece thoroughly.

21. To give the piece a final polish, rub it rapidly with a buffing stick to which rough has been applied. Scrub again with detergent, rinse, and dry. The piece is completed.

Projects You Can Do

The following projects are all simple ones, designed to introduce both of the casting techniques covered here. Having once produced a piece in either of the methods described, it will be possible to make increasingly complicated and larger pieces or one that combines the two casting techniques. The possibilities are endless.

STEAM CASTING: BAND RING

1. Have ready a wooden dowel rod, one that is as close in size as possible to the diameter of the finger, but never larger.

Figure 24. Cut several pieces from a wire coat hanger, and file shapes into the tips. Use a knife and straight edge to cut a wax strip. Then, press the tips into the wax to create a design.

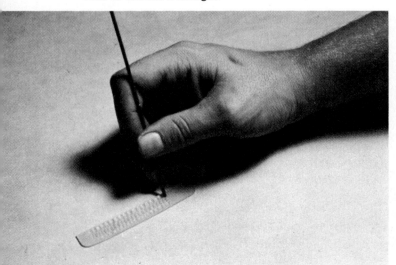

2. Wrap the rod with masking tape until it is the size of the diameter of the finger.

3. Cut a coat hanger into several three-inch pieces, and file shapes into the tips.

4. With a knife and a straight edge, cut a one-half inch strip of wax and press the filed tips into the wax sheet to create a texture or pattern.

5. Bend the strip tightly around the dowel rod. Where it overlaps, make a cut.

6. Flow hot wax in the seam, joining the two ends smoothly. Continue the texture over the seam to hide it.

7. Take wax wires or narrow wax strips and work them into the pattern to echo some of the pressed-in shapes. This will yield a variation in the levels of the ring which were formed by the depressions from the coat hanger, the original surface of the sheet, and the raised edge of the wires. Do not make the wax wires stand up too high or the ring will be uncomfortable to wear.

8. To add more interest to the design, heat the tip of the filed coat hanger, and push it all the way through the wax strip, making holes. Be careful not to make too many holes or to put them too close together — this would weaken the ring and it might crack with wear.

9. Smooth out all rough edges and carefully remove the ring from the dowel rod.

Figure 25. Wrap a wooden dowel rod with masking tape and bend the wax strip around the taped portion. Cut the strip to fit the diameter of the dowel rod and seal the seam with hot wax.

Figure 26. Narrow wax wires can be worked into the wax strip to raise the depressions formed by the pieces of coat hanger (above). After the rough edges have been smoothed, sprue the model and cast it. The addition of the wax wires creates variations in the levels of the ring design (right).

10. Check the inside of the ring for lumps that can be smoothed out with the wax tool. Flow some hot wax into the inside of the seam to fill it.

11. Sprue up the model. (See "Basic Procedures.")

STEAM CASTING: PENDANT

1. Lay out a piece of sheet wax approximately two inches square.

2. Cut strips of sheet wax of varying widths and apply them flat or on edge to the surface of the square.

3. Extend some of the strips slightly beyond the edge of the piece.

4. Pierce the surface of the wax sheet. Try out some of the techniques learned from experimenting with the wax.

Figure 27. Cut wax strips of varying widths and apply them in an irregular fashion to the surface of the piece. Pierce the top of the pendant to create an interesting effect (left). Cut two pieces of wax wire, and attach them in a U-shaped loop to the bottom of the pendant (right).

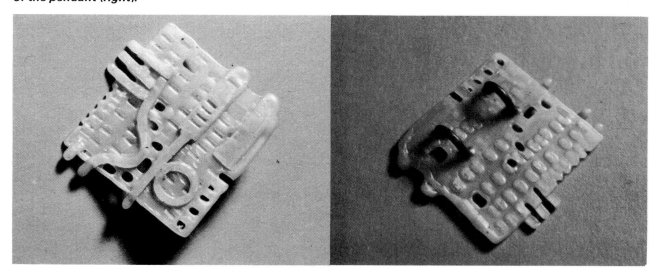

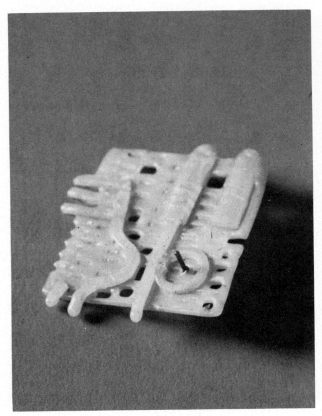 

Figure 28. Half-drilled cultured pearls are inexpensive and can be purchased from a jewelry supplier. To add them to the pendant, cut a small piece of wire and attach it at a right angle to the surface (left). After the pendant has been cast, apply glue to the peg and pearl to secure the mounting (right).

5. Turn the piece over. Make two U-shaped pieces from 14-gauge wax wire, and attach them straight up and down and side by side, about one-third of the way down from the top of the piece. These loops will hold the pendant level and keep it from tipping forward when it is hung on a chain or cord. Make sure that the loop openings are at least 3/16 inch wide, so that a cord or chain can pass easily through them.

6. To mount a pearl in the pendant (optional), attach a small piece (about one-quarter inch long) of 20-gauge wax wire perpendicular to the surface of the model. After the piece is cast, the pearl will be mounted on the peg. Inexpensive cultured pearls, which are often sold at jewelry supply houses, can be ordered half drilled. Then, by applying a small amount of epoxy glue to the peg and into the half drilled hole, the pearl may be mounted in place and allowed to dry until set. Do not mount any stones or pearls, however, until the piece has been completely finished — cast, filed, snaded, oxidized, and polished. Otherwise, there

is the risk of damaging the stone or pearl. Cord, clasps, and chain may all be purchased at jewelry supply stores.

SAND CASTING: BUTTON

1. Take a block of hard File-Wax and saw off a piece about 3/8-inch thick.

2. Saw the thin piece into a 1¼ inch square.

3. With a half-round hand file, file the corners away until an oval or a circle is shaped.

4. With knives and needle files begin to file and carve away areas to create the design. Remember, do not make any holes or undercuts that will make it difficult to remove the model from the sand mold later.

5. With coarse to fine sand paper, sand the model as smooth as possible.

6. After casting, drill two small holes through the piece so that it can be sewn to fabric. Remember to allow room for this in the design, or better yet,

Figure 29. After the first button is finished, the wax model or the metal button itself can be used to make a complete set. Begin by rounding out a circle from a piece of file wax, and then carve a design on the surface (left). After the piece has been cast, drill two holes through the button (right).

work the space where the holes will be into the design.

7. Cast the button in the sand mold.

8. With a hand drill and a 1/16-inch drill bit, drill two holes in the button.

9. Finish the button according to the directions in "Basic Procedures." Now, using the wax model again, or the metal button as the model, it is possible to make several buttons as a complete set for a coat or jacket.

For Additional Reading

Bovin, Murray, **Jewelry Making,** privately published, 1964.

Morton, Philip, **Contemporary Jewelry,** Holt, 1970.

Pack, Gretta, **Jewelry and Enameling,** Van Nostrand, 1961.

Untracht, Oppi, **Metal Techniques for Craftsmen,** Doubleday, 1968.

Von Neuman, Robert, **The Design and Creation of Jewelry,** Chilton, 1972.

Flower Making
and Preserving

Flower making and preserving are creative activities for those interested in making artificial flowers or in preserving fresh flowers, weeds, or plants.

Throughout the world, man has tried for centuries to duplicate flowers in one form or another. One of the earliest forms of duplication were bone china flowers. The bone china composition process was discovered and developed in England around 1750. Some of the earliest forms of floral bone china, such as flower encrusted vases and figurines, can be seen in the British Museum. Today, most department stores sell bone china flowers in the form of bouquets in a basket, as separate flowers on wire stems, or as decorations on vases or other china pieces.

Another type of artificial flower is found in the Botanical Museum of Harvard University. *The Ware Collection of Glass Models* represents the artistic and scientific efforts of two German brothers, Leopold and Rudolph Blaschka, who created the flowers over a period of nearly 50 years. They were not only artists by trade, but naturalists as well. With the financial backing of Mrs. Elizabeth C. Ware and her daughter, the Blaschka brothers accepted a contract with Harvard University, and from 1887 until 1936 created thousands of glass models for display. No other museum in the world contains comparable collections.

Like the pendulum of a clock, craft trends go from one extreme to another in popularity. For instance, tissue paper was first used to make flowers as long ago as the 1880s. Until that time, wrapping had been the primary use of tissue paper. However, two sisters named Heath began to crumple it, cut it, fringe it, and flute it — with surprisingly interesting results.

Then, in 1887, crepe paper was accidentally discovered. A superintendant, walking through a tissue paper mill, came upon a heap of strangely crinkled, discarded paper. The operator explained that too much water had mistakenly gotten into the paper and as a result, crepe paper was discovered. It was first imported from England in 1892. (Crepe paper has a great advan-

Figure 1. This Victorian style arrangement (opposite) shows the colors and shapes of summer flowers, dried and preserved for year-round enjoyment. (Courtesy, Georgia Vance; photo, Kenneth Bergeron.)

Figure 2. These realistic looking orchids (above) and apple blossoms (below) are glass arrangments from the Ware collection at the Harvard Botanical Museum. (Courtesy, Shostal Associates, New York.)

tage over tissue in making realistic flowers because it can be so easily manipulated to simulate real flowers.)

The art of drying and preserving live plants and flowers was conceived centuries ago and is undoubtedly as old as civilization itself. The early Greeks and Romans decorated their banquet tables with garlands of preserved flowers. The monks in medieval times dried flowers using a "hanging" method. The early settlers in America had flowers, foliage, and plants hanging from the beams in their barns in order to preserve the summer and fall beauty through the winter months. The first straw flowers arrived in England in the sixteenth century and were cultivated into the type which exist today. Chinese lanterns also decorated many English homes at this time and many other dried pods and flowers enhanced British interiors.

Pressing live flowers can be labeled Victorian art, for as early as 1850 delicately arranged, pressed flowers and leaves were mounted for keepsakes by Victorian ladies. Seaweed was then gathered at low tide and brought home to be pressed between blotting paper in books. In 1849, the Rev. Lansborough published a book entitled "A Popular History of British Seaweeds," which guided Victorian enthusiasts in the hobby of pressing flowers and weeds for preservation.

One of the most popular uses today for pressed flowers is a floral arrangement mounted under glass and used as a picture. Modern designs can be achieved by the addition of ferns or leaves or by separating petals and forming a design or border.

Common Terms Used In Flower Making and Preserving

Cupping: the particular way of stretching crepe paper between thumb and forefinger to form a cupped shape; used for making petals.

Pressing: the placing of flowers between blotters and weighing them down.

Tinting: restoring lost color with watercolors.

Tying: binding with fine tying wire.

Wrapping: the wrapping of stem wire with floral tape.

Basic Equipment And Supplies

Following is a list of materials needed for flower making and preserving. They are easily obtainable and none are expensive.

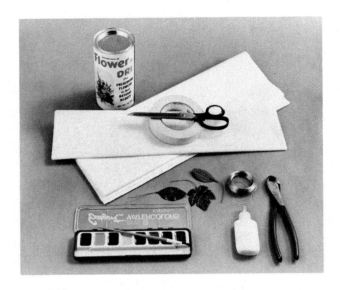

Figure 3. The supplies needed for flower making and preserving are available in craft departments.

1. Tying wire. A fine wire, usually sold in a spool. Wire sold for hanging pictures is a suitable substitute.

2. Stem wire. A stiff heavy wire should be used for large flowers which would ordinarily have a heavy stem such as large roses, dahlias, or peonies. Lightweight coat hangers may also be used for this purpose. A medium-weight wire can be used for carnations, pompon chrysanthemums, and small sprays. Fine wire, which is slightly heavier than tying wire and stands alone, can be used for stems of separate small flowers such as pansies or violets. For smaller buds and flowers which will be attached to a main stem, a fine wire such as tying wire may be used.

3. Flower centers. Most craft departments or stores carry small packages of flower centers in assorted colors and varieties. If the stamens are at each end of a bunch, they should be folded in half or cut in half and then tied with tying wire into smaller groups.

4. Leaves. Some stores will carry packages of readymade leaves in assorted shapes and sizes. Instructions for making leaves are given later in the chapter.

5. Floral tape. A green tape 1/2" wide which comes in a flat roll. It can be made either of crepe paper or of a plastic self-adhering material. The plastic floral tape requires no gluing.

6. Silica gel (or Flori Dry). A granular mixture for preserving flowers, approximately four pounds should be purchased initially. In addition to the above, other necessary items include: (1) wire cutters; (2) white glue; (3) crepe paper; (4) tissue paper; (5) blotting paper, such as the kind used for a desk blotter, for pressing flowers; (6) scissors; (7) masking tape for reinforcing the petals of dried or preserved flowers; (8) tweezers; and (9) watercolors.

Basic Procedures

For each of the techniques discussed here for working with flowers, there are a few introductory steps which should be taken. For artificial flower making, first collect all the materials necessary for making the flowers. For pressed flowers, construct a temporary press to hold the flowers and select those which seem attractive. For making pictures, leaves and foliage are important for filling in backgrounds and borders. The only materials necessary, other than the press

Figure 4. A mass of crimson spreads over this Chinese import bowl. The arrangement features real flowers, preserved to form a traditional creation. (Courtesy, Georgia Vance; photo, Kenneth Bergeron.)

on the "gathering day," is a sharp knife or scissors for cutting and trimming. When flowers and foliage are completely dry, select the background and frame and have the remaining supplies ready.

To prepare for flower preserving, have air-tight containers and sufficient Silica Gel ready so that flowers may be imbedded as soon after cutting as possible. Have tying wire, stem wire, wire cutter, and scissors available. After flowers are removed from silica gel, carefully store them in a box or other container until enough have been collected for a bouquet. Have tools and supplies ready for assembling.

ARTIFICIAL FLOWERS

When cutting crepe paper petals, the grain of the paper is important because the paper will stretch in only one direction. All patterns shown here have an arrow pointing in the direction of the grain. Be sure the lines of the paper run in this direction.

Cutting Crepe Paper

Do not unfold the package unless instructed to do so. If the package has a heavy label, use it as a cutting guide; if not, measure and draw a line for the desired width and cut right through the package.

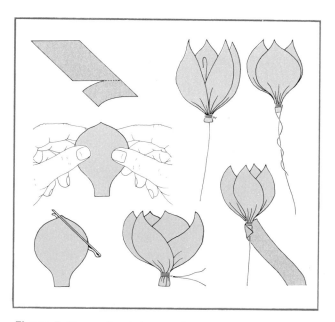

Figure 5. Several petals may be cupped at the same time. To roll the edges, place bobby pins over upper edge of petal. Roll under and remove pin. To fasten, twist wire two or three times and fold ends.

Cupping the Petals

Several petals may be cupped at the same time — be sure the grain of each petal runs in the same direction. Stretch each petal between thumbs and forefingers, pulling out slightly and stretching paper through center.

Rolling the Edges

Place a bobby pin or knitting needle over the upper edge of the petal. Roll under, then remove pin.

Fastening With Tying Wire

Cut off about 4" to 6" of wire and tie it around the base of the flower, about 1/2" from the end. Be careful to keep the tying wire high and tight enough so it will not slip off. Twist the wire tightly 2 or 3 times, then fold down ends. Do not cut wire.

Attaching Stem Wire

Some instructions call for making a small hook at the end of the stem wire and forming a flower over wire; other methods call for placing the stem next to the base of the flower and twisting the tying wire around the stem wire. A drop of glue can be dabbed on the base of the flower to strengthen the joining.

Wrapping Wire and Adding Leaves

If floral tape is not available, cut a 1/2" width of moss green crepe. Cut through the folded package.) Cut pieces of floral tape into not more than 6" to 8" lengths — shorter lengths are easier to work with. Cut the ends on the diagonal. If paper floral tape is used, place a small amount of glue on one end. Place the glued end over the base of the flower to cover and wrap tape around the stem wire on the *diagonal*, stretching the tape and twisting the wire with one hand and holding the tape with the other, keeping the tape smooth. When a leaf is to be added, place it next to the stem wire and wrap the two wires together as one. If self-adhering floral tape is used, follow the same method as above but omitting the glue.

Making Leaves

Trace a leaf pattern onto lightweight cardboard and cut out the leaves using green crepe paper. Place glue on a piece of fine wire (heavier than tying wire) and press down the center back of leaf. Hold until completely dry. If heavier leaves are desired, place another leaf over the wrong side of the first leaf and glue it in place. If desired, mark veins by drawing them with a knitting needle, using a firm stroke.

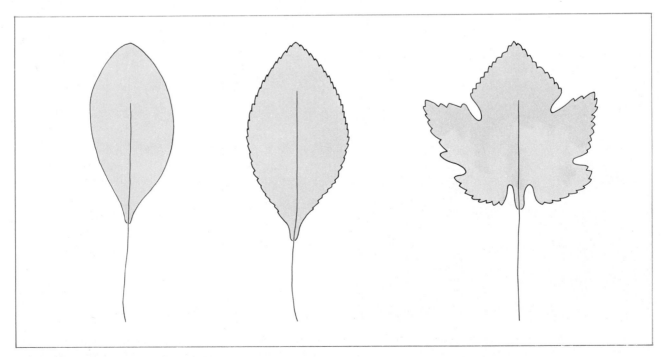

Figure 6. These basic leaf patterns may be used for most paper flower arrangements. Fine wire is glued to leaves that are cut out of green crepe paper.

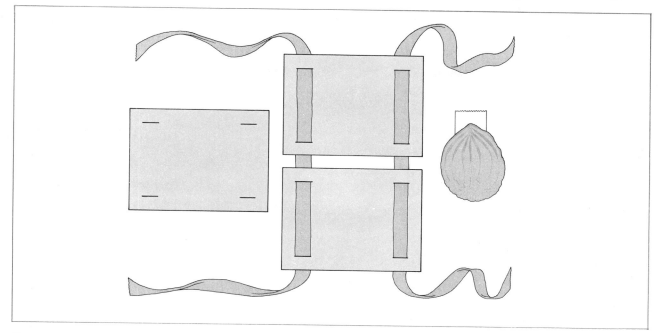

Figure 7. A temporary press can be made with heavy cardboard and ribbon. Blotters and newspaper should be placed between the two pieces of cardboard to protect the flowers. The press is most helpful while out collecting flowers. It will secure and separate the blossoms as well as begin the pressing of the flowers.

PRESSED FLOWERS

Some of the more common wildflowers which press well are buttercups, daisies, goldenrod, late purple asters, black-eyed susans, and trumpet weed. Do not try to press thick, heavy flowers such as thistle — these can be preserved in their natural state. Ferns, grass, and leaves are, of course, easy to press because they are flat.

To make a temporary press, take 2 sheets of heavy cardboard about 9" x 12" or larger and make 4 horizontal slits in each. Draw ribbon through slits. When going to collect flowers, take along a few sheets of newspaper and 2 blotters. Place a blotter over each piece of cardboard. Place the first layer of flowers on one blotter and place a double piece of newspaper over the flowers. Make additional layers with newspaper between, ending with the second blotter. Close the press and tie the ribbons. (When placing flowers between layers of newspaper, be sure the flowers are the same thickness in each layer.)

After arriving home, open the press and add fresh newspaper between each layer of flowers. If some flowers, such as daisies, have a thick center, take a few pieces of a blotter the size of the flower and cut out a hole in the center. Place enough of these around the flower center until they are built up to the same level. Place a heavy weight, such as several books, on top and leave for several days. Check flowers and add fresh paper. Again, place weights on top of press and leave for another week. Continue this method until flowers are completely dry. This process may take anywhere from a week to a month.

After flowers are completely dry, separate those which need to have color restored. Most flowers lose some of their natural color in drying. Some of these may also need some reinforcing. If a flower is about to fall apart, remove the petals and place each petal on a piece of cellophane tape or masking tape and press in place. Carefully cut around each petal, leaving a small piece of tape at the center of the flower. Now, put the flower back together again, being careful to hide the tape.

To restore color, place a few drops of liquid detergent into a small container of water. Using water color paints, a small brush, and the detergent-water, paint color onto petals. If the flowers are completely dry, only the pigment in the paint will penetrate the petals and the color should dry quickly.

PRESERVING FLOWERS

There are several methods for preserving flowers. As just described, they can be placed between layers of papers and pressed, or they can be hung up to dry, placed in a sand and borax mixture, or placed in a granular drying agent such as silica gel. Instructions for the latter three methods follow.

Figure 8. A wealth of actual plant material has been preserved to create these lovely bouquets. The abstract arrangement "Africa" (left) was designed by Mrs. Myles H. Reynolds. The dramatic bursts of color are well suited to the curved leaf pattern. Included in the delightful bouquet above are peonies, lilies, roses, goldenrod, zinnias, and celosia. The attractive bouquet (opposite) is in a place of honor in one of the reception rooms of the State Department. It is a graceful arrangement of foliage and flowers that preserves their original color and freshness. (Courtesy, Georgia Vance; photos, Kenneth Bergeron.)

Drying Flowers, Plants, and Weeds Upside Down

Cut the stems to desired length. Remove all unnecessary parts, dead leaves, or insect eaten leaves, but do not strip them completely. Stems may be curved *before* drying by bending and tying in the direction desired.

Figure 9. To dry flowers, plants, and weeds, hang them upside down, allowing air to circulate freely on all sides. Keep them out of direct sunlight and dampness. (Courtesy, Georgia Vance; photo, Kenneth Bergeron.)

Group 3 or 4 stems together and tie them securely, or place an elastic band around them because they shrink while drying. Thick stems should be hung alone. Hang them upside down, allowing air to circulate around all sides. They can be hung on a clothes line, but should be placed in a shed, garage, cellar, or attic and, kept out of direct sunlight and dampness. After about 8 to 10 days they should be stiff to touch and the stems should snap easily when completely dry. A longer drying period may be necessary during humid weather. Weeds, pods, straw flowers, Japanese lanterns, cockscomb, and money plant are examples of plants which dry well in this manner. This method, of course, requires no extra materials or equipment.

Drying Fresh Flowers With Silica Gel

All flowers should be cut when they reach full bloom or are about to open. Cut flowers on a bright sunny day, but not after a rainfall — the least amount of moisture is desirable. Place flowers immediately into silica gel (instructions follow). If this is inconvenient, use a jar of slightly tepid water to hold the flowers until ready to use.

Figure 10. Fresh flowers are preserved in an air-tight container such as this cake tin and supported by about a two-inch layer of silica gel. (Courtesy, Georgia Vance; photo, Kenneth Bergeron.)

Choose a container such as a cake tin, plastic box, or any shallow air-tight container. Remove all but 1" or 2" of the flower's stem. Pour about 2" of silica gel into the container. Using fingers, make a small well in the center. Carefully place the fresh flower faceup in this well. Push silica gel up under petals to be sure they are supported. Fill a cup with silica gel and gently trickle the crystals onto and around the flower. It is important to slowly trickle the crystals as the petals cannot support a great amount of sudden weight. Build up the crystals slowly to keep the flower in its natural shape. Continue sprinkling the silica gel until the flower is completely covered. Several flowers can be placed in the same container, providing they do not touch each other.

Place the lid on the container and be sure it is air-tight. Do not open it for at least 3 days. Dense, heavy flowers may require longer to dry. To be certain the flowers are completely dry, tilt the container and check. If the top layer is still moist, again trickle silica gel until the flower is covered and seal container.

To remove the flowers from the container, slowly pour the crystals into another container until the flowers are exposed. Using curved-nosed tweezers, pick up the flower at its base and lift it out. If any petals have loosened and dropped off, they can be secured with a drop of white glue or silicone sealer.

Slowly trickle sand-borax mixture onto flowers as in the silica gel method. The container need not be covered. With this mixture, flowers will take 3 weeks or longer to dry, but they may be left in sand indefinitely without harm to flowers.

Figure 11. To remove flowers from the container, slowly pour crystals into another container until all the flowers are exposed. Lift out each flower base with a curved-nose tweezers. (Courtesy, Georgia Vance; photo, Kenneth Bergeron.)

Drying Fresh Flowers With Borax-Sand Mixture

To 3 parts borax, add 1 part heavy, clean, finely-sifted sand; or, to 3 parts pure white sand, add 1 part borax. As this is a less expensive method of preserving flowers, larger containers with more depth may be used. Stem wire can be attached before the flowers are dried by making a small hook at the end of the wire and inserting the straight end into the center, hooking the wire into the flower. Flowers with many petals, such as zinnias, marigolds, or carnations, may be tied together with tying wire or cellophane tape at the base of the flower to hold the petals securely while drying.

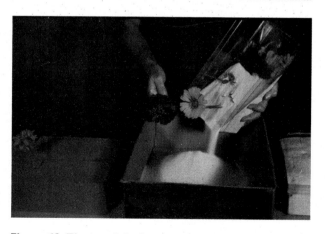

Figure 12. The sand drying method takes three weeks to dry the flowers. Gloriosa daisies (top) are dried face down while delphinium and larkspur (center) are dried in a horizontal position as sand is trickled over them. The uncovering technique (bottom) is the same as the silica gel method. (Courtesy, Georgia Vance; photo, Kenneth Bergeron.)

Making a Bouquet

Having dried sufficient flowers and foliage to make a bouquet, place flowers on stem wires by laying the wire next to the stems of the flowers and wrapping these with floral tape. Flower colors may be protected against the humidity by spraying them with a clear acrylic such as Krylon or Gard's Spra-tone. The surface will be moist, but will quickly dry without absorbing moisture.

Storing Dried Flowers for Later Use

Carefully wrap air-dried flowers in tissue paper and lay them in a box. To store silica gel dried flowers, place them in a large air-tight container with about 4 tablespoons of silica gel placed in a small tin or a pyrex custard cup. Check periodically to be sure the crystals are still blue and if necessary dry the silica gel by removing only the custard cup and placing it in a warm oven (250°) for about 20 minutes. Reseal the container.

Choosing Colors of Flowers for Drying

Violets and purples tend to either darken too much or fade; harsh magentas, however, become a more favorable color. Yellow keeps its original color and may even become more intense. Marigolds in particular look almost fresh after drying. Blue does not retain its color too well and is not easily found. Some available blue flowers are delphiniums, larkspur, and hydrangea. Red can be preserved with a fast-drying method, such as silica gel. It is wise to choose orange-reds or deep pinks rather than blue-reds. Foliage usually dries to a soft gray-green, especially lilac and rose foliage. Remember, too, that white is important in a large, mixed bouquet. White larkspur, sweet peas, daisies, or Queen Anne's lace are some of the more attractive white flowers.

Figure 13. Flowers preserved in silica gel must be stored in an air-tight container. The flowers shown above are safely stored in a plastic bag. (Courtesy, Georgia Vance; photo, Kenneth Bergeron.)

Projects You Can Do

Because original flower pressing and preserving projects are easily decided upon, the suggestions offered here deal only with making bouquets of artificial flowers. The following material gives step-by-step procedures for making several kinds of individual flowers.

BOUQUET I: DELPHINIUMS, POMPON CHRYSANTHEMUMS, AND ROSE OF SHARON

Although this bouquet is time-consuming, the effort will be worthwhile and the results rewarding.

Delphiniums

Materials required are one package of pastel crepe paper, floral tape, yellow stamens, tying wire, stem wire, and three daisy leaves for each spray.

To begin the buds, cut through the package of crepe paper to make a 2″ width of folded paper. Cut through both ends to make separate pieces. Trace a pattern for a circle onto a light piece of cardboard and cut it out. Using the pattern, cut out circles for buds. Then, to cut the flowers, trace a pattern for the flower onto a light piece of cardboard and cut it out. Using the pattern, cut out two pieces for each flower.

Figure 14. Delphiniums, pompon chrysanthemums, and rose of sharon make a delightful paper flower arrangement.

To make the buds, place one circle over the end of a pencil and mold the bud. Remove the pencil and tie a 4" piece of tying wire around the base, being careful not to crush the buds. Make about seven or eight of these for each spray.

To make the flowers, place two flower pieces together, turning the top piece so the petals do not match. Fold two stamens in half if they are tipped at both ends or use four stamens. Make a *small* hole in the center of the flower with the end of a pair of scissors and push the ends of the stamens through it. Press flower and stamens together and tie with a 4" piece of tying wire around the base of the flower. Make about 18 flowers for each spray.

Cut several 2" pieces of floral tape to wrap flowers and buds. If paper tape is used, spread some glue onto a dish or piece of cardboard so it will be handy. Dip one end of the tape into the glue and wrap each stem of buds and flowers, covering the wire (see "Basic Procedures").

To assemble the spray, tie three buds together with tying wire, having the center bud slightly higher. Wrap as one piece. Add two or three more buds and tie these together below the first group. Tie and wrap the stems as one. Tie group of buds to a 12" piece of stem wire with tying wire. Add three flowers below the group of buds and tie and wrap for 1 inch. Continue to add a group of three flowers an inch apart down the stem until the spray is the desired length. Add the three daisy leaves which have been cut (see "Basic Procedures"), or make leaves and wrap the remainder of the stem. If the spray does not turn to one side when completed, bend wire slightly.

Pompon Chrysanthemums

Materials required are: one package each of white and moss green crepe paper, floral tape, stem wire, glue, stapler, and pliers.

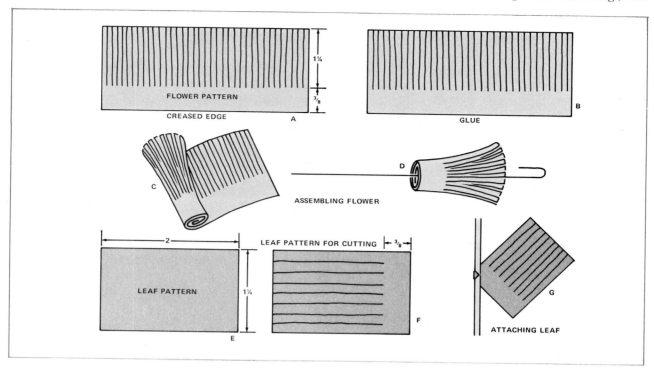

Figure 15. Pompon chrysanthemums (above) are simple to assemble, as shown in this diagram. Buds, flower centers, and flowers can be created from the diagram for delphiniums (opposite page).

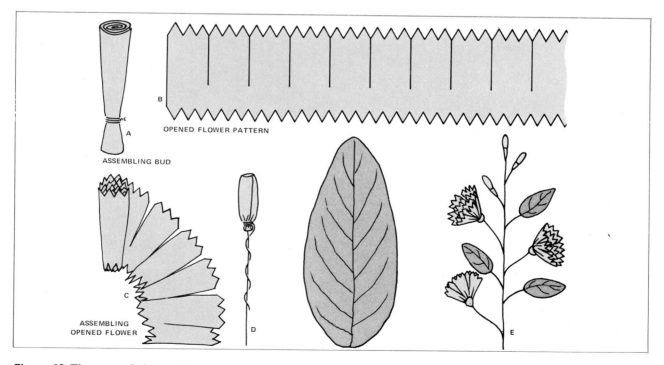

Figure 16. The rose of sharon blossom is excellent for large or small arrangements. A floral spray is assembled by placing a bud at the end of a piece of stem wire. Twist the wire several times. Alternate leaves and buds along the wire according to the directions.

Cut through the packages of crepe paper, making 2½" widths of folded paper. Unfold these and cut them into 12" lengths for each flower. Now fold each strip in half lengthwise to make a 1¼" width double strip 12" long. Crease the edge sharply. Bring ends together to make a 6" length, then fold again to make a 3" length. Even the creased edges and secure them either with 2 staples placed about 1/4" from the creased edge, or with paper clips. Cut a very fine fringe along the open edge within 3/8" from the creased edge. Carefully remove the staples, leaving the strip folded.

To make the flower, spread glue along the strip on the top side only. Starting at one end, roll the strip tightly to the end. Glue the remaining layers at the end. To assemble, make a small hook with a pair of pliers at one end of an 8" length of stem wire. Carefully push the straight end down through the center of the pompon until the hook catches.

Next, make the leaves. Cut several pieces of green crepe paper (2 for each flower) into 2" x 1-1/4" pieces. Cut one edge into 8 sections, cutting to within 3/8" from opposite edge. Wrap floral tape around the 3/8" base of flower, continuing tape down the wire for about 1 inch. Cut and glue tape. Place glue along the uncut edge of the leaf and wrap diagonally down the stem. Wrap the remainder of the wire with floral tape.

Rose of Sharon

This is an extremely simple flower to make. It can be attached to tree branches for decorating a large area or several can be placed on stem wire for a floral spray. Materials required are: one roll of fluted streamers in bright rose, pink, or fuscia; floral tape; stem wire; tying wire; glue; and daisy leaves. If the sprays are to be attached to tree branches, omit the stem wire.

Cut 6" lengths of streamers for the buds. Cut 10" lengths for partially opened flowers and 18" lengths for opened flowers. Cut tying wire into 6" lengths.

To make buds, roll a 6" length of paper and tie it with tying wire. Cut floral tape into 3" lengths. Starting at the base of a bud, wrap the bud and tying wire (see "Basic Procedures"). Set buds aside.

To make opened and partially opened flowers, cut between every third notch on one edge of a fluted strip to within 1/2" from the opposite edge. Roll approximately a 2" strip for the center of the flower, then loosely gather the remainder of the strip around the center, turning the flower while gathering. Tie with tying wire and wrap with floral tape. Carefully spread out the petals.

To assemble these for a floral spray, place a bud at the end of a 12" piece of stem wire. Twist the tying wire around the stem 2 or 3 times. Cut the floral tape into several 3" lengths and wrap the wires together. Attach 1 or 2 more buds down stem as desired. Leaving 1" of covered tying wire extended, attach a partially opened flower, then 3 or 4 opened flowers and leaves down the stem (see "Basic Procedures" for attaching leaves). To assemble the flowers for attachment to tree branches, it is not necessary to make sprays. Buds and flowers may be attached directly to the branches by tying them with tying wire or stapling them in place. Be sure to wrap the buds and flowers with floral tape before attaching.

BOUQUET II: DAISIES, TULIPS, JONQUILS, AND GLADIOLI

This is another bouquet project. It is, of course, up to the individual what kinds of flowers will go into a bouquet — they can be mixed or can be a bouquet of only one kind of flower.

Daisies

Materials required are white typing paper or white duplex crepe paper; tying wire and stem wire; yellow crepe paper; white covered tying wire; glue; daisy leaves; and floral tape.

From typing paper, cut pieces 3" x 4" for daisy petals. Cut pieces of covered wire into 2½" lengths — 12 for each daisy. Cut tying wire into 4" lengths. For the centers, cut through the package of crepe paper, making a 1" width. Cut through each end. Fold each strip in half, then in half again. Cut a fine fringe 1/2" deep, along one edge. Gather together and tie with tying wire. Spread out fringe.

To make the petals, fold a piece of white typing paper in half to make a folded piece 1½" x 4". Open up the fold and spread glue across one half

Figure 17. Daisies, tulips, jonquils, and gladioli make a bright bouquet for use in spring and summer.

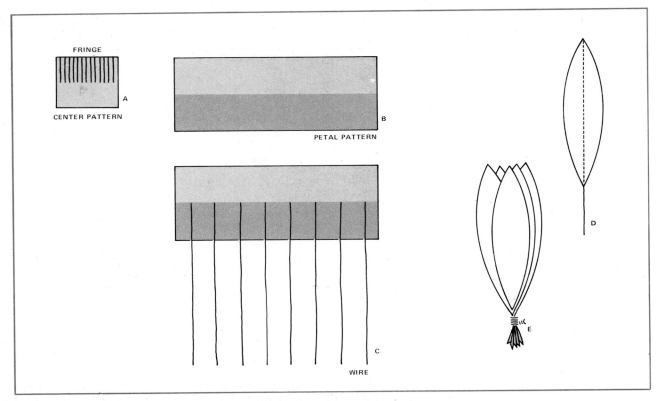

Figure 18. White typing paper may be substituted for crepe paper when making daisies. This pattern gives the actual size of the daisy petal.

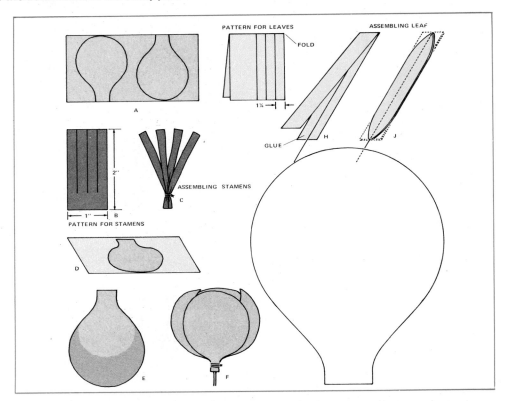

Figure 19. Using two-tone duplex crepe paper gives more contrast to these tulips. Crayons may also be used to shade the outer portions of the petal.

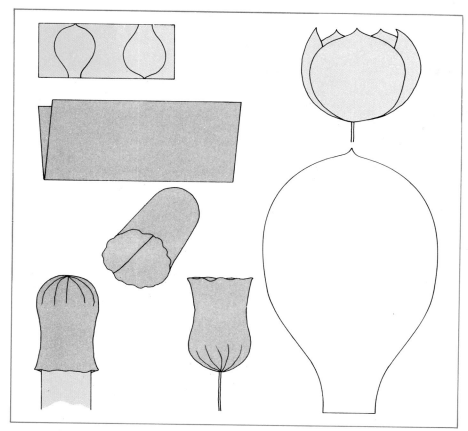

Figure 20. A broomstick handle is helpful in molding the tubular portion of the jonquil. The double petals can be attached to the rounded center.

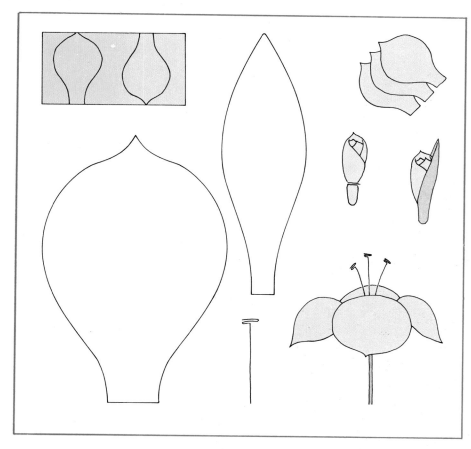

Figure 21. Gladioli are made from this basic petal pattern. Each bud requires three double petals. Gladiolus buds are most effectively used in a spray.

of paper only. Place pieces of covered wire 3/4" apart across glue, having wires end at the fold line. Fold down the other half of the paper and press together. Smooth out around the wire and cut out petals, having the wire as the center spoke. A pattern is given for the actual size but it is not necessary to draw each petal.

To assemble, place 12 petals around a center and tie these together with tying wire. Place a piece of stem wire next to the daisy and tie with tying wire, placing a drop of glue on the base of the daisy. Wrap the stem with floral tape for about 2" inches. Place a leaf next to the stem and wrap remainder of stem, adding another leaf about 1" below.

Tulips

Materials required are 1 package of 2-tone rose duplex crepe paper, 1 package each of green and black regular crepe paper, 12" lightweight stem wire for leaves, 12" medium weight stem wire, tying wire, glue, and crayons or pastels.

To cut the petals, trace the pattern for the petal onto lightweight cardboard and cut it out. Cut through the package of rose crepe paper, making a 3" width and cut through each end. Trace the pattern onto several layers and cut out 4 petals for each tulip.

To make the stamens, cut through the package of black crepe paper, making a 2" width and cut through each end. Cut a strip in half, then in half again. Cut each 1" x 2" piece into 4 sections, leaving 1/2" uncut at edge. Roll the stamens together and tie with 4" piece of tying wire.

Next, place a petal on a piece of cardboard with the wide end of the petal toward you. With crayon or pastels shade the outer part of the petal, using yellow on the light pink side or orange on the rose side. Cup petals, having shaded side away from you (see "Basic Procedures").

To assemble, tie stamens with tying wire to the medium weight wire. Place a small amount of glue on the base of the stamens to prevent the wire from slipping. Place 4 petals, shaded side out, around the stamens and tie them with tying wire. Wrap the base of the tulip and the entire stem with floral tape.

To make the leaves, cut off several folds from the package of green paper (do not cut through this package). Fold piece in half to make a 10" depth. Now cut folded piece into 1¼" widths. Apply glue down 10" of the inside of strip. Place a piece of lightweight stem wire down the center, leaving 2 inches extending. Press the other half of the strip in place to make a two-layered leaf with wire between. Taper each end. Place leaf next to the stem of the tulip and wrap the 2" extension of the leaf wire together with the stem wire. Make one leaf for each tulip.

Jonquils

Materials required are 1 package each of yellow and moss green crepe paper, 12" lengths of green covered medium weight stem wire, 12" lengths of uncovered lightweight stem wire, glue, and tying wire.

For the petals, cut through the package of yellow paper making a 3" width of folded paper. Cut through each end. Trace pattern onto lightweight cardboard and cut it out. Trace pattern onto several pieces of yellow paper and cut out the petals. For the centers, cut through the package of yellow paper, making a 4" width. Cut through each end. Fold a strip in half lengthwise and crease sharply. Then ruffle the folded edge by stretching the paper.

To make the jonquil, place glue on one edge of a 4½" folded strip and glue together, overlapping 1/4". Place tubular piece over a broomstick with ruffled edge down. Press the paper over the end of the broomstick to round it off and then glue the folds in place. Allow this to dry completely. Next, make a small hook at the end of the green covered wire with pliers and place the hooked end through the center. Place a drop of glue on the end of the hook to hold it in place. Glue 2 petals together to make double petals; make 5 double petals for each jonquil. Hold flower center and wire upside down. Glue 5 petals around the rounded end of the center, overlapping the petals. For leaves, follow the instructions for tulip leaves, making one for each flower.

Gladioli

Materials required are 1 package each of orchid and moss green crepe paper, white covered tying wire, glue, black marking pen, and 14" heavy stem wire.

Figure 22. The brilliant poppies spill over a lustrous bowl. The texture of the crepe paper gives the flowers a realistic appearance. (Courtesy, Dennison Co.)

Cut through the package of orchid paper making a 3" width of folded paper. Cut through each end. Trace pattern for petal onto lightweight cardboard and cut it out. Using pattern, cut out petals: each flower requires 4 double petals (two placed together but not glued). Each bud requires 3 double petals.

To make the calyx, cut through the package of green paper, making a 3" width. Cut through each end. Trace the pattern for the calyx and cut it out — 1 for each flower and 1 for each bud. To make the stamens, cut the white covered wire into 3" lengths. Bend one end of wire into 2 small folds about 1/4" long and squeeze these together. With the marking pen, blacken the folded end. Make 3 stamens for each flower.

For buds, roll 3 double petals together, overlapping 3/4 of the petals and tying these together (see illustration). Place glue along the long edge of the calyx and wrap around bud. Wrap the remainder of the bud with floral tape. Make 3 or 4 buds for each spray.

For flowers, tie 3 stamens together with tying wire. Cup each double petal and place 4 of them around the stamens with the petals cupping out. Tie with tying wire. Glue a calyx over the base of the flower, as on the bud. Wrap the remainder of the stem with floral tape. Make about 7 flowers for each spray.

Finally, tie one bud to the end of the 14" wire. Wrap this with floral tape for 1 inch. Tie on another bud and wrap for 1 inch. Add 1 or 2 more buds 1" apart, then add flowers 1" apart. Wrap the remainder of the stem with floral tape. For leaves, follow the instructions for tulip leaves. Make 1 or 2 for each spray.

For Additional Reading

Beautiful Flowers 'n Things, Craft Course, 1970.

Dennison Flower Book, Dennison Manufacturing Co., 1963.

Hamel, Esther Veramae, **Creative Designs With Dried and Contrived Flowers,** Simon and Schuster, 1971.

McDowall, Pamela, **Pressed Flower Pictures,** Scribner, 1969.

Pantz, Phillis, **Decorating With Plants and Natural Materials,** Doubleday, 1971.

Squires, Mabel, **The Art of Drying Plants and Flowers,** Bonanza Books, 1958.

Dough Art

The popular folk art of making decorative objects from various kinds of edible and inedible bread dough owes its beginnings to ancient bakers who first began to sculpt and mold the pliable substance while preparing the "daily bread."

The knowledge of bread making is as old as recorded history; bread is also man's first formulated food. Since the first baker pushed his fist into a soft mound of dough and gave a brief thought to the resulting shape, bread dough has been explored as an artistic medium as well as a nutritional one.

The earliest evidences of bread making come from the Neolithic Age. Ancient graves, dating from 6000 B.C., were found to contain small fragments of bread-like material. The first breads were probably made of crushed grain mixed with water and formed into paddies which were left to dry in the hot sun. Later, the grain was crudely milled, resulting in a slightly finer product.

Figure 2. The stylistic Madonna and Child on this "baked Christmas card" was designed by Ray Ameijide. (By permission from Lithopinion 32, *the graphic arts and public affairs journal of Local One, Amalgamated Lithographers of America and lithographic employers, New York, © 1973 by Local One, A.L.A.)*

The Egyptians are credited with the discovery of a leavening agent and, in time, they also invented the first baking ovens. Wheat is believed to have been raised first in ancient Abyssinia. The grain was carried by boat down the Nile to Egypt. The

Figure 1. This quaint house was made from baker's clay. Dough art is sometimes called "poor man's ceramic" because no expensive equipment is required to create decorative objects.

archeological explorations at Deir-el-Bahari have turned up ancient loaves of bread, either round or triangular in shape, which had been baked in ovens and which represented the finest bread product of that period.

Bread became an important factor in the success of Egyptian civilization and a symbol of its bounty. Bread was ceremoniously cast upon the waters of the Nile in tribute to the gods and has been discovered in Egyptian tombs, where it was placed to sustain the departed spirits of the dead. Often bread was used for money. At the end of a work day, laborers were paid their due in bread.

The developing Greek civilization borrowed much from the Egyptian culture, including the secret of leavened bread. Realizing the importance of bread, the Greeks came to worship it much as the Egyptians had done. Demeter was named "Goddess of Bread," and the "Celebration of Bread" became one of the more important Greek festivals. Eventually, the Greeks began to use bread dough for decorative as well as for religious and ceremonial purposes.

The circular millstones for grinding grain were invented by the Romans, who also saw the practicality of enlarged baking ovens where bread could be prepared on a commercial level. Roman bakers, in business by 168 B.C., were careful to mark each loaf with their own personal sign. Loaves of bread, left baking in beehive-shaped ovens at the time of the catastrophic eruption of Mt. Vesuvius in 79 A.D., have been found in the ruins of Pompeii.

As European cultures developed during the Middle Ages, bakers' guilds were formed. Substances other than bread dough were developed for decorative and artistic baking purposes during this time. One of the more successful ones, marzipan — a sweet, pliable material — was made from crushed almonds and pressed into molds or freely sculptured. While too expensive at first for widespread use by the common people, this new, highly popular substance triggered the production of a vast variety of molds for candy and breads.

Various kinds of fancy baked goods became traditional fare for market places, village fairs, and large festivals. Individual regions featured their own specific design, often commemorating some locally famous event or story. Large honey biscuits and delicate honey cookies, decorated with biblical parables, family coats of arms, historical captions, sayings, and tales, were proudly displayed before being consumed.

Inedible forms of bread dough evolved along with the edible, probably appearing first in Yugoslavia and later in other parts of Europe. South America

Figure 3. These intricately detailed ornaments of bread dough illustrate the skill developed by Ecuadorian craftsmen.

and Mexico developed a highly decorative form of bread dough art, utilizing brilliant color and minute detail. The folk art of Ecuador included highly ornamented mirrors, picture frames, figurines, and nativity scenes as well as a wide variety of jewelry made from bread dough which has the lasting power of ceramics. Today, the tourist in Bolivia, Peru, Columbia, Ecuador, and Mexico will be dazzled by the vast array of designs in both utilitarian and decorative baked objects produced by local craftsmen.

In the United States, the contemporary movement is back to nature, back to harmonious, organic living, and back to the more simple pleasures of folk art. The bread dough medium, in all of its varieties, represents a fundamental link with man's earliest beginnings.

Figure 4. Mushrooms, molded of bread dough, were combined with tree bark, strawflowers, and a pine cone in this decorative wall plaque.

Figure 5. This Christmas wreath, which has been fashioned from bread, is an attractive wall decoration.

Figure 6. The "stained glass" cookie (left) was created from cookie dough and hard candy. The stained glass effect is achieved by filling cut out areas in the cookie with finely crushed candy before baking. The candy melts during baking and spreads to fill out the spaces. The Raggedy Ann and Andy (right) are made of baker's clay, which becomes hard as rock after baking. Such figures, which have parts several layers thick, tend to warp during baking.

Figure 7. This close-up view of the clown shown in Figure 3 illustrates the elaborate detail possible in dough art.

Figure 8. This elaborate and colorful necklace is made of baker's clay. Although usually long lasting, such dough items, like items made of porcelain, will break if they are handled carelessly.

Common Terms Used In Dough Art

Acrylic: an odorless, quick drying, water-based paint made from plastic polymers; also acts as a strong adhesive.

Baker's Clay: a clay-like material made of salt, water, and flour; must be baked in order to become hard.

Bread Dough: a substance made with bread, white glue, and a small amount of glycerin or liquid detergent; hardens without baking.

Creative Clay: a mixture of cornstarch, baking soda, and water which is cooked briefly to form a pliable material.

Dough Appliqué: the process of applying several layers of dough over a foundation layer.

Glazing: the brushing of the surface of a baker's clay item with mayonnaise, canned milk, or egg yolk before it is baked. By glazing, a surface may be made to appear smooth, glossy, crackled, or browned and antiqued.

Sealer: a clear acrylic or shellac applied in several light coats over any finished dough project to prevent the absorption of moisture and to add a protective, glossy, or matte coating to the surface; may be sprayed on or painted with a brush.

Tempera: an inexpensive type of water-based paint which can be used to tint the uncooked dough or to decorate the finished product.

Basic Equipment And Supplies

One of the greatest appeals of this medium is that it is relatively inexpensive. Most of the varying dough recipes, both edible and inedible, use reasonably priced ingredients from the grocery store; many of the shaping tools and extra equipment may be found in an ordinary kitchen. Sometimes referred to as a "poor man's ceramic," dough art requires none of the expense of clay, potter's wheel, kiln, and glazes as does actual ceramic work. Yet the dough material has the plasticity of clay, the lasting quality of ceramics or porcelain, is nontoxic, and displays a warmth and beauty all its own.

THE DOUGH

There are a variety of dough recipes, each one calling for slightly different ingredients and techniques of preparation. One recipe may be suitable for very tiny, fragile items while another is best for larger, sturdier projects. Some types of inedible doughs will not be longlasting while others will hold up for years. Various doughs can be stored in plastic bags in the refrigerator and used over a period of weeks while others must be used within hours of preparation. While guidelines for the handling of various doughs will be given during the course of this article, personal experimentation is highly recommended.

Flour

The flour called for in some of the recipes can be of nearly any kind as long as it is white. It does not need to be "self-rising" or "enriched" and does not require sifting before use. Generally, the least expensive flour available is perfectly satisfactory.

Salt

The salt, which does not have to be iodized, can be any brand available as long as it is of the table salt variety.

Water

Comfortably warm water from the faucet is recommended for those doughs requiring kneading. The warm water gives the dough a pleasant feel and seems to speed up the kneading process. It appears to make no difference if the water is "hard" or "soft."

Baker's Clay Mix

A ready-made dry mix of salt and flour may be available at craft stores for those who do not care to make their own. However, the water must still be added in correct proportions and the dough kneaded until the desired consistency is attained, so very little time and effort are saved by buying the mix.

Bread

Several recipes call for the use of white bread. Generally, fresh bread is preferable but older bread, when placed in the freezer for several days and then thawed, is also adequate.

Glue

Any brand of general-purpose white glue can be used. Several recipes call for the glue to be mixed with pieces of bread; this causes the bread to change back into a doughy substance. When kneaded properly, the bread and glue mixture will not be sticky. White glue, which is colorless when dry, is often mixed with water to give a porcelain-like surface to the finished project.

Glycerin

Easily purchased at any drugstore, glycerin is added to the bread and glue recipes to improve the plasticity of the dough. It is also helpful to moisten the hands with glycerin periodically while working with the dough. A few drops of liquid detergent may be tried as a substitute for the glycerin, and hand lotion can be used to keep the hands from drying.

Whitening Agent

Several additives may be used to enhance the whiteness of the dough. Small amounts of white acrylic paints, white tempera, or tube watercolors are recommended.

Cornstarch

Several recipes use cornstarch as a basic ingredient rather than flour or bread. Often the cornstarch recipe, containing baking soda, is used as "play dough" in nursery schools and kindergartens. It is safe for small children, is easily made and worked, and stores well for long periods of time.

EQUIPMENT

Most of the equipment required for the basic dough recipes is readily available in well-stocked kitchens, with only a few special items needed from a hardware or paint store. The following supplies are not required for all dough recipes, nor are they necessary for all projects.

Garlic Press

A garlic press, while not necessary, is a handy gadget to use with dough. Such items as string-like hair, manes, and tails can be produced from the long, thin, "noodles" of dough squeezed through a press. A garlic press can be purchased chased at hardware or department stores containing a section for gourmet cooking ware.

Shaping Tools

The kitchen drawer is the first place to look for dough tools. A small paring knife is probably the most versatile tool available and may be the only one needed. Other tools might be a rolling pin, melon-ball shaper, potato ricer, pastry wheel, vegetable peeler, ice pick, pieces of dinner ware, or a nut cracker. Check the "stray items" drawer for pencils, toothpicks, popsicle sticks, bottle lids, golf tees, manicure scissors, or anything else with which to jab, poke, prod, or pinch. Cookie cutters are excellent tools for cutting and shaping, while a child's toy box may yield various tools and molds for play dough. A wide variety of wood, plastic, or metal specialty tools for clay and dough sculpting are also available at craft and hobby supply stores.

Figure 9. Although a variety of special tools are available, practically all of the equipment necessary for dough art can be found in the home. A paring knife is almost indispensable. Other utensils that might be useful include a pastry wheel, tweezers, and cookie cutters.

Other Household Equipment

Aluminum foil is indispensable for projects using dough which must be baked. When making several small projects, it is easiest to form each one on a separate piece of foil, then slide the foil onto a cookie sheet and place in the oven. Wax paper may be employed as a surface on which to work when using the materials which are dried in air.

Several of the doughs respond well to being pressed into molds. Antique and Jell-O molds as well as candy, cookie, and marzipan molds might be considered. A variety of molds for plaster, resin, and candles are offered by local craft shops. Stoneware cookie molds pressed into small rounds of dough make interesting imprints, as do ornamental metal and wooden buttons and costume jewelry with interesting surfaces. Some materials, such as metal buttons, hard seeds and nuts, some pasta products, odds and ends of old jewelry, beads, and chains, can be pressed into the soft dough and baked in.

Color Additives

Color may be added to the various doughs either before using or after, depending upon the type of dough prepared and the particular project being attempted. Baker's clay, after being baked in an oven, turns delicately brown and closely resembles an edible dough. The natural coloring of this type of dough is one of its charming qualities. However, the addition of some color to a project after baking is quite acceptable. Tempera paint is most easily handled — it is applied with a small brush — and can be used by anyone. Acrylic paint is somewhat more expensive but perfectly satisfactory. Felt-tip markers may be used, but the surface of the baked dough is often so uneven that the color from such markers is not satisfactory. Vegetable dyes may be employed, added either before the dough is used, during the mixing process, or afterward. The same is also possible with a variety of other commercial dyes.

Dough made from bread and glue is often colored before use, generally by the addition of small amounts of tempera paint or tube watercolors. Projects made from bread dough can be decorated with pigment after completion as well. Other dough recipes should be experimented

Figure 10. Commonly used cooking ingredients, such as Worcestershire sauce, canned milk, egg yolk, and mayonnaise, provide a variety of finishes when brushed over the unbaked dough. Such pre-bake glazing is not essential, however.

with by adding color either before or after baking or drying in order to arrive at the most satisfying results.

Wire

Dough material lends itself to the making of hanging ornaments. A light grade of wire, cut into 1- or 2-inch lengths and then twisted around a pencil, makes a good hanger for an ornament. A non-rust steel or aluminum alloy wire is recommended. The wire loop (or paper clip, bobby pin, etc.) should be inserted while the dough is soft.

Another type of wire, #9 green-covered wire, is ideal for use with bread dough when designing small flowers requiring stems. Heavier wire or a fine grade of chicken wire or wire mesh can be used for support when larger, heavy projects are undertaken.

Sealer

All dough art work will last longer and look better if it is protected by a sealer. The dough containing salt absolutely requires sealing to avoid softening and crumbling. Depending upon the product used, a nearly invisible matte finish is possible, as is one of high gloss. Clear acrylic and shellac come in spray-type containers and are easily handled. Craft shops carry a variety of other types of transparent sealants as well. In some instances, shellac or lacquer can be applied by brush. All surfaces, front and back, should be sealed.

Basic Procedures

Working in dough is a pleasant pastime for everyone. It is an ideal project for children of all ages and for various clubs, organizations, and fund-raising groups.

Generally speaking, the resulting objects improve in quality as one's skill increases, but the medium does not require great expense, concentration, time, or special ability. Moreover, the craft imparts a satisfying feeling of achievement regardless of the artistic worth of the end product.

Of the half-dozen or more dough recipes found in craft magazines, two of them are the most satisfactory. Other recipes appear to be simply variations of these basic two, but all should be tried if one is interested in achieving unusual results or is seeking some quality not present in the master recipes.

Baker's clay, made with flour and salt, is an inedible, nontoxic dough which closely resembles edible dough when baked. It smells pleasant while baking and puffs up slightly, softening edges and details, and turns light brown. If it is baked too long, it becomes dark and will catch on fire if forgotten in a hot oven. If coated with a matte finish sealant after baking, the dough will continue to resemble any regular cookie or bread dough product. This type of dough is excellent for all projects with the exception of the most delicate. It is extremely longlasting but subject to breakage, as is any ceramic or porcelain item. However, the unused dough does not save well and begins to deteriorate within hours of being prepared.

Bread dough, consisting of white bread and glue, works particularly well for small projects requiring minute detail and fragile edges. It is used primarily for making small, delicate flowers because the material is highly pliable and elastic; it can be pressed and gently pulled until very thin. The finished products are sturdy and longlasting. The unused dough can be successfully stored in a sealed, plastic bag in the refrigerator for several weeks.

BAKER'S CLAY

Baker's clay is most satisfactory if used right after preparation and baked as soon as each project is completed. When the dough is allowed to remain unbaked for an hour or more it begins to get sticky; covering the dough in a container will not remedy this problem. Often, more flour can be kneaded into the softening dough. However, such treated dough has a greater tendency to expand and crack while baking, often distorting pertinent details of the design.

Preparation of the Dough

The very first step in working with baker's clay is to allow time enough for the dough preparation, the creative process, and the baking of the finished piece. The master recipe calls for 4 cups of flour, 1 cup of salt, and 1½ cups of water.

Mix the flour and salt together in a flat-bottomed plastic bowl. A spatula or wooden spoon may be used for mixing, but the hands are best. Wear plastic gloves to protect the hands from excessive drying. Add warm water slowly, stirring constantly. As soon as the dough has formed enough to pull away from the sides of the bowl, turn it out onto a floured counter. Knead it vigorously, adding more flour if it becomes too sticky or more water if it is dry and crumbly. Continue to knead for seven to ten minutes or until the dough resembles heavy, thick clay with a smooth, elastic surface. (If salt granules show, the dough is too dry. If there is any tendency for the dough to stick to the fingers or counter, it is too wet.) Place the material immediately in a covered, plastic container or bag and remove only small pieces at a time while working with the dough.

Working the Dough

Baker's clay may be rolled out with a rolling pin and cut into shapes with cookie cutters. Like clay, it may be handled and shaped into sculptured figures and built up on chicken wire foundations or, for larger projects, on a metal armature. Or, it can be formed over crushed balls of aluminum foil. It can be molded into forms and have forms molded into it. It can be squeezed, pinched, stretched, or cut. One piece can be sealed to another by lightly wetting the two surfaces.

Figure 11. Baker's clay consists of flour, salt, and water. Use a wooden spoon and a large bowl to mix the correct amount of each ingredient (above left). When the mixture pulls away from the sides of the bowl, turn it out onto a floured surface (above right). Then, knead the dough (below left) until its surface is smooth and elastic (below right).

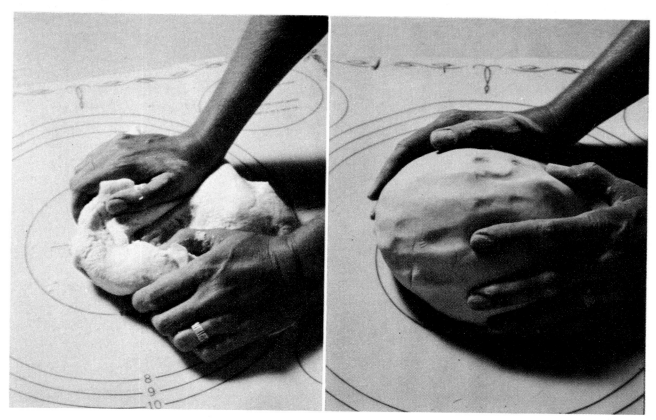

A variety of surface effects can be achieved by coating the dough with a number of substances before or during baking. Mayonnaise applied several times during the baking process will result in a crackled, rich, warm brown color. A canned milk coating causes a deep brown, semigloss surface which can be utilized for highlighting. Other colors and textures are created by using egg yolk, egg white, weak solutions of tea or coffee, lemon juice, and shoe polish. Before using, the dough can be colored with vegetable or powdered dyes; generally, however, color is added after baking.

Baker's clay cannot be attached to other surfaces before baking. As a general rule, the dough will not cook well if parts of it are more than several inches thick. Dough which is too soft may enlarge and crack during baking, and dough which is too dry may develop an unpleasant granular surface.

Baking the Dough

The purpose of baking this material is two-fold: (1) to "set" the dough, driving out the moisture and leaving a hard, sturdy substance; and (2) to achieve the color and appearance of a real dough product. When the dough creation is relatively thin — under 1/2" in thickness, for example — the dough browns as it dries and becomes evenly hardened. When items to be baked vary in thickness or are 1 to 3 or more inches thick, problems can arise. Generally, the larger or thicker the item, the longer it must bake and at a slower temperature.

Most small projects such as ornaments the size of cookies, which are relatively thin, can be cooked in a 350° oven for approximately 30 minutes. Figures or constructions from 1/2 to 2 inches thick will probably require an hour or more and should be baked at 300° or 325°. Larger projects require longer baking. A baker's clay project is done when it has baked through completely and is rock hard. If items must be cooked for long periods of time, it is sometimes helpful to lightly cover the item with aluminum foil. The foil reduces the speed of browning so that an item which must cook three hours or more will not come out of the oven too dark to be attractive.

Figures with long legs, arms, hair, or shapes made of several thicknesses of dough tend to warp during baking. This problem can be offset to some degree by placing the item, before baking, on the surface of the stove after the surface has been warmed by the oven. The warm metal of the stove seems to dry out the underneath surface of the dough creation and, in most cases, helps in cutting down or eliminating the tendency to warp.

Thin areas or the uppermost surfaces on dough projects will brown faster than the main body. Sometimes, as in the mane and tail of a lion design or the fur on a dog, this is desirable. However, this early browning can be controlled by careful placement of small pieces of aluminum foil, covering only those areas which are darkening too rapidly.

All projects should be constructed on aluminum foil and baked on cookie sheets or other large, flat metal pans.

Finishing the Dough Project

After the dough piece has thoroughly baked, been removed from the oven, and cooled, it can be finished in a variety of ways. If the surface color is entirely satisfactory and attractive, perhaps nothing more should be done to enhance it. In this case, several coats of a matte finish sealer will protect the item, yet will be scarcely visible as a coating over the surface.

Color can be applied at this time, either as a highlight or as a covering of the entire surface. Tempera is inexpensive and easily used. Any of the other coloring agents previously mentioned deserve experimentation. All pieces must be sealed as a final step.

An interesting surface can be achieved by antiquing a finished piece. After completely sealing a project with several coats of clear, acrylic spray, brush on a coat of wood stain, such as oak, walnut, or teak. Then, after letting the piece dry briefly, rub the stain off with a soft cloth. Several more coats of sealant will bring back a slight gloss to the finished product.

Dough sculptures can be mounted on wooden plaques, driftwood, barn siding, cork board or used in ecology boxes and miniature scenes. A dependable adhesive is epoxy glue, particularly the quick-set type. Once set, the glue will hold indefinitely, and there is no danger of the dough creation coming loose from its wooden backing.

BREAD DOUGH

Made primarily of bread and glue, this dough can be successfully formulated from several recipes. It stores well when placed in a sealed container and refrigerated, and can be used over a period of several weeks.

Preparation of the Dough

The master recipe for bread dough calls for 6 slices of white bread (if extremely soft, allow to dry in air for several hours); 2 tablespoons of white glue; and 2 teaspoons of glycerin (or liquid detergent). Other additives include 6 drops of lemon juice and 6 drops of white paint (tempera or tube watercolor) or white shoe polish.

Remove crusts from the bread and tear or cut the bread slices into small pieces. Mix the crumbs and glue together in a small bowl, kneading the mixture with the hands until a small, pasty ball is formed. Work in the remaining ingredients and continue working the material with the hands until the dough is firm, smooth, and not sticky. If it seems too sticky, add more bread crumbs; if too dry, mix in more glue. Place the dough in a plastic bag and store until needed.

Figure 12. When making bread dough, first remove the crusts from slices of white bread and tear the bread into small pieces (below). Next, mix in some white glue (top right) and form a ball of dough. Blend in glycerin, lemon juice, and paint (center right), and knead until the dough is firm and smooth. If the dough is too sticky (bottom right), add more bread. If the dough is too dry, add more glue. Store the dough in a plastic bag.

Coloring the Dough

Color may be added to the dough either before use or after a project is completed. Probably the easiest method of tinting is to mix the individual colors desired into the fresh dough, later adding more color to the completed project if necessary. Tempera paint or vegetable colors are best to use when tinting fresh dough. Color only small amounts of material at a time unless planning a very large project containing only one or two major colors.

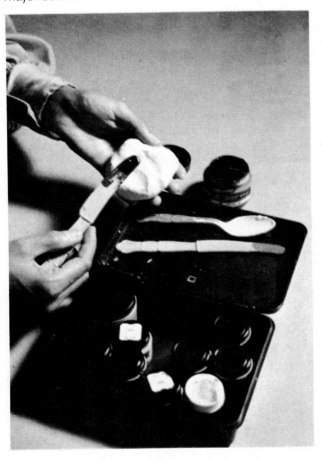

Figure 13. When coloring bread dough with tempera paint, flatten a small ball of fresh dough and add the paint. Work the paint into the dough by kneading and squeezing; mix thoroughly.

Make a ball about 1" in diameter and flatten it on a on a piece of paper. Apply tempera color with a popsicle stick or brush, or carefully add vegetable color drop by drop. Work the color into the dough by kneading and squeezing, taking care to mix it thoroughly. If the color develops darker than desired, add uncolored, white dough to lighten the shade. Repeat this process with each color and store each ball of dough in a separate sealed container. Marbleized dough may be created by partially mixing balls of different tints together.

Working the Dough

Anytime the dough is being worked for the first time or has just been taken from the refrigerator, it is helpful to knead it for several minutes to render it pliable and to bring it approximately to room temperature. Keep a container of hand lotion or glycerin handy and occasionally put a few drops on the hands to keep them moist. When one piece of dough is to be added to another, it must be glued. Merely sticking the damp ends together will not result in a permanent seal. To adhere the surfaces, the same white glue used in the preparation of the dough may be employed. If, however, the dough creation will receive hard wear and tear, as in the case of rings, pins, and brooches, a regular cement must be used to join surfaces.

A bread dough project cannot be hurried. When it consists of many separate, assembled pieces, such as the petals of a rose or decorations or an ornament, it must be allowed to dry thoroughly between steps. Work on wax paper so that the dough object may be carefully laid down to dry without the problem of sticking to surfaces. Often a block of styrofoam can be used as a base and the wire stems of flowers placed in it as the flowers dry.

Occasionally, bread dough will shrink and crack as it dries, especially if the dough was too dry to begin with. It may be helpful to brush a light coat of equal parts water and white glue over each object when the design is completed and the drying process ready to begin. This procedure will give a glossy finish to the creation as well as retard cracking.

Finishing the Project

After a project has been completed and allowed to air-dry entirely, the finishing touches can be added. Color may be applied by using tempera, acrylic, or oil paints or by using vegetable and commercial dyes. Wood stains and shoe polish may be used to give an antiqued finish. All dough pieces should be sealed with a lacquer or shellac as a final step.

Projects You Can Do

Four projects are suggested here, each using either baker's clay or bread dough. Although the last project is the most detailed, none is difficult and each should be fun.

BAKER'S CLAY ORNAMENTS

Probably the easiest project for someone new to the art of working in dough is making cookie-cutter ornaments, either as Christmas decorations or as jewelry to be worn. The ornaments are easily decorated with tempera paint or felt-tip pens, just as one might use frosting on real cookies.

The materials needed are prepared baker's clay dough, an assortment of cookie cutters, rolling pin, thin wire cut into 1½" lengths and twisted to form small loops, cookie sheet, tempera paint (or other paint) in a variety of colors, small brushes or magic markers, and spray sealant.

Start with about 1/3 of the prepared dough, forming a ball and then flattening it slightly with the hands. Using a rolling pin, roll the dough out on a slightly floured counter to about 1/4" thick. Cut the dough with the cookie cutters, dipping each cutter into flour occasionally to prevent the dough from sticking. Before placing each shape on a cookie sheet, insert a wire loop in the soft dough, taking care that the wire ends do not protrude.

Bake the cookies in a 350° oven for 20 to 30 minutes or until the cookies are rock hard and the desired shade of brown. Some shapes tend to expand and puff up slightly, making the resulting ornament either more attractive or unusable.

Figure 14. Before beginning baker's clay ornaments, make hangers for them from short lengths of wire that have been twisted around a pencil to form loops (top left). Prepare the baker's clay and roll out one-third of it (top right). Use cookie cutters to cut the dough, place the pieces on a cookie sheet, and insert a hanger in each piece (bottom left). Bake the ornaments and then paint them if desired (bottom right).

Sometimes a light covering of aluminum foil while baking helps prevent excessive puffing of the dough and produces a flatter cookie.

The cookie ornaments can be decorated after they have cooled. They may be completely covered with paint or merely outlined and only slightly decorated. Because the natural color of the dough is part of its charm, leaving part of the natural surface exposed will result in a finished ornament which more closely resembles a real cookie.

The final step is that of applying several light coats of spray sealer to both sides of the baked dough — allowing 15 to 30 minutes drying time between coats, depending on the brand and type of spray used.

plaque, driftwood, barn siding, tree bark, pressed cork or other mounting material; and a strong adhesive.

The dough to be pressed into molds should be on the stiff side without being crumbly. When making the dough, knead in extra flour and work the material ten minutes or longer to achieve a stiff, smooth, yet pliable substance.

Lightly sprinkle the mold with cornstarch to prevent sticking, shaking out excessive, loose cornstarch before applying the dough. Press a ball of

Figure 16. Baker's clay can be pressed into molds. When used in this way, the dough should be slightly stiff. First, dust the mold with cornstarch so that the dough does not stick (top). Note that the dough is kept in a plastic bag until needed. Firmly press a ball of the stiff dough into the mold (bottom). The choice of molds is limited only by the imagination of the craftsman.

Figure 15. These Christmas tree ornaments were cut out of baker's clay. Paint was used to add decorative touches.

USING A MOLD WITH BAKER'S CLAY

Materials needed are prepared bread dough; white glue; paint (tempera or watercolor in tubes); brush; floral tape; stiff wire (#9 green-covered wire if available); shaping tools; toothpicks; knife; cuticle or découpage scissors; and sealer, either matte or gloss finish.

Materials needed are prepared baker's clay dough; mold; cornstarch; kitchen paring knife; various substances for glazing, if desired (see discussion of glazing in section on common terms); cookie sheet; paint or stain; sealant; wooden

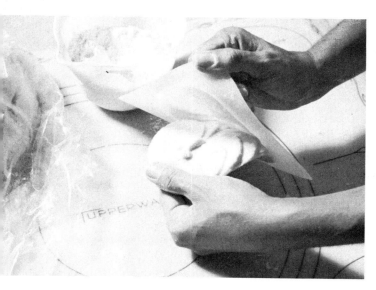

Figure 17. The baker's clay must be removed from the mold very carefully: start at one edge and gently pull back the dough (above). Place the molded dough on a flat surface and examine it; trim off any excess dough and reshape any distorted areas. With the mold on a piece of foil or a cookie sheet, apply a pre-bake glaze (right). Bake, cool, and paint the molded dough.

Figure 18. The molded dough, painted or stained if desired, must be sealed. Brush on several coats of shellac or clear acrylic. Mount the object on a wooden plaque, a scrap of lumber, a slab of tree bark, or some other material; use a strong adhesive.

dough firmly into the mold, filling all corners and crevices. Lift out the dough gently, starting at one edge and carefully pulling back. Thicker dough may be tapped out or a dough ball may be pressed into the back of the molded dough and used as a handle.

Examine the molded dough carefully, trimming off excess dough with the fingers or paring knife and gently reshaping if necessary. Thick dough may be inconspicuously pierced in several places with a pin to help prevent distortion and warping during baking.

Now is the time to apply a prebake glaze, if desired. Place the object on a cookie sheet and bake at 300° to 325° until done. Rapid browning can be slowed by a covering of aluminum foil. After the molded form has cooled, it may be painted, stained, antiqued, or left its natural color. As with all dough projects, the item must be sealed with a shellac or clear acrylic.

Many molded items are especially attractive when mounted on a background. Wooden plaques, available at hardware stores and craft shops, can be stained, painted, antiqued, or covered with material such as burlap. Weathered siding or lumber scraps along with tree sections, slabs of firm tree bark, or pressed cork are examples of other material with potential as background mountings. A strong adhesive is necessary to permanently glue the dough design to the background material. Various types of wood glue or quick-set epoxy glue are recommended.

MAKING A BASKET OF DOUGH

Lovely and unusual baskets that can be made from this versatile material are occasionally found for purchase in the more expensive gift shops; however, they can be made at home quite easily. The basket, which is woven, baked, and covered with sealant, can be used in flower arrangements, as an Easter basket for holding decorated eggs, or as a container for real bread and rolls. It is longlasting when stored in a dry place and can even be cleaned with a slightly damp cloth.

Materials needed are prepared baker's clay dough, a metal bowl to be used as a mold, rolling pin, ruler, sharp knife, orange shellac, gloss varnish, and a small brush.

Prepare the dough by working it until warm, soft, and smooth. Using approximately 1/2 of the dough, roll it out on a slightly floured surface until about 1/4" thick. Cut the dough into strips of equal width and long enough to fit over the bowl. Strips may be extended by attaching two or more together at the ends, moistening and gluing each contact surface.

Cover the outside surface of the bowl with aluminum foil, tucking the edges over the rim. Invert the bowl on the cookie sheet. Lay the dough strips over the bowl, in one direction, spaced evenly. Weave in an equal number of strips at right angles, moistening and gluing the strips at each junction. Trim away all excess dough around the rim of the inverted bowl.

Bake the construction (still supported on the bowl) in a 300° to 325° oven for 1 to 1½ hours or until cooked through. The basket may be covered with aluminum foil if it darkens too rapidly. Cool completely before gently inverting the metal bowl and sliding the basket off.

A decorative rim can be made by twisting the remaining strips of uncooked dough together and attaching them to the basket by moistening and gluing all the adjoining surfaces. Place the dough

Figure 19. Use baker's clay for a woven basket. Cut strips from the dough (top left). Twist some strips to make a rim and weave the others, shaping them over an inverted bowl (top right). Join the rim and woven strips with toothpicks (bottom left). Remove bowl after dough cools (bottom right).

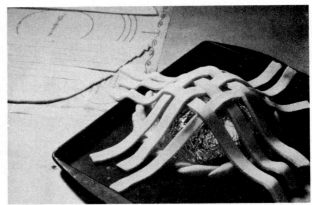

basket in a loose wrapping of aluminum foil, leaving the rim and interior of the basket exposed. Put the basket with its foil protection back into the oven, baking just long enough to brown and set the rim.

The completed basket must be sealed with more care than the previous projects if it is to be used and expected to last. Equal amounts of orange shellac and gloss varnish can be mixed and carefully brushed on the basket; allow complete drying between coats. Do not allow drips to harden. Cover completely with a final coat of pure varnish for a high-gloss effect.

Although the basket can be cleaned with a damp cloth, do not allow it to remain damp for any length of time and do not set it down on a wet counter surface. Store the dough basket in a dry, cool place.

FLOWERS FROM BREAD DOUGH

Bread dough is particularly suited for small, delicate projects although it may be used successfully for larger ones. However, a full loaf of bread does not produce a large quantity of dough and, when large projects are contemplated, the other dough recipes will probably be more satisfactory. Bread dough cannot be surpassed for making small doll house-sized miniatures, jewelry, picture frame and mirror decorations, and flowers, all of which have the appearance of a porcelain material.

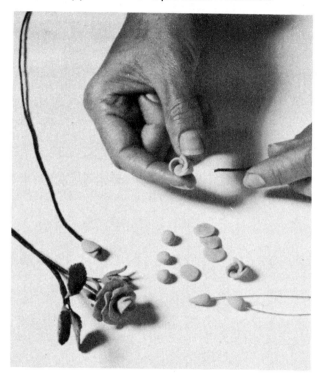

Figure 20. These baker's clay baskets have been sealed with several coats of a mixture of orange shellac and gloss varnish. Clean dough baskets with a damp cloth and store these versatile pieces in a cool, dry place.

Figure 21. To make the center of a rose from bread dough, flatten and form several small balls of dough into a petal shape. Then roll together three of these pieces (top). Use either a real rose leaf or a plastic one as a mold (bottom).

Figure 22. The rose center should be completely dry before petals are added. Shape each petal so that it resembles one from a real flower.

Before beginning a project of making flowers, it is advisable to consult a good flower book with many clear color plates. These pictures can serve as guides to shape, tint, and relative size of numerous flowers and will help in achieving a natural looking dough design.

Materials needed are prepared bread dough; white glue; paint (tempera or watercolor in tubes); brush; floral tape; stiff wire (#9 green-covered wire if available); shaping tools; toothpicks; knife; cuticle or découpage scissors; and sealer, either matte or gloss finish.

A rose is a good flower for the beginner because it is easily made, each petal being pressed from a small ball of dough and then wrapped around the stem. The first step is to color the dough. Divide the dough into walnut-sized pieces, add color to each, then work the ball until the desired shade is evenly mixed throughout.

Work with small amounts of dough at a time, keeping the remaining material covered in a plastic bag. Roll a number of small, pea-sized balls of dough and flatten each one, forming a petal shape and making sure the edges are particularly thin. Overlap three petals using a small amount of white glue to form a seal. (Because this dough does not adhere to itself well, all joints must be glued.) Roll the petals together, forming the center of the rose. Cut a length of #9 wire or cover a piece of wire with green floral tape and gently insert one end into the base of the rose cen-

ter, pinching the dough around the stem and sealing with a small dab of glue. The glue in the center must dry for 12 hours before more petals are added. A small drinking glass, a lump of clay, or a styrofoam block can be used to hold the stem and rose upright while it is drying.

The petals are added in rows of three, with each row having petals which are slightly larger and broader than the previous one. Apply a small amount of glue to the base of the rose and add the first petal, allowing it to flair slightly. Lightly curl back the upper edge, copying an actual rose or a picture of one in order to approximate a natural look. Attach the remaining two petals. Start on the second row of petals in the same manner, using glue to attach them and curling and waving each one. Alternate the second row of petals with the first row, as one finds in nature. Allow the glue in each row of petals to dry before attaching the next row.

A third row of five petals finishes the rose, which will now measure about 1" in diameter. Natural color gradation can be achieved by adding small amounts of white dough to the basic color as each row of petals is made, causing the rose to become deeper in color towards the center.

A calyx is a small collar of green leaf segments arranged around the base of a blossom. One may be devised for the rose by forming a small, flattened teardrop of green dough and cutting it, from the smaller end, into five, tapering segments. Do not cut the dough completely through to the far end. Roll the teardrop between the fingers and gently separate and flair each section, cutting tiny nicks along the edges with cuticle scissors. Slide the calyx up the stem of the rose and attach it to the base of the flower with white glue.

Leaves may be formed by using either a real rose leaf or a plastic one as a mold. Form a small amount of green dough into the general size and shape of the desired leaf. Press it onto the underside of the leaf chosen to serve as a mold. Squeeze out and thin the edges of the dough to conform to the appearance of the real leaf. The dough material will pick up the natural vein pattern of the leaf and appear quite realistic. Peel the dough leaf off carefully and glue the base to a length of green wire, pressing the base slightly around the wire. Cut teeth into each leaf with scissors.

Figure 23. It is difficult to distinguish the real rose (top) from the bread dough one (bottom). Always study natural flowers — size, color, etc. — before attempting to make them from dough.

After the finished flower has dried completely, seal it either with a spray gloss or matte lacquer or brush on several coats of glue mixed with equal parts water. A gloss is produced by placing the item in a 350° oven for a few minutes after applying the final coating of glue and water.

The leaves of a rose are assembled in threes, using floral tape. The three-leaf sections are then attached to the rose stem with the same tape. Cut away excess wire when assembling the leaves to avoid an overly thick, bulky stem.

All types of flowers can be designed with bread dough, either following the basic directions given for the rose, by adding each petal separately, or by cutting the flower petals from a single, flattened round of dough. An oxeye daisy, black-eyed susan, or any other flower with numerous, similar petals can easily be constructed by cutting a whorl of petals from a single piece of dough. Interesting centers for such flowers are made by pushing the dough into a tiny mesh such as netting or nylon stockings. For each flower attempted, always return to nature and observe the form, size, shape, color, and arrangement of the petals, calyx, leaves, and stems.

Bread dough flowers look elegant when arranged in small baskets, antique china dishes, sugar bowls, and vases. They may be placed on brooches, pins, and earrings or even serve as place-card holders for fancy dinner parties. Flowers, mushrooms, small animals, and insects — all from bread dough — can be attached to plaques, jewelry boxes, mirrors, frames, and shadow-box pictures.

For Additional Reading

Andreas, Liza, "Bread Basket," **Family Circle,** May 1974.

Chernoff, Goldie Taub, **Clay-Dough, Play-Dough,** Scholastic Book Services, 1974.

Du Pont, Ana, **Bread Dough Artistry,** Craft Course, 1968.

Gerhard, Mae, "Balthasar," **Life Magazine,** Dec. 15, 1972.

Johnson, Ilse, "Cookies and Cathedrals Glazed with Good-to-Eat Glass," **Life Magazine,** Dec. 15, 1972.

Lanier, Ruth Asawa, "Christmas Claybake," **Ladies Home Journal,** Dec. 1964.

Mergeler, Karen, **Too Good to Eat: The Art of Dough Sculpture,** Folk Art Publications, 1972.

Sommer, Elyse, **The Bread Dough Craft Book,** Lothrop, Lee and Shepard, 1972.

Weber, Elizabeth, **From Bread to Flowers in the Palm of Your Hand,** Cunningham Art Products, 1972.

Williams, Greta, **Bread Dough Miniatures,** Craft Course, 1973.

Antiquing

Using paints, glazes, and finishes to produce an antique look can provide a creative approach to furniture decoration.

When paint was first used to decorate and brighten the gloom of the family cave is a fact lost in the history of man. However, it is known that paint made its first appearance as a means of decorating furniture among the Egyptians and, not long afterwards, among the classical Greeks and Romans.

Following the time of the Crusades, the walls of medieval halls and castles were brightened by painted decoration. The prosperity of the late medieval churches, however, enabled them to hire artists who were highly skilled. These artists became famous for their work in gold leaf and their ability to create illusions with the paint brush.

Figure 1. The early American side chair (opposite) is a fine example of the Hitchcock
tradition of craftsmanship. (Collection, Mr. and Mrs. John Gordon.) The Kas (above)
was painted to create the illusion of relief sculpture. (Courtesy, The Monmouth
County Historical Association; photo, George J. Evans, Sr.)

Figure 2. Paint has been used for centuries to decorate furniture. Contemporary furniture designers combine modern techniques with traditional design. The secretary (left) and magazine rack (below) reflect the influence of early Chinese craftsmen.

Figure 3. Throughout history nature has provided a source of inspiration for the craftsman. Intricate designs from nature add a special touch of beauty to the lacquered chair (below) and the cabinet (right).

Constant observation of lovely painted church furniture led the common people to desire aesthetically pleasing furniture in their own homes. France and Italy became flourishing centers of painted decoration, and knowledge of this craft eventually spread throughout the other European countries.

Whereas the furniture of the royal palaces in seventeenth-century France depended heavily on gilding (see "Common Terms"), people of the upper nobility used furniture that was painted white and embellished only with gold trim. This furniture, after it had been polished for generations, developed a delightful patina and an off-white look of age. It is this effect which "French antiquing" strives for.

Another step in the seventeenth-century development of painted finishes came with the sudden desire of European people to own Chinese lacquer furniture, which was becoming extremely popular and quite scarce. Europeans soon became skillful in simulating lacquer finishes and used these to tastefully complement the graceful Queen Anne furniture produced in the first half of the 1700s.

Among all the Europeans, however, it was the French who became leaders in the art of decorative furniture. French upholsterers, cabinetmakers, and finishers reached almost perfect harmony in their combined skills: finishers were able to make their work harmonize with upholstery fabrics by using colored varnishes and, at the same time, to enhance the design of the cabinetmakers. These combined skills peaked at the time of the French Revolution, and never again was such perfection reached. Indeed, the furniture pieces remaining from this period now command the highest prices on the antique market.

The next major development in the art of decorating furniture occurred in the United States. Throughout the American colonial period, decorated furniture had been imported from Europe. However, in the early 1800s, native craftsmen began to furnish many homes, often traveling from house to house to do their work.

These pieces were, for the most part, excellent copies of the European formal pieces. Then, about 1815, a native style of decoration was developed. This style was mainly restricted to chairs referred to as "Hitchcock" chairs or "Fancy Chairs." The method of decoration was to apply a base coat of a reddish color and, after this had dried, to apply a black or brown coat. The second coat was then partly wiped away, giving the wood a resemblance to rosewood.

In addition to this basic decoration technique, many of the ring turnings on the chairs were striped with gold or other metallic colors. The larger cross slats of the chair backs were embellished with elaborate stenciled designs in various colors. From these great traditions evolved the modern craft of antiquing — the application of a painted finish and glaze, both of which are covered with a protective finish, to create an antique look.

Common Terms Used In Antiquing

Bleeding: a showing, or "bleeding," of dye through the base coat.

Distressing: depositing flecks and spots of the glazing medium by snapping a partly loaded brush a short distance from the piece.

Flow: the tendency of paint and varnish to flatten or flow over the brush marks and hide them, causing the finished surface to be smooth.

Gilding: decorating by gold bronzing or gold leafing.

Grain: the direction in which the most prominent lines run in a piece of wood; also the direction in which a piece of wood will split.

Highlighting: bringing some areas of a piece into prominence by removing particular areas of glaze.

Runs: lumps of paint caused by using a brush that contains too much paint.

Scuff Sanding: a light sanding with a relatively fine paper (220 to 500 grit).

Teeth: a very fine scratching produced in a glossy finish by scuff sanding; allows for better adhesion between coats.

Basic Equipment And Supplies

When considering the purchase of supplies, one

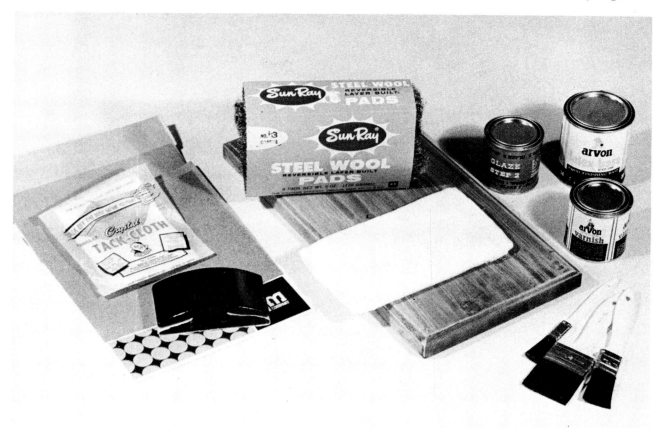

Figure 4. *Some of the supplies needed for antiquing include sandpaper and a sanding block, steel wool, brushes, a tack cloth, cheesecloth, and a trial board to experiment with the base and glaze coats.*

may either buy an antiquing kit or buy supplies separately. Either alternative is available in paint stores, hardware stores, and some department stores. The kits usually contain the following items: one can of low-gloss enamel or latex base coat; one can of antiquing glaze; cheesecloth or burlap; #120 and #220 grit sandpaper; and, of course, instructions.

For the beginner, the kits offer certain advantages: the materials are all compatible and the cost is the same or only slightly higher than buying the ingredients separately. The disadvantages are the unavailability of "custom" colors and the necessity of buying certain quantities and items that may not be needed.

Following is a list of necessary supplies if one chooses not to purchase a kit:

1. Bronzing liquid. This is either a slow-drying lacquer or varnish which is used as a base for bronzing powder.

2. Bronzing powder. This is used with the bronzing liquid to tone or stripe the furniture item with gold.

3. Brushes. 1- or 2-inch sizes of average quality are adequate. For especially good varnishing results, purchase a quality varnish brush that is tapered.

4. Cheesecloth. This is an open-weave, lint-free cloth used for wiping the glaze coat.

5. Clean cloth. This cloth can be either open or close weave, and should be free from all grease and dirt and, preferably, lint-free. Cloths that have been washed many times usually do not have any lint.

6. Cleaning solution. Any commercial cleaner that will remove wax and dirt will do. Or a mixture of 1/2 gallon of water, 1/4 cup of detergent, and 1/4 cup of household ammonia will work. The solution is used to clean the object before antiquing, regardless of

whether the furniture has a clear finish, is painted, or is unfinished.

7. Coarse woven burlap. This should be a burlap with a weave comparable to that of burlap bags. Obtainable in upholstery or fabric shops, it is used to wipe and texture the glaze coat. The textured effect is accomplished by pressing the burlap directly onto the glaze coat.

8. Drop cloth. In order to protect the floor or carpet, place old newspapers or cheap material about 10 feet square under the piece being antiqued.

9. Excelsior. These are curled shavings used to create certain effects on the glaze coat. They can be obtained at no charge from places that unpack furniture and appliances.

10. Glaze. This is a pigmented slow-drying varnish or lacquer with other additives; it is used to cover the base coat. When partly dry, it may be wiped to achieve different effects.

11. Latex base coat. This paint is for the first coat applied.

12. Mixing stick. This is a broad, flat piece of wood for mixing paint and is obtainable free at paint stores. It is preferable, however, to have the paint mixed at the store in a mechanical shaker.

13. Paint can opener. This small device for opening paint cans is available free at most paint stores.

14. Plastic wood. This is a filling material available clear or in colors.

15. Putty knife. This blunt knife, which has a broad, thin surface and shape, is used for transferring such soft materials as putty and plastic wood from their containers to the places to be filled. It can then be used to level and pack in the fillers.

16. Safety glasses. This hard-plastic eye protection will protect the eyes from sharp objects and spilled liquids.

17. Sandpaper. Beige-colored adalox is recommended, either #120 or #220 grit. The sandpaper is used to smooth the old surface and to produce "teeth" in a varnish coat for correct adhesion of the antiquing base coat.

18. Satin varnish. This nonglossy type of hard varnish protects the somewhat delicate finish of the glaze coat. The low luster of the varnish also enhances the depth of the finish.

19. Sealer. This enamel primer is available in cans or as a spray; used to prevent "bleeding."

20. Semigloss enamel base coat. This is an oil-based paint which can be used as the base coat. It requires a cleanup with turpentine.

21. Spackling paste. This powder can be purchased in most paint stores. When mixed, it is used to fill small dents and scratches.

22. Tack cloth. This commercially available sticky cloth, also called tack rag, is saturated with varnish and turpentine and then squeezed out. It is purchased in a plastic con-

Figure 5. This table was stripped to the bare wood because it had been painted several times and the surface was in poor condition.

tainer and, when not in use, must be kept in a clean, airtight jar.

23. Trial board. This is any piece of board used for experimenting with glaze coats.

24. Varnish. This hard, clear, protective finish seals wood and the antiqued finish.

Basic Procedures

Antiquing is not only one of the easiest crafts to learn but also one of the most helpful in developing several basic skills in a gradual and interesting way. None of the skills is difficult; each is useful in the everyday care of furniture. Basically, what will be explained here are the techniques for using paint and varnish brushes.

CLEANING THE OLD FINISH

One advantage of antiquing is that it is not necessary to remove the old finish — it is, however, necessary to clean the old finish. Dirt and wax must be removed or the antiquing base coat will not adhere.

Wear rubber gloves; dip a clean rag, sponge, or scrubbing brush into a cleaning solution. Then, with a scrubbing motion, go over one section of the piece at a time. As soon as one section is completed, dry it with a clean rag. Use a turning and mopping motion — the cleaner only loosens the dirt and wax; the clean cloth removes it from the surface. (*Note:* If there is veneered wood on the piece, use lukewarm water and only a slightly damp sponge or rag. Quickly wipe dry.) Let the piece dry several hours if necessary.

Look the piece over carefully for runs or sags from the previously applied varnish or paint. These can be removed with a sharp knife or by sanding (first with #120 sandpaper and then #220). If there are several dents and scratches, decide whether to fill all, some, or none.

FILLING DAMAGED AREAS

Open a can of clear plastic wood and, using a putty knife to remove a small amount from the can, press the plastic wood down in the spot to be filled. It is best to make the fill a little higher than the wood surface as the plastic wood tends to shrink as it dries. If the spots are rather small,

Figure 6. After the surface area has been cleaned, the damaged areas should be filled with plastic wood or spackling paste. Use the flat side of a putty knife to smooth the filler (left). Some of the dents and scratches can be left to create a distressed appearance. For those areas that are to be filled, apply the filler so that it is slightly higher than the wood surface (right).

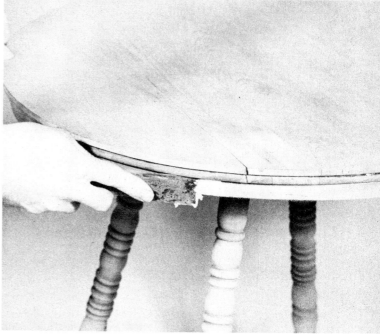

Figure 7. Allow the filler to dry before sanding. Put the sandpaper in a sanding block and smooth the filled areas. Then, smooth the entire surface. Use a small piece of sandpaper for hard-to-reach places.

spackling paste may work better. The only disadvantage in using the latter is that it must be mixed; plastic wood comes premixed.

Allow whatever drying time is recommended on the package. Refill the spots if the fills have shrunk below the wood surface. Wait the proper time, then sand the fill level with the surface.

SANDING THE OLD FINISH

After sanding the fills, go over the entire piece with #220 sandpaper held in a sanding block. In hard-to-reach places, the sandpaper may be folded four ways and used without the block. The purpose of sanding the old finish is to create "teeth," a slight scratching of the previous surface for better adhesion between coats.

APPLICATION OF THE BASE COAT

Before beginning, it is a good idea to experiment with the base coat paint on a trial board. A great deal more is learned by experimenting than merely by reading directions. Be sure that the paint is well mixed. At this point the paint can be transferred with an old ladle or tablespoon from the can to a more convenient container. Check the directions on the base coat can to see if the paint should be diluted. Before starting to apply the paint, however, dust off the piece with a brush that will get into crevices, then with a clean cloth, and finally with the tack cloth.

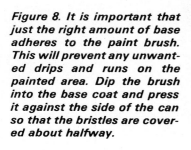

Figure 8. It is important that just the right amount of base adheres to the paint brush. This will prevent any unwanted drips and runs on the painted area. Dip the brush into the base coat and press it against the side of the can so that the bristles are covered about halfway.

Figure 9. Use a 2-inch brush to apply the base coat to large surface areas. Smaller areas, such as the table rim and legs, require a smaller brush. Finish brushing in the direction of the wood grain.

Next, dip the bristles of the brush about halfway into the paint; remove any excess paint by pressing the brush against the side of the paint container. If using a latex base coat, keep a water-dampened rag handy; if using an enamel base paint, the rag should be dampened with turpentine.

Start the application of the base coat paint on the trial board. This gives the paint a chance to work evenly into the bristles of the brush. A second tip is to start on the side of the piece least exposed to view. In this way there is time to perfect the brushing technique before doing the front sections.

If working on a chair, turn it upside down and use something to support it in this position. Paint all parts that are reachable in this position and then paint the outside of the chair (if the outside were done first, it would have to dry completely before the inside could be done).

If working on a chest of drawers, take out the drawers, remove all the hardware, and use masking tape to cover brass or other areas not to be painted. Prop the chest up so the bottom can be easily reached.

If the piece has a large panel, start the brush strokes in the middle and brush toward an edge. Then brush toward the opposite side from the middle, overlapping the thicker paint on the previous brush stroke. At this point it is permissible to brush crossways or in any other direction, but always finish in the direction of the grain and with progressively lighter strokes. Always check for runs and sags on the edges or carvings — these can be removed with the dampened cloth and then recoated. Continue to inspect the piece as work progresses.

A 2-inch brush will suffice for most of the work, but a 1-inch brush may be necessary for small places. Keep watching for any sign of bleeding. If there is any indication of discoloration, wipe the spot off with the damp cloth and then spray or brush on enamel sealer. In fact, the sealer can be used as a first coat to insure against all possibility of bleeding.

Let the base coat dry according to directions and clean the brushes. If, after it has dried, the base coat does not entirely conceal the color of the original finish, it is necessary to recoat the piece. This often happens when a light color is used over a dark old finish. Scuff sand the base coat with #220 sandpaper before applying the second coat.

APPLICATION OF THE GLAZE

Stir the glaze mixture thoroughly and dip a clean, dry brush about halfway up the bristles. Remove any excess glaze by pressing the brush against the side of the container. Brush a liberal coat of the glazing material on the trial board, then wipe the wet glaze with a soft, lint-free cloth. Work the cloth in circles and scrub a little. Finally, using a clean cheescloth, wipe the glaze all one way, following the original grain direction.

Figure 10. After the base coat has dried, brush the glaze on the wood surface (above left). When the glaze has partially dried, it can be wiped with steel wool to produce the desired texture (above right). A tack cloth is used to wipe the surface areas after the glaze has dried (right).

Recoat the trial board with glaze several times and experiment with burlap, excelsior, and dry brushes for a wood grain effect. Pressing a sponge on the surface can also create unusual patterns. To try a new technique, recoat with the glaze. It can always be wiped off.

Once a glaze effect has been selected, coat a section of the piece with glaze, wipe off the excess with the lint-free cloth, and texture the glaze as desired (cheesecloth is probably the favorite medium for this purpose). Remember to clean the brush when you are finished.

APPLICATION OF GILDING

There are three methods of applying gilding to furniture: (1) brushing on prepared gold paint, which is cheap in cost; (2) using bronzing liquid plus bronzing powder; or (3) doing traditional gold leaf work. The last two give excellent results. Gold leafing, however, is expensive and not recommended for beginners.

Bronzing liquid is a slow-drying liquid with a varnish-type base. It is applied like any varnish, but only to those areas that are to be covered with bronzing powder.

Pour some bronzing powder onto a piece of soft, dark cloth that is about 4" to 6" square. Slip a small piece of the same cloth over a fingertip. Use the cloth-covered fingertip to transfer the gold or bronze powder from the large cloth to the areas that have been covered with bronzing liquid. The powder may be tapped on or rubbed on. It may be rubbed partly off by using another cloth over the fingertip. After the bronzing liquid has set the powder, use a small syringe or a tapping motion to dislodge any excess powder. Clean all containers when you are finished.

APPLICATION OF SATIN VARNISH

After having created the desired glaze effect and perhaps having applied some gilding, add a protective hard finish over the rather delicate glazes. It is also important to use a varnish that is not shiny: satin varnish has that property and also has the added advantage of not showing fingerprints very clearly.

In many of today's homes, the temperatures are slightly lower than is advisable for good varnishing. To offset these lower temperatures, the following procedure is suggested. Select a clean 8-ounce jar, preferably one that is calibrated in ounces. Before pouring or handling varnish or turpentine, it is wise to put on safety glasses. Transfer the varnish from the original can to the container by means of an old spoon or ladle. Add turpentine or mineral spirits if directed. These two solvents are usually interchangeable but not always; it is safer to follow the directions exactly. Then, to offset the cool house temperature, immerse the jar in a saucepan of warm water, covering about half the jar. The water should be replaced as it cools.

The piece to be varnished should be elevated, if possible, so that its surface is not chilly and it is easier to reach. Go over the surface with a tack rag; then dip the brush into the varnish mixture about halfway up the bristles. Press the brush against the side of the container in order to eliminate any excess varnish. Make a few trial strokes on an old newspaper in order to work the varnish into the brush and to get the feel of the brush. It is a good idea to apply some varnish strokes on the trial board, starting in the middle and drawing the brush toward one edge. Next, start from the middle and brush to the opposite edge, overlapping the previous stroke where the varnish is thicker.

Use very light pressure on the brush — varnish should be flowed on rather than brushed on. Finish by using progressively lighter pressure. A light stroke can be acquired by holding the brush so that the fingers touch the metal clasp (the *ferrule*) around the bristles.

Figure 11. Transfer the varnish from its original container into a clean glass jar and add turpentine or mineral spirits. With light brush strokes, apply the varnish in the direction of the original wood grain so that the previous coats are not disturbed.

Figure 12. Base and glaze coats were applied to the natural wood to create an antiqued finish. The glaze was worked into certain areas to produce highlights and a wood-grained appearance.

The varnish is applied, in the direction of the original wood grain, of course. Because this same direction was followed in the application of the base and glaze coats, there is little risk that the coat of varnish will disturb the previous coats. Always check for runs and sags on the edges. These can either be brushed out or rubbed out with a turpentine rag. Remember to clean brushes and utensils in turpentine when you are through using them.

Projects You Can Do

The following projects can be done with a minimum of expense and time. They include examples of antiquing unfinished furniture; antiquing over clear, varnished finishes; and antiquing over painted finishes. All projects are illustrated step-by-step, enabling the beginner to develop the basic skills necessary for achieving satisfactory results.

ANTIQUING A PAINTED CHAIR

Almost every home has old wooden chairs which, in many cases, have been relegated to the attic or basement because of their shabby appearance. Most contain several coats of paint.

Preparation for Antiquing

First, check the item carefully for any loose parts, rough chips knocked out of the previously painted surface, or nails and screws showing plainly through the old paint cover. Unscrew the latter, if any, and remove the surface under them by drilling. Screw them back in, cover the holes

Figure 13. Use an appropriate sized brush to apply the base coat (left). After the base has dried, brush on a coating of glaze. Then, work in the glaze with a cloth until the desired effect is achieved (below).

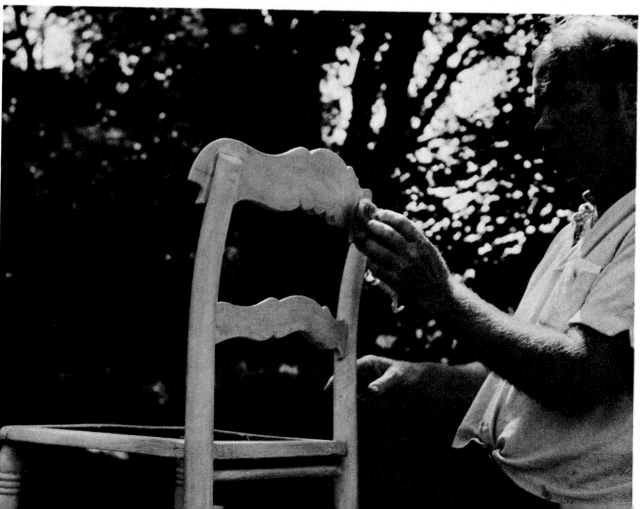

Figure 14. It is necessary to thoroughly clean the surface of the chair before the finish is applied (above). The antiqued effect was achieved by sealing the base and glaze coats with a satin varnish (right).

with plastic wood, and, after it dries, sand the fill so that it is level with the wood surface.

Sand any chipped edges with #120 sandpaper. Then apply enamel primer to these spots to prevent poor adhesion and to help make the level of the chipped out spots even with the main surface. Finally, fix any loose pieces with glue, wash the

chair with cleaning solution, and let it dry for several hours.

Brushing on the Base Coat

After stirring the base coat thoroughly, follow the application method described under "Basic Procedures." (Note particularly the explanation of how to apply the base coat when working on a chair.) Allow the chair to dry for about four hours. Clean brushes and containers. Inspect the base coat after it has dried. If it has completely concealed the previous coat, it is time to glaze.

Brushing on the Glaze

Brush on the glaze coat. Use a clean, dry, lint-free cloth to wipe off the excess glaze, and then use a cheesecloth to achieve a misty effect if desired. Let the chair dry overnight.

Brushing on the Satin Varnish

Prop the chair in the upside-down position and start applying the varnish. Do the inside, then set the chair right side up and varnish the outside. It is especially important to clean the varnish brush with turpentine when you are finished.

ANTIQUING AN UNFINISHED STOOL

Begin by sanding the surface, first with #120 sandpaper and then #220. Go over the surface with a damp sponge to raise any fuzzy grain fibers that might later come up in the base coat. Then resand with #220 sandpaper and wipe the surface with the tack rag.

Apply the base coat as described for the preceding project. Let it dry for at least four hours. When drying is complete, check the piece for skips and runs. Clean brushes and utensils.

Figure 15. Check the stool for damaged areas (top); then, sand the wood until it is smooth (below left). The varnish is applied after the base and glaze coats have dried completely (below right).

Next, brush on the glaze coat in the usual manner, wipe off the excess, and use a dry brush to simulate the grain of the wood. Leave to dry overnight. Finally, apply the satin varnish coat as described above.

ANTIQUING AND GILDING A PICTURE FRAME

Picture frames are sold in many colors and finishes, but it is often difficult to find one that is exactly the right color. Antiquing not only solves the color problem but also allows for creativity.

Wash the frame with the cleaning solution. If the surface has a high sheen, dull it down with #220 sandpaper. Apply the base coat as detailed in "Basic Procedures," remembering to clean brushes and utensils. Apply the glaze coat in the usual manner and let dry. Again, clean brushes when you are finished.

Apply the gilding as follows. Cut two pieces of soft material, one about 5 inches square, the other about 2 inches square. Next, apply the bronzing liquid according to directions on container, and only to those areas to be gilded. When the bronzing liquid reaches the stage where it is no longer wet but sticky, pour some bronzing powder on the large piece of fabric and put the small piece over a fingertip. Dip the fingertip into the powder and tap or rub the powder gently on the areas where there is bronzing liquid.

When the desired effect is achieved, blow away any excess powder and allow the piece to dry for several hours. Finally, apply the satin varnish. Let dry under as dust-free conditions as possible.

Figure 16. After the base coat has dried, use a soft cloth to work in the bronzing liquid. Apply the liquid only to those areas that are to be gilded (left). Gilding lends a rich finish and adds highlights to the grain of the wood (right).

For Additional Reading

Cennini, Cennino, **The Craftsman's Handbook,** Dover, 1933.

Johnstone, James B., and the Sunset Editorial Staff, **Furniture Finishing,** Lane Books.

Kuhn, H. W., **How to Refinish Furniture,** Fawcett-Haynes.

O'Neil, Isabel, **The Art of the Painted Finish for Furniture and Decoration,** William Morrow, 1971.

Wright, Florence E., **How to Stencil Chairs,** Cornell Univ. Press.